SHIP ARREST HANDBOOK

OTHER TITLES IN THIS SERIES:

Shipbuilding Contracts
SECOND EDITION
by Malcolm A. Clarke
1992

Time-Barred Actions
SECOND EDITION
Edited by Francesco Berlingieri
1993

Liability for Damage to the Marine Environment
Edited by Colin de la Rue
1993

The York-Antwerp Rules
SECOND EDITION
by N. Geoffrey Hudson
1996

Bill of Lading: A Document of Title to Goods
by Michael Bools
1997

Shipbrokers and the Law
by Andrew Jamieson
1997

SHIP ARREST HANDBOOK

EDITED
BY
PAUL SMITH

LLP

LONDON HONG KONG
1997

LLP Limited
Legal & Business Publishing Division
69–77 Paul Street
London EC2A 4LQ
Great Britain

SOUTH EAST ASIA
LLP Asia Limited
Room 1101, Hollywood Centre
233 Hollywood Road
Hong Kong

British Library Cataloguing in Publication Data
A catalogue record for this book
is available from the
British Library

ISBN 1–85978–139–X

Typeset in 10/12 Plantin
by Mendip Communications Ltd
Frome
Printed in Great Britain by
WBC Limited
Bridgend, Mid-Glamorgan

PREFACE TO SHIP ARREST HANDBOOK

The arrest of a ship is not something that should be undertaken without careful consideration of the consequences which may ensue. To detain a VLCC or container ship in port, even for a day beyond its scheduled stay, may cost an owner or operator many thousands of dollars. It is therefore highly unlikely that any kind of commercial relationship can be restored between the respective parties once an arrest order has been obtained.

On many occasions, arrest is used as a tool to force a defendant to consider, and hopefully settle, a liquidated claim which he most probably would have otherwise ignored. Alternatively, a ship may be arrested in order to obtain security for a maritime claim. In this context it is worth quoting the definition of arrest as set out in the Brussels Arrest Convention 1952 (the International Convention for the Unification of Certain Rules Relating to the Arrest of Sea-Going Ships, Brussels, 10 May 1952): "Arrest means the detention of a ship by judicial process to secure a maritime claim, but does not include the seizure of a ship in execution or satisfaction of a judgment."

Two of the principal considerations when contemplating an arrest are the location of the ship and, once located, whether an arrest in a particular jurisdiction is possible or desirable. If the claim is one for which an arrest can be made, practical considerations then need to be taken into account, e.g. whether the claimant needs to give security for costs, damages and interest and how quickly an arrest order can be obtained. The costs of the arrest (and whether they can ultimately be recovered from the defendant) are also an important factor in deciding whether or not to proceed. The consequences of a wrongful arrest must also be considered since they differ from one jurisdiction to another.

This volume will provide claimants with information on whether their claim is one for which a ship may be arrested in major maritime jurisdictions. It will also answer many of the practical questions which, in ITIC's long experience of arresting ships worldwide on behalf of Members, are considered to be relevant.

Many of the countries which have supplied the information have ratified the 1952 Brussels Arrest Convention and for convenience the full text is set out in Appendix 1 (page 243) together with a list of the parties who have ratified the Convention. It should, however, be noted that at the time of going to press a joint UNCTAD/IMO Inter-Governmental Group of Experts on Maritime Liens and Mortgages is meeting with the object of revising the 1952 Convention. In particular, the current draft includes a new definition of a maritime claim. If adopted, this will have the effect of substantially increasing the categories of claims in respect of which ships may be arrested. For example, claims for unpaid insurance premiums and Club calls, agency fees and stevedoring charges—all of which are, beyond doubt, of a maritime nature but which have not, up to now, enjoyed the status of other maritime claims—could be secured by means of arrest of the ship which has incurred the debt.

Finally, although many of the replies to question 9 provide an estimate for the costs of a typical arrest, caution should be exercised since each case can be very different in terms of its complexity. It is therefore always prudent to obtain a separate estimate on each and every occasion. These estimates were provided during 1996 and inflationary factors should therefore be taken into account.

PAUL G D SMITH

ACKNOWLEDGEMENTS

I wish to express my appreciation to all the lawyers and correspondents around the world who are listed below and without whose co-operation this book would not have been possible.

PAUL G D SMITH

Omar Khelifa, Algeria
Edye, Roche, De La Vega & Ray, Argentina
Norton Smith & Co., Australia
Kegels, Roosendaal, Keyzer, Straatman & Berckmans, Belgium
Clyde & Co., Brazil
Owen Bird, Canada
Cave Y Compañia Limitada, Chile
Sinclair Roche & Temperley, China
Peter Schaumburg-Müller, Denmark
Eldib & Partners, Egypt
Andrew M. Jackson & Co., England and Wales
Rembauville Bureau Martel Lalanne Lescop & Associés, France
Blaum Dettmers Rabstein, Germany
John G. Hadjis Law Offices, Greece
Ng & Partners, Hong Kong
McCann Fitzgerald, Ireland
S. Friedman & Co., Israel
Studio Legale Mordiglia, Italy
Braun Moriya Hoashi & Kubota, Japan
Kim, Shin & Yu, Korea
Skrine & Co., Malaysia
Fenech & Fenech, Malta
Den Hollander, The Netherlands
Chapman Tripp Sheffield Young, New Zealand
Wikborg, Rein & Co., Norway
Carreira Pitti P.C. Attorneys, Panama
Kancelaria Adwokacka, Poland

Medeiros Cosme Graça Sardinha, Portugal
Henderson Boyd Jackson W.S., Scotland
Khattar Wong & Partners, Singapore
Adams & Adams, South Africa
Albors, Galiano & Co., Spain
Setterwalls, Sweden
Clifford Chance, United Arab Emirates
Chalos & Brown, United States of America

For full details of contributors please refer to Appendix 2 (page 249).

ABOUT THE AUTHOR

Paul Smith has had a background of 22 years in the management of maritime intermediary Clubs. He qualified as a solicitor in 1975 and became a partner in the London firm of Hedleys. In 1986 he joined Tindall Riley & Co. where he was involved in the management of CISBACLUB (the Chartered and International Shipbrokers P & I Club Ltd). In 1992 he joined the board of the management company of ITIC (International Transport Intermediaries Club) as head of marketing.

He has a close involvement with a number of international maritime organisations and is the vice-chairman of the chartering and documentary committee of FONASBA and a member of BIMCO's documentary committee. He is also a member of the Institute of Chartered Shipbrokers, the Chartered Institute of Arbitrators, the Baltic Exchange and The Law Society.

Paul Smith has recently set up a consultancy business (Paul Smith Associates) providing assistance and advice to ship agents, ship managers and shipbrokers. This includes the organisation of corporate loss prevention seminars.

CONTENTS

THE QUESTIONNAIRE

(1) What are the types of claim for which a ship may be arrested in your country?

(2) Is there a distinction between claims which give rise to a maritime lien and other types of claim?
If so please elaborate.

(3) (a) What pleadings, affidavits and documents must be presented to the court when applying for an arrest and in what language?
(b) Which documents must be notarised or otherwise authenticated?

(4) Is it possible to arrest a ship solely in order to obtain security for a claim which will ultimately be determined in another jurisdiction?

(5) What kind of security is normally acceptable to enable the ship to be released from arrest?

(6) In what circumstances can a claimant be made to give security and what security is acceptable?

(7) In the event that the arrest was ultimately shown to have been wrongful, can a claim be made for wrongful arrest and what must be established in order to successfully maintain such a claim?

(8) What are the court fees which must be paid in order to make an arrest? Are they recoverable in the event of a successful claim?

(9) How are the lawyers' fees calculated?
If possible please estimate the costs of a typical arrest.

(10) Are all or any part of the lawyers' fees recoverable in the event of a successful arrest?

(11) How quickly can a ship be arrested after the local lawyer is fully instructed?

(12) Is there a minimum amount in dispute for which a ship may be arrested?

(13) Is it possible to arrest a sister ship or a ship in "associated ownership"?

(14) What is the order of priorities in the event of the distribution by the court of the proceeds of sale of the ship?

(15) Are the claims in respect of which a ship may be arrested subject to a

time bar (or prescription) and, if so, are these different according to the nature of the claim?

(16) Is it possible to apply for the arrest of a ship outside the normal working hours of the court?

(17) Please provide any other information which you believe is relevant in deciding whether or not to arrest a ship in your jurisdiction.

CHAPTER 1

ALGERIA

(1) What are the types of claim for which a ship may be arrested in Algeria?

The types of claim for which a ship may be arrested in Algeria are generally related to cargo damages found by the receiver during the discharge of goods.

From time to time, there may be a claim initiated by a foreign creditor against a shipowner, taking advantage of the presence of a ship in an Algerian harbour.

(2) Is there a distinction between claims which give rise to a maritime lien and other types of claim?

There is no distinction between claims which give rise to a maritime lien.

(3) (a) What pleadings, affidavits and documents must be presented to the court when applying for an arrest and in what language?

Written pleadings and all documents or affidavits establishing the claim must be given and presented in the Arabic language.

All documents translated from English to Arabic are to be authenticated.

(b) Which documents must be notarised or otherwise authenticated?

No documents need be notarised.

(4) Is it possible to arrest a ship solely in order to obtain security for a claim which will ultimately be determined in another jurisdiction?

Yes, it is possible to arrest a ship solely to obtain security for a claim which will ultimately be determined in another jurisdiction.

(5) What kind of security is normally acceptable to enable the ship to be released from arrest?

Generally a bank guarantee is the sort of security acceptable to the cargo underwriter to enable the ship to be released from arrest.

(6) In what circumstances can a claimant be made to give security and what security is acceptable?

Generally, a claimant is never asked to give security.

(7) In the event that the arrest was ultimately shown to have been wrongful, can a claim be made for wrongful arrest and what must be established in order to successfully maintain such a claim?

If the arrest was ultimately shown to have been wrongful, you have the right afterwards to issue a writ against the arrestor to claim interest-damages. However, you can only do this after giving security to enable the arrest to be lifted.

(8) What are the court fees which must be paid in order to make an arrest? Are they recoverable in the event of a successful claim?

The court fees are not high and can be paid by the lawyer.

However, in the recent past, the court bailiff who is no longer a civil servant asks for fees calculated on a percentage of the claim amount.

We have not paid this kind of fees as they are normally applicable only in the event of a cash payment, whereas in our case we are only dealing with security and not cash.

The court fees are not recoverable.

(9) How are the lawyers' fees calculated? If possible please estimate the costs of a typical arrest.

The lawyers' fees are calculated on time spent. A typical arrest will range from US$1,000 to US$2,000 in Algiers if it proves difficult to obtain the arrest.

If the arrest takes place out of Algiers, in other ports, the fees will be higher to take account of the time spent by the lawyer out of Algiers.

(10) Are all or any part of the lawyers' fees recoverable in the event of a successful arrest?

The lawyers' fees are not recoverable in the event of a successful claim.

However, the arrestor may obtain interest-damages in addition to the principal.

(11) How quickly can a ship be arrested after the local lawyer is fully instructed?

A ship may be arrested five days after the lawyer is fully instructed.

(12) Is there a minimum amount in dispute for which a ship may be arrested?

There is no minimum amount in dispute for a ship arrest.

(13) Is it possible to arrest a sister ship or a ship in "associated ownership"?

Yes.

(14) What is the order of priorities in the event of the distribution by the court of the proceeds of sale of the ship?

The proceeds of sale of a ship have never been distributed in Algeria to date.

There is an order of priorities in the event of the distribution by the court of the proceeds of sale of the ship.

(15) Are the claims in respect of which a ship may be arrested subject to a time bar (or prescription) and, if so, are these different according to the nature of the claim?

Yes, the claims in respect of which a ship may be arrested are subject to a time bar.

These are different according to the nature of the claim. The time bar relating to a cargo claim or a charterparty is one year, whereas the time bar for general average is two years.

However, the time bar can be opposed upon a judgment rendered by a court.

(16) Is it possible to apply for the arrest of a ship outside the normal working hours of the court?

No.

(17) Please provide any other information which you believe is relevant in deciding whether or not to arrest a ship in your jurisdiction.

Generally, when a ship is arrested in Algeria, which is done upon an *ex parte* action with the Chairman of the first court, the vessel is always compelled to provide a guarantee notwithstanding the validity of the claim.

The validity of the arrest will be monitored by a judge in the merits proceedings which must be issued by the arrestor within 15 days of the order for arrest. Otherwise, if these proceedings are not issued in time, the arrest will be nullified.

CHAPTER 2

ARGENTINA

(1) What are the types of claim for which a ship may be arrested in Argentina?

In accordance with the Argentine Navigation Act, ships may be arrested for preferred claims (maritime liens).

(a) The Act makes a distinction between the arrest of ships of national flag and foreign ships.
(b) Foreign ships anchored at ports of the Argentine Republic may be arrested: (1) for preferred claims, for maritime claims, i.e. for debts deriving from the activity of the ship, or for claims which have no relation whatsoever to said activity, whenever such claims are enforceable before the courts of the country, and (2) for debts assumed in the national territory for the benefit of the same ship, or of another ship belonging to or which had belonged to the same owner at the time the debt was created (Art. 532 Nav. Act).
(c) Ships of national flag may be arrested at any port of the Argentine Republic for preferred claims, and may be arrested for any other type of claims at the port where the owner is domiciled or where he has his main place of residence (Art. 531 Nav. Act).
(d) The arrest for claims alien to the vessel, to her exploitation or the navigation must meet the requirements provided for by the procedural law in order to be admissible (Art. 531 in fine Nav. Act).

(2) Is there a distinction between claims which give rise to a maritime lien and other types of claim?

The arrest for judgment execution is admissible against any ship of the debtor (Art. 535 Nav. Act).

(3) (a) What pleadings, affidavits and documents must be presented to the court when applying for an arrest and in what language?
(b) Which documents must be notarised or otherwise authenticated?

When applying for an arrest, you must present to the court the documentation supporting the claim duly translated into Spanish, if written in a foreign language.

The arresting party must justify his legal capacity, i.e. if he invokes a legal representation, he must attach a power of attorney granted before a Notary Public.

In the case of preventive arrests for maritime claims, the court admits a document justifying the verisimilitude of the claim, even if its existence is not *prima facie* proved. This provision reflects the need for the distinction mentioned under (1)(c).

(4) Is it possible to arrest a ship solely in order to obtain security for a claim which will ultimately be determined in another jurisdiction?

Yes. The arresting party must make the appropriate clarification because, in accordance with our law, the court with jurisdiction to order the arrest also has jurisdiction to judge the claim on the merits (Art. 612 Nav. Act).

(5) What kind of security is normally acceptable to enable the ship to be released from arrest?

A surety, which according to the plaintiff or the court's criterion, shall cover the claim amount.

Generally, this will be a guarantee from a bank or from a person, who according to the court's opinion, is sufficiently solvent.

(6) In what circumstances can a claimant be made to give security and what security is acceptable?

The courts generally require a security to cover the damages which may arise in case the arrest has been wrongful.

(7) In the event that the arrest was ultimately shown to have been wrongful, can a claim be made for wrongful arrest and what must be established in order to successfully maintain such a claim?

The answer is yes, and if one has not acted maliciously the liability should be limited to the damages arising out of the detention of the ship until the time her creditor is compelled to substitute the arrest for a guarantee and the expenses deriving therefrom.

(8) What are the court fees which must be paid in order to make an arrest? Are they recoverable in the event of a successful claim?

One must pay 3 per cent of the arrest amount as court tax and a fee to the coast guard in order to make an arrest.

They are recoverable depending on the case circumstances.

(9) How are the lawyers' fees calculated? If possible please estimate the costs of a typical arrest.
(10) Are all or any part of the lawyers' fees recoverable in the event of a successful arrest?

In accordance with our law, the lawyers' fees are calculated according to the claim amount and are fixed at a percentage which varies depending on the claim amount.

In principle, they would not be recoverable because the purpose of such costs is to obtain a guarantee. In certain cases, they might be recoverable. See question (8) above.

If the admissibility of an arrest is disputed and the arrest is admitted or denied, the costs of that issue would be paid by the unsuccessful party, unless he is exempted by the court on the grounds that he was right in raising that issue.

(11) How quickly can a ship be arrested after the local lawyer is fully instructed?

Immediately, i.e., on the day when everything is ready, and it depends on the urgency and the possibility that the ship might leave the port. It is not enough to instruct the local lawyer, the documentation mentioned under question (3) must be submitted.

(12) Is there a minimum amount in dispute for which a ship may be arrested?

No.

(13) Is it possible to arrest a sister ship or a ship in "associated ownership"?

The answer is yes; it has been set out above at (1)(b) and (d).

The jurisprudence has considered the subject of the economic groups *vis-à-vis* one-ship companies, but special requirements must be met to justify "piercing the veil of the legal entity".

(14) What is the order of priorities in the event of the distribution by the court of the proceeds of sale of the ship?

The order of priorities is as follows: first of all, the preferred claims of first rank, then the mortgage and then the preferred claims of second rank. The general claims are ranked last.

(15) Are the claims in respect of which a ship may be arrested subject to a time bar (or prescription) and, if so, are these different according to the nature of the claim?

Yes, and if the claim is time-barred, the arrest shall not be admissible.

(16) Is it possible to apply for the arrest of a ship outside the normal working hours of the court?

Yes, in cases of justifiable urgency. This generally implies raising the issue in court beforehand.

(17) Please provide any other information which you believe is relevant in deciding whether or not to arrest a ship in your jurisdiction

It is worth emphasising that this subject is governed by our Navigation Act in Arts. 531 to 541, that Argentina has not adhered to the 1952 Convention; and see J. D. Ray, *Derecho de la Navegación I* (1992), Chapter XXI, page 492.

CHAPTER 3

AUSTRALIA

(1) What are the types of claim for which a ship may be arrested in Australia?

Proceedings *in rem* including an ancillary application to arrest a ship may only be brought under the Admiralty Act 1988 (Cth) (the "Act").

Proceedings *in rem* may be brought on a maritime lien or other charge or on a "maritime claim". A maritime claim is either a "proprietary maritime claim" or a "general maritime claim".

Maritime liens are defined as "including" liens for:

(i) salvage;
(ii) damage done by a ship;
(iii) wages of the master, or of a member of the crew, of a ship; or
(iv) master's disbursements.

Whilst it is possible for Australian courts to hold that other maritime liens exist they have not yet done so.

Proprietary maritime claims are defined as:

(a) a claim relating to:
  (i) possession of a ship;
  (ii) title to, or ownership of, a ship or a share in a ship;
  (iii) a mortgage of a ship or of a share in a ship;
  (iv) a mortgage of a ship's freight;
(b) a claim between co-owners of a ship relating to the possession, ownership, operation or earnings of the ship;
(c) a claim for the satisfaction or enforcement of a judgment given by a court against a ship or other property in a proceeding *in rem* in the nature of a proceeding in Admiralty; or
(d) a claim for interest in respect of a claim referred in paragraphs (a), (b) or (c).

General maritime claims are defined as:

(a) a claim for damage done by a ship (whether by collision or otherwise);
(b) a claim in respect of the liability of the owner of a ship arising under Part II or IV of the Protection of the Sea (Civil Liability) Act 1981

or under a law of a State or Territory that makes provision as mentioned in subsection 7(1) of that Act;

(c) a claim for loss of life, or for personal injury, sustained in consequence of a defect in a ship or in the apparel or equipment of a ship;

(d) a claim (including a claim for loss of life or personal injury) arising out of an act or omission of:

  (i) the owner or charterer of a ship;

  (ii) a person in possession or control of a ship; or

  (iii) a person for whose wrongful acts or omissions the owner, charterer or person in possession or control of a ship is liable; being an act or omission in the navigation or management of the ship, including an act or omission in connection with:

    — the loading of goods onto, or the unloading of goods from, the ship;

    — the embarkation of persons onto, or the disembarkation of persons from, the ship; and

    — the carriage of goods or persons on the ship;

(e) a claim for loss of, or damage to, goods carried by a ship;

(f) a claim arising out of an agreement that relates to the carriage of goods by persons by a ship or to the use or hire of a ship, whether by charterparty or otherwise;

(g) a claim relating to salvage (including life salvage and salvage of cargo or wreck found on land);

(h) a claim in respect of general average;

(i) a claim in respect of towage of a ship;

(j) a claim in respect of pilotage of a ship;

(k) a claim in respect of goods, materials or services (including stevedoring and lighterage services) supplied or to be supplied to a ship for its operation or maintenance;

(l) a claim in respect of the construction of a ship (including such a claim relating to a vessel before it was launched);

(m) a claim in respect of the alteration, repair or equipping of a ship;

(n) a claim in respect of a liability for port, harbour, canal or light tolls, charges or dues, or tolls, charges or dues of a similar kind, in relation to a ship;

(o) a claim in respect of a levy in relation to a ship, including a shipping levy imposed by the Protection of the Sea (Shipping Levy) Act 1981, being a levy in relation to which a power to detain the ship is conferred by a law in force in Australia or in a part of Australia;

(p) a claim by a master, shipper, charterer or agent in respect of disbursements on account of a ship;

(q) a claim for an insurance premium, or for a mutual insurance call, in relation to a ship;

(r) a claim by a master, or a member of the crew, of a ship for:
   (i) wages; or
   (ii) an amount that a person, as employer, is under an obligation to pay a person as employee, whether the obligation arose out of the contract of employment or by operation of law, including the operation of the law of a foreign country;

(s) a claim for the enforcement of, or a claim arising out of, an arbitral award (including a foreign award within the meaning of the Arbitration (Foreign Awards and Agreements) Act 1974) made in respect of a proprietary maritime claim or a claim referred to in one of the preceding paragraphs;

(t) a claim for interest in respect of a claim referred to in one of the preceding paragraphs.

(2) Is there a distinction between claims which give rise to a maritime lien and other types of claims? If so please elaborate.

Yes. Maritime liens and proprietary maritime claims (which are in essence statutory maritime liens) "attach" to the vessel concerned and survive changes in ownership which is not the case for general maritime claims.

(3) (a) What pleadings, affidavits and documents must be presented to the court when applying for an arrest and in what language?

When applying to arrest a vessel it is necessary to prepare the following documents:

(i) Writ of Summons in Rem containing details as to the ship or property the subject of the proceedings, the amount claimed or any other relief sought and particulars of the claim;

(ii) Application for Arrest Warrant;

(iii) Affidavit to Support the Application for Arrest Warrant (this is usually prepared by the solicitor for the claimants certifying that no caveats against arrest are in force and normally providing particulars of how the claim falls within Admiralty jurisdiction. Whilst not necessary, it is preferable that the Affidavit annexes copies of supporting documentation for the claim);

(iv) Arrest Warrant.

All of these documents must be in the form specified in the Admiralty Rules and the Rules of the Court in which the proceedings are commenced and must be in English.

(b) Which documents must be notarised or otherwise authenticated?

None of these documents.

(4) Is it possible to arrest a ship solely in order to obtain security for a claim which will ultimately be determined in another jurisdiction?

Yes. Where it appears to the Australian court that the proceedings ought to be stayed or dismissed on the ground that the claim should be determined by arbitration or by a court of a foreign country, the court may order that the proceedings be stayed on the condition that the ship, or property, under arrest be retained by the court as security for the satisfaction of any award or judgment that may be made in the arbitration or foreign proceedings. The power of the court to stay or dismiss proceedings includes the power to do so on such conditions as are just, including a condition:

(a) which relates to the institution or prosecution of the arbitration or proceeding in the court of the foreign country; and
(b) that equivalent security be provided for the satisfaction of any award or judgment that may be made in the arbitration or in the foreign court.

As a practical matter, unless the defendant shipowner seeks the dismissal or a stay of the proceedings, the proceedings will continue in Australia. Whilst it is possible for the claimant to seek a stay, this application will prove difficult if the defendant opposes it.

(5) What kind of security is normally acceptable to enable the ship to be released from arrest?

A guarantee from an Australian trading bank, a letter of undertaking from an international group P & I Club or a cash payment into court or into the trust account of the claimant's solicitor.

(6) In what circumstances can a claimant be made to give security and what security is acceptable?

Unlike in an application for an interlocutory injunction (for example a Mareva type injunction) where the claimant will normally be required to give an undertaking to pay the damages of any person affected by the injunction should the claimant ultimately fail in his case, no such undertaking has to be given by a claimant seeking the arrest of a ship.

Where the claimant is ordinarily resident outside of Australia, he may, on the application of the defendant, be required to provide security for the defendant's costs of the proceedings. Such security is normally provided by way of a guarantee from an Australian trading bank or a cash payment into court or into the trust account of the defendant's solicitor.

(7) In the event that the arrest was ultimately shown to have been wrongful, can a claim be made for wrongful arrest and what must be established in order to successfully maintain such a claim?

Yes, a person who obtains an arrest "unreasonably and without good cause" will be liable to a person who is a party to the proceedings or to a person who has an interest in the ship or property and who has suffered loss or damage as a direct result.

In order to obtain damages it is necessary to prove that the vessel was arrested unreasonably and the vessel was arrested without good cause. It is not necessary to establish bad faith or gross negligence.

(8) What are the court fees which must be paid in order to make an arrest? Are they recoverable in the event of a successful claim?

Court filing fees are in the order of A$500. The Admiralty Marshal (who is responsible for the practical aspects of arrest) may require certain costs up-front; however, this is at his discretion. It is prudent to assume that the Marshal would require an up-front payment in the order of A$2,000 to cover his initial costs. In applying for the arrest of a ship the claimant also gives an undertaking to the court to pay to the Marshal, on demand, the Marshal's fees and expenses in relation to the arrest.

Often the Marshal will require that the vessel be insured whilst under arrest. The cost of insurance will vary depending on the type of vessel involved and length of cover sought.

All of the Marshal's fees and expenses and court filing fees are recoverable in the event of a successful claim.

(9) How are lawyers' fees calculated? If possible please estimate the costs of a typical arrest.

Normally charged at an hourly rate. The cost of a typical arrest would be in the order of A$2,000.

(10) Are all or any part of the lawyers' fees recoverable in the event of a successful arrest?

Approximately two thirds of lawyer's fees are recoverable in the event of a successful arrest.

(11) How quickly can a ship be arrested after the local lawyer is fully instructed?

Normally, that day.

(12) Is there a minimum amount in dispute for which a ship may be arrested?

No.

(13) Is it possible to arrest a sister ship or a ship in "associated ownership"?

Yes, sister ship arrests (or surrogate ship arrests as they are known in Australia) are permitted under section 19 of the Admiralty Act so long as the following conditions are satisfied:

(a) a relevant person in relation to the claim was, when the cause of action arose, the owner or charterer of, or in possession or control of, the first mentioned ship; and
(b) that relevant person is, when the proceedings are commenced, the owner of the second mentioned ship.

The "second mentioned ship" is called a "surrogate ship". As section 19 of the Act is limited to general maritime claims, the right to proceed against a surrogate ship does not extend to proprietary maritime claims, nor does it extend to a ship which is chartered, be it by demise, voyage or time charter, by the relevant person.

"Relevant person" means the person that would be liable *in personam*. To illustrate, if at the request of the time charterers a stevedore provides services to ship A and is not paid, then the time charterers are the "relevant person", i.e. they would be liable *in personam*. However, the stevedores could not proceed *in rem* against ship A unless the time charterers had become either the owners or demise charterers of ship A. Whilst this is possible it does not happen very often. However, if the time charterer owns another ship B then the stevedore can proceed *in rem* against ship B. This will be so even if the time charterer of ship A is no longer the time charterer of that ship or did not become the owner of ship B until after the cause of action arose.

(14) What is the order of priorities in the event of the distribution by the court of the proceeds of sale of the ship?

There are no statutory provisions which set out the priorities of claims in the event of the distribution of the proceeds of a judicial sale but generally:

— the Marshal's fees and sale expenses of the court will take first priority; these fees may include preparing the vessel for sale, dock or harbour dues and supplies for crew whilst the vessel is under arrest
— the costs of the arresting party will take next priority
— followed by any rewards for salvage and master's and seamen's wages and master's disbursements
— a security interest in the vessel will take next priority even though it attaches by operation of law and does not evolve out of a possessory interest
— those claiming possessory interests, i.e. a ship repair person, are next in line

— followed by any legal and executable mortgages and statutory rights *in rem*.

(15) Are the claims in respect of which a ship may be arrested subject to a time bar (or prescription) and, if so, are these different according to the nature of the claim?

Yes, claims in respect of which a ship may be arrested are subject to a three-year time bar so long as no time bar applies by force of another Act or contractual terms. For example, claims brought pursuant to a bill of lading must be brought within the usual one-year time bar period and claims arising out of collisions or salvage services rendered subject to a two-year limitation period.

(16) Is it possible to apply for the arrest of a ship outside the normal working hours of the court?

Yes, although it is easier if the Registrar/Duty Judge has been "put on notice" that an application will be made at a particular time.

(17) Please provide any other information which you believe is relevant in deciding whether or not to arrest a ship in your jurisdiction.

(i) *In rem* proceedings can also be brought against demise chartered vessels. Section 18 of the Act permits a claim against a ship where the relevant person was, when the cause of action arose, "the owner or charterer, or in possession or control, of the ship" and is, when the proceedings are commenced, "a demise charterer of the ship". In other words, the Act permits arrest for demise charterers' liabilities.

(ii) It is not necessary to commence *in rem* and arrest proceedings in the place where the ship is to be arrested. As the Federal Court of Australia has admiralty jurisdiction, proceedings can be commenced in any registry of that court and the ship arrested at any place in Australia. To illustrate, *in rem* proceedings and an application for arrest can be filed in Sydney and the ship arrested in Melbourne.

CHAPTER 4

BELGIUM

Belgian law makes a fundamental distinction between conservatory measures and measures of enforcement.

Measures of enforcement are always and necessarily based upon a title, a judgment, an arbitration award or a notarial deed.

In essence this procedure is similar to the normal procedural rules for the forced sale of other assets of a debtor, his furniture, his house, his shares and other belongings.

Conservatory measures to the contrary do not prejudice the rights of the party and intend to protect, secure and preserve alleged rights without pronouncing upon the right itself.

(1) What are the types of claim for which a ship may be arrested in Belgium?

Belgium approved the 1952 Convention by law dated 24 March 1961 and incorporated in its new Procedural Code the principles of the Convention.

Article 2 of the 1952 Convention says that a ship may be arrested in respect of any maritime claim but in respect of no other claim.

A conservatory arrest is thus possible only for the maritime claims listed in Article 1 of the 1952 Convention:

— damage caused either in collision or otherwise;
— loss of life or personal injury caused by any ship;
— salvage;
— the use or hire of any ship by charterparty or otherwise;
— agreement relating to the carriage of the goods;
— loss of or damage to goods;
— general average;
— bottomry;
— towage;
— pilotage;
— supplies to a ship for her operation or maintenance;
— construction, repair or equipment or dock charges and dues;
— wages;

— master's disbursements including disbursements made by shippers, charterers or agents on behalf of a ship or an owner;
— dispute as to the title to or ownership of the ship;
— disputes between co-owners as to ownership, possession, employment or earnings;
— mortgage or hypothecation.

A conservatory arrest of a ship is not possible for other claims.

(2) Is there a distinction between claims which give rise to a maritime lien and other types of claim?

Claims other than the maritime claims listed above do not entitle a conservatory arrest of a seagoing vessel.

Such other claims, e.g. insurance premiums, are subject to the normal procedural laws but not to the 1952 Convention. However, once a title is obtained the normal procedural rules apply and a vessel can be arrested in execution for satisfaction of such title whatever the nature of the claim.

(3) What pleadings, affidavits and documents must be presented to the court when applying for an arrest and in what language?

Belgian courts are not formalistic and do not need any authentication. The arrestor will, in Chambers, present his claim and the documents at hand without necessity for official translation, affidavits or original documents.

Such request to the court is presented by a lawyer who drafts the required request and presents it together with the documents at hand.

(4) Is it possible to arrest a ship solely in order to obtain security for a claim which will ultimately be determined in another jurisdiction?

A ship can be arrested in order to obtain security only and without influencing the competent jurisdiction for the judgment of the claim. There is thus no link between the conservatory arrest and the jurisdiction.

(5) What kind of security is normally acceptable to enable the ship to be released from arrest?

Once a vessel is arrested the security to obtain release can be either a deposit in the State bank (nearly never used) or the issuance of a guarantee.

In theory the guarantee must be issued by a first class Belgian bank. The arrestor cannot be obliged to accept the guarantee of a Club but nothing forbids him from accepting such guarantee if proposed.

Other securities such as guarantee-cheques, and personal undertakings of agents, cannot be used for obtaining the release.

(6) In what circumstances can a claimant be made to give security and what security is acceptable?

The facility for obtaining the arrest (allegation of a claim) persuades the judges to ask for a counter-security in favour of the owner. Such counter-security had to guarantee the potential indemnity the owner would claim for damages resulting from an unjustified arrest.

The counter-guarantee, when imposed, must be a bank guarantee issued by a first class Belgian bank.

However, in more recent times, judges often refrain from imposing a counter-guarantee on the arrestor. Statistics show that the number of wrongful arrests are extremely rare. If a counter-security is imposed it is generally equal to 65 Belgian francs per ton deadweight, an amount assumed to represent the economic loss suffered by the owner in a case of wrongful arrest, but if the owner can show evidence that his losses will actually be higher than 65 francs per ton, he is entitled to ask the judge for an increase.

(7) In the event that the arrest was ultimately shown to have been wrongful, can a claim be made for wrongful arrest and what must be established in order to successfully maintain such a claim?

A wrongful arrest entitles the victim to claim for damages. This is, however, an action in tort and the claimant (owner of the vessel) has to prove that the arrestor committed a fault and in addition that this fault caused damages.

Belgian law indeed ignores liability without fault and the 1952 Convention remains silent on this point.

(8) What are the court fees which must be paid in order to make an arrest? Are they recoverable in the event of a successful claim?

The expenses of making an arrest consist of:

(a) the court expenses;
(b) the costs of the bailiff who arrests the vessel;
(c) lawyers' fees.

Items (a) and (b) are fully recoverable under Belgian law. Item (c) is not.

(9) How are lawyers' fees calculated? If possible please estimate the costs of a typical arrest.

Lawyers' fees are subject to agreement between the parties. There are norms at the Belgian bar but they can be discussed freely. The timetable system can be applied, or the traditional system of result.

The total of the recoverable expenses can be estimated at about £1,000 sterling, depending on the complexity of the matter; indeed once a vessel is arrested the owner can lodge an opposition before the same judge and an appeal is possible, even an action before the Supreme Court (Cour de Cassation), on a case of principle.

Bf 50,000 are the normal expenses likely for arresting a vessel, inscription in the ship's register, lifting of the arrest and release from the ship's register.

(10) Are all or any part of the lawyers' fees recoverable in the event of a successful arrest?

Lawyers' fees: see (9) above.

(11) How quickly can a ship be arrested after the local lawyer is fully instructed?

Once a local lawyer is fully informed it is theoretically possible to arrest in a couple of hours, even during the weekend. Judges, at least in the main ports, are prepared to hear the arrestor outside office hours.

(12) Is there a minimum amount in dispute for which a ship may be arrested?

There is no minimum amount for arresting a ship.

(13) Is it possible to arrest a sister ship or a ship in "associated ownership"?

The sister ship position

Sister ships, defined in the 1952 Convention, when all the shares therein are owned by the same person, can be arrested.

Although Belgian law recognises the independence of patrimonia of companies and the validity and existence of foreign companies, judges can pierce the so-called corporate veil when they become convinced that the aim or consequences of such legal constructs are to bypass legitimate claims of third parties. In such circumstances legal constructs can be considered as fraudulent and set up with a view to avoiding justified claims.

The legal background

It is the claimant who has to prove that the single-ship legal construct does not represent the actual situation and that the different companies must be considered as though they were one and the same company.

(14) What is the order of priorities in the event of the distribution by the court of the proceeds of sale of the ship?

When a vessel has been arrested, in execution or satisfaction of a title, and has been auctioned publicly the proceeds of the sale shall be distributed in accordance with the rules of the International Convention of Brussels, 10 April 1926.

The order is as follows:

(a) the maritime liens in the following order:
  (i) law costs due to the State:
  expenses incurred in the common interests of the creditors;
  tonnage, harbour and other dues;
  pilotage dues;
  (ii) claims for wages;
  (iii) remuneration for assistance, salvage and contribution in general average;
  (iv) indemnities for collisions, accidents of navigation, damage caused to docks, harbours, navigable ways;
  indemnity for personal injury to passengers or crew;
  loss and damage to cargo;
  (v) claims resulting from contracts entered into by the master, away from the vessel's own port for the preservation of the vessel;
(b) the mortgages;
(c) the non-preferred claims.

(15) Are the claims in respect of which a ship may be arrested subject to a time bar (or prescription) and, if so, are these different according to the nature of the claim?

The action for arresting a vessel is not subject to any time bar but the action for the claim can be: nearly any action is subject to a time bar.

For example:

— collision: two years
— cargo claims under bill of lading: one year
— charterparty disputes: three years.

The time bar, however, is subject to the law of the contract.

(16) Is it possible to apply for the arrest of a ship outside the normal working hours of the court?

Yes. See (11) above.

(17) Please provide any other information which you believe is relevant in deciding whether or not to arrest a ship in your jurisdiction.

In Belgium it is possible to arrest a ship for a claim against a person other than the shipowner.

The vessel is considered as security for the maritime claim, without consideration as to whether the debtor *in personam* was the owner or the demise charterer, or the voyage charterer, or any other person. The creditors have at their disposal a right *in rem* against the vessel, besides an action *in personam* against the debtor of the maritime claim.

Bunkers ordered for a vessel by a charterer allow the oil company to arrest a ship. Harbour dues incurred by a charterer must be secured by the vessel. Cargo claims under bills of lading issued by a charterer must be secured by the vessel.

The owner must guarantee the debt of the charterer and his guarantee must cover claims he did not cause directly in order to release the ship.

CHAPTER 5

BRAZIL

(1) What are the types of claim for which a ship may be arrested in Brazil?

Any type of unfulfilled monetary claim. In theory, the claim should not be unliquidated, but in practice we have been involved in many arrests where the claim has been unliquidated (such as cargo claims) under the Commercial Code route (see (2)(a) below).

(2) Is there a distinction between claims which give rise to a maritime lien and other types of claim?

Yes, although the concept "maritime lien" does not exist as such in Brazil. There are, however, certain types of claim which survive a change of ownership of the vessel.

Essentially, there are two types of ship arrest in Brazil.

(a) Commercial Code arrest

This applies to "privileged" claims, generally associated with the last voyage of the vessel. In practice, courts often disregard the requirement for claims to have originated on the last voyage in the case of non-Brazilian vessels. These claims survive a change of ownership of the vessel, and include:

- — wages for salvage and pilotage
- — port fees and navigational taxes
- — warehouse and keeper's fees
- — debts for necessaries supplied at last port
- — officers' and crews' wages
- — hull/freight insurance covering last voyage
- — funds lent to Captain for necessaries, repairs, and insurance premiums during last voyage
- — claims for short delivery of cargo, in particular average, insurance premiums, and everything associated with last voyage
- — moneys owed to shipyard for construction or repair of the vessel
- — moneys owed for purchase of the vessel.

(b) Procedural Code arrest

This is strictly speaking an attachment order, called an "*arresto*", preventing the ship from being sold until the respective claim (which should be determinable and unliquidated) has been satisfied, or suitable security (cash or bank guarantee covering the full claim) deposited at the court. In practice, this often prevents the vessel from sailing and so amounts to an arrest. The Procedural Code arrest does not survive a change of ownership.

(3)(a) What pleadings, affidavits and documents must be presented to the court when applying for an arrest and in what language?

In an application for the arrest, the following documents should be attached:

- document of title/proof of debt (e.g. invoice)
- relevant contract (if any)
- Power of Attorney
- document of constitution of plaintiff company (best to include, but not vital).

These documents should be translated into Portuguese, if time allows, by an official translator.

(b) Which documents must be notarised or otherwise authenticated?

At the arrest stage, none. Fax copies will suffice. The Power of Attorney should be notarised by a notary approved by the nearest Brazilian Consulate and then "consularised" (authenticated) by the Brazilian Consulate itself. This must be lodged at the court within 15 days of the arrest application (usually extendable for a further 15 days if necessary).

(4) Is it possible to arrest a ship solely in order to obtain security for a claim which will ultimately be determined in another jurisdiction?

In theory an action on the merits must be commenced in Brazil within 30 days of the arrest or the ship will be released. However, in practice, it is generally possible to negotiate security for the dispute to be resolved in another jurisdiction, and the claim in Brazil to be dropped within the 30-day period.

(5) What kind of security is normally acceptable to enable the ship to be released from arrest?

A cash deposit or bank guarantee should be lodged at court. In practice, one would probably negotiate for the claim in Brazil to be dropped in return for satisfactory security elsewhere (e.g. Letter of Undertaking from owner's P & I Club).

(6) In what circumstances can a claimant be made to give security and what security is acceptable?

A foreign claimant will often be required to provide counter-security for the costs of the defendant. This is usually for an amount up to 20 per cent of the total claimed in the form of a cash deposit or bank guarantee issued by a Brazilian bank.

(7) In the event that the arrest was ultimately shown to have been wrongful, can a claim be made for wrongful arrest and what must be established in order to successfully maintain such a claim?

Yes. The arresting party must indemnify the defendant for losses caused by wrongful detention (usually where there were no proper grounds for arrest or more likely where facts were concealed), which is decided by the court either *per se* in the arrest action, or when the claim in the main (subsequent) action is denied. If a would-be wrongful arrest claimant was not party to the arrest proceedings (e.g. a subcharterer), he could bring an action under Brazilian civil law. This establishes a general obligation to indemnify for losses caused by wrongful acts, in relation to fault, negligence and recklessness. However, we are aware of only a very few attempts to seek damages for wrongful arrest in Brazil.

(8) What are the court fees which must be paid in order to make an arrest? Are they recoverable in the event of a successful claim?

It depends on the court and the size of the claim. Typically, $600 for a claim of $50,000. They are not recoverable.

(9) How are lawyers' fees calculated? If possible please estimate the costs of a typical arrest

Generally, as a percentage of the claim. Say, 12 per cent plus costs (e.g. on a claim of $50,000: $6,000 plus costs). However, for higher value claims, a smaller fixed fee would be acceptable.

(10) Are all or any part of the lawyers' fees recoverable in the event of a successful arrest?

Only at the conclusion of the main action, if the claim is successfully pursued in Brazil.

(11) How quickly can a ship be arrested after the local lawyer is fully instructed?

On average, 48 hours. It can be done more quickly in some instances.

(12) Is there a minimum amount in dispute for which a ship may be arrested?

No.

(13) Is it possible to arrest a sister ship or a ship in "associated ownership"?

Sister ship

Only under the Procedural Code system.

Associated ship

As above, but only if the managers are the contractual carriers (e.g. if they issued the bill of lading).

(14) What is the order of priorities in the event of the distribution by the court of the proceeds of sale of the ship?

(i) Costs of the auction.
(ii) Fiscal and labour debts.
(iii) "Privileged" claims, as per the International Convention on Privileged Claims on Vessels (e.g. mortgages and other encumbrances).

(15) Are the claims in respect of which a ship may be arrested subject to a time bar (or prescription) and, if so, are these different according to the nature of the claim?

Yes. It depends on the nature of the claim. Under the Brazilian Commercial Code, the time limit for all claims brought on commercial contracts is 20 years (Art. 442). However, cargo and most maritime claims are subject to a one-year time bar (Art. 449).

Under the Brazilian Civil Code, the general rule for all civil actions between persons is that the time limit is 20 years, unless otherwise specified.

(16) Is it possible to apply for the arrest of a ship outside the normal working hours of the court?

Usually, no.

(17) Please provide any other information which you believe is relevant in deciding whether or not to arrest a ship in your jurisdiction.

The practice of the court differs from port to port. Most judges are inexperienced in maritime matters.

CHAPTER 6

CANADA

(1) What are the types of claim for which a ship may be arrested in Canada?

A ship may be arrested in Canada for maritime lien claims, mortgage claims and various types of claims for which a statutory right of arrest is given.

The law with respect to maritime liens closely follows that of the United Kingdom. Maritime liens include claims against ships for salvage, property damage and personal injury claims, wages of seamen and master and a master's disbursements.

A statutory right of arrest is given for contractual claims such as those involving necessaries (provision of goods and services to a ship), ship repairs, towage, cargo damage, claims by charterers, claims for marine insurance premiums and general average. With the exception of general average, the beneficial owner of the ship at the time of commencement of the proceedings must also have been the owner when the cause of action arose. The shipowner must also be contractually liable to the claimant.

(2) Is there a distinction between claims which give rise to a maritime lien and other types of claim?

There is a distinction between claims which give rise to a maritime lien and other types of claims.

A maritime lien against a ship is not normally lost as a result of a change in ownership unless by laches. Cargo claims and other *in rem* claims which do not give rise to a maritime lien cannot be exercised against the ship after a change of ownership, if legal proceedings have not earlier been commenced. However, pilotage and general average, although not traditional maritime liens, may survive a change in ownership.

(3) (a) What pleadings, affidavits and documents must be presented to the court when applying for an arrest and in what language?

If a ship is arrested by proceedings commenced in the Federal Court of Canada, the documents required include a Statement of Claim, an Affidavit to Lead Warrant and draft Warrant for Arrest. The language in the Federal

Court may be in English or French. Outside Quebec, they are normally filed in English.

(b) Which documents must be notarised or otherwise authenticated?

The affidavit must be sworn before a Commissioner for taking Affidavits. There is no requirement that documents attached to an affidavit be notarised. A Canadian lawyer may normally swear the affidavit on the basis of information provided by the client. In some instances, supporting documentation is attached to the affidavit as an exhibit.

(4) Is it possible to arrest a ship solely in order to obtain security for a claim which will ultimately be determined in another jurisdiction?

The Federal Court has allowed arrest of a ship in Canada solely to obtain security for a claim being dealt with in another jurisdiction. However, whether a court will as a condition of staying proceedings require security to be posted, depends on the circumstances. If litigation or arbitration has not been commenced elsewhere, while a claimant may be able to arrest in Canada, there is a risk that the shipowner may accept the jurisdiction of the court, in which case for the claimant, in the absence of agreement of the parties, this may result in his claim being dealt with in Canada.

(5) What kind of security is normally acceptable to enable the ship to be released from arrest?

A P & I Club letter of undertaking from a member of the international group is normally acceptable to claimant's counsel and their clients. Alternatively, if a Club letter of undertaking is not acceptable to the claimant or forthcoming from the P & I Club, security by way of cash, a bank letter of guarantee from a Canadian chartered bank or bail bond would be required by the Federal Court.

(6) In what circumstances can a claimant be made to give security and what security is acceptable?

A claimant may be required to give security by way of costs if it ordinarily resides out of the jurisdiction, if it is suing for the benefit of another person and there is reason to believe it will be unable to pay costs, or it has changed its address during the course of the proceedings with a view to evading consequences of the litigation. The security is to be given as the court may direct and is normally in the form of a bond unless agreement is reached by counsel as to another form of security.

(7) In the event that the arrest was ultimately shown to have been wrongful, can a claim be made for wrongful arrest and what must be established in order to successfully maintain such a claim?

If an arrest is ultimately shown to have been wrong, a claim may be made for wrongful arrest. While there are very few cases in which such a claim has been made, the party whose vessel was wrongfully arrested would likely be entitled to recover the provable damages which might reasonably have been foreseen to arise from the arrest. If a bail bond is posted following an arrest and the action is subsequently dismissed, the claimant will be liable for the cost of posting the bond.

(8) What are the court fees which must be paid in order to make an arrest? Are they recoverable in the event of a successful claim?

The Federal Court fees vary between $20 and $150 to issue a Statement of Claim and obtain a Warrant, depending on the amount claimed. Additional charges must be paid to the sheriff to carry out the arrest for which a deposit is normally required of at least $350. The costs are recoverable in the event of a judgment against the ship.

(9) How are the lawyers' fees calculated? If possible please estimate the costs of a typical arrest.

The lawyers' fee is normally calculated on the basis of the amount of time spent although the amount involved may affect the fees. The cost of a typical arrest without complications is in the range of $1,500 to $2,500 plus disbursements.

(10) Are all or any part of the lawyers' fees recoverable in the event of a successful arrest?

A part of the lawyers' fees are recoverable in the event that a judgment is obtained against the shipowner. While some of those fees may pertain to the cost of arrest, they are not recoverable until a decision has been made on the merits of the claim or the defendant has admitted liability.

(11) How quickly can a ship be arrested after the local lawyer is fully instructed?

After the local lawyer is fully instructed, a ship may be arrested within hours, depending on its location in relation to the court registry where the warrant is issued.

(12) Is there a minimum amount in dispute for which a ship may be arrested?

There is no minimum amount for which a ship may be arrested.

(13) Is it possible to arrest a sister ship or a ship in "associated ownership"?

It is possible to arrest a sister ship. However, it is a condition of arresting a sister ship that at the time the action is commenced, the named ship has the same shipowner that existed at the time the cause of action arose. The owner of the sister ship must also be the same owner of the named ship. Partial ownership of another ship is insufficient to allow the ship to be arrested as a sister ship.

(14) What is the order of priorities in the event of the distribution by the court of the proceeds of sale of the ship?

The order of priorities in the event of distribution by the court of the proceeds of sale of a ship is as follows:

(a) certain governmental claims allowing seizure for dock and harbour charges, wreck removal and pollution;
(b) maritime liens;
(c) pilotage;
(d) mortgages;
(e) claimants having statutory rights of arrest who are treated as unsecured creditors.

Where there is a conflict of law issue as to whether there is a lien, as opposed to a statutory right of arrest, Canada, unlike the United Kingdom, will recognise the law of the place where the lien arose in determining whether or not a lien exists, following which priorities will be determined as above. If bunkers were supplied to a ship in the United States which gave rise to a maritime lien under US law, the Canadian courts would recognise the claim as a maritime lien, even though it would only have the status of a statutory lien if supplied in Canada.

(15) Are the claims in respect of which a ship may be arrested subject to a time bar (or prescription) and, if so, are these different according to the nature of the claim?

The claims in respect of which a ship may be arrested are subject to time bar but the bar differs according to the nature of the claim. Normally, the time bar will range from one year to six years. In the case of cargo claims, it is normally one year. Contractual claims are normally two years or six years. Claims in tort are normally two years although the time limitation in force in the country where the tort or contractual obligation occurred may be of relevance.

(16) Is it possible to apply for the arrest of a ship outside the normal working hours of the court?

Arrest of a ship outside the normal working hours of the court may be applied for in circumstances where the ship is expected to leave port before the normal business hours of the court the following working day.

(17) Please provide any other information which you believe is relevant in deciding whether or not to arrest a ship in your jurisdiction.

A ship in Canada may normally be arrested quickly following receipt of the information required to issue a Statement of Claim. Application is normally made by filing documents with the Court Registry and a hearing before a judge is rarely required prior to an arrest. Apart from the court and legal fees, no other charges are normally incurred to arrest a ship. Unlike some jurisdictions, the sheriff or marshal does not normally stay aboard the vessel following the arrest or take possession of the ship. There is therefore no need to post a bond or enter into an indemnity agreement with the sheriff.

CHAPTER 7

CHILE

(1) What are the types of claim for which a ship may be arrested in Chile?

Basically an arrest can be requested and granted if the arresting party has some credit against the ship. These credits can be of two types:

(a) Privileged credits: these are defined in Articles 844, 845 and 846 of Book III of the Chilean Code of Commerce. A free translation of the text of these articles can be found in the Annex to this chapter.

(b) Credits other than those mentioned in (a) above: in this case the arrest is a precautionary measure under the Civil Code (common law), not necessarily relating to maritime matters (Article 1240 of Book III of the Code of Commerce).

(2) Is there a distinction between claims which give rise to a maritime lien and other types of claim?

The distinction mentioned in the preceding question is relevant:

(a) When a *privileged credit* is invoked, if it attaches antecedents which constitute presumption of the right being claimed, the tribunal must accede to the petition without further formality and, if these antecedents are not sufficient or the petitioner states they are not yet available to him, the tribunal may require that security be provided for the eventual damages which may be caused if, subsequently, it is found that the petition lacked basis (Article 1231). In other words, except for the aforementioned supposition, the tribunal must accede to the arrest and it is not necessary to constitute a guarantee.

(b) On the contrary, if the arrest is petitioned by invoking a *credit other than privileged ones*, the general rules of the Code of Civil Procedure are applicable, this being an alternative which gives rise to two possibilities, albeit the first one is the most probable in view of the urgent nature of the arrest:

(i) petition the arrest as a *pre-judicial precautionary measure* (prohibition from sailing), that is to say, in order to safeguard the exercise of the future action. In this event, without prejudice to concurrently existing motives considered to be serious and qualified, the value of the assets upon which the precautionary measure falls must be determined and, most particularly, a security or another guarantee considered sufficient in the opinion of the tribunal should be lodged, in order to respond to the damages which may arise or fines which may be levied (Article 279 of the Code of Civil Procedure);

(ii) petition the arrest as a *precautionary measure together with filing the suit itself*, in which event the arrest also means the specific measure called "prohibition from sailing"; for this course of action it is necessary that the financial means of the defendant do not offer sufficient guarantee or that there is reason to believe that he will try to conceal his assets (Article 295 of the Code of Civil Procedure) without the need to lodge a guarantee. In this event, supporting documents which may constitute at least a serious presumption of the right being claimed, should be attached (Article 298 of the Code of Civil Procedure) without prejudice to the fact that when dealing with serious and urgent cases the tribunal may grant the measure, even if the required supporting documents have not yet been produced, for a term not exceeding 10 days, until the supporting documents are presented, and will demand in this event a security to respond to the resulting damages.

(3) (a) What pleadings, affidavits and documents must be presented to the court when applying for an arrest and in what language?

The arrest, whether it is petitioned in accordance with the legal system of the Code of Commerce or the general system of the Code of Civil Procedure, must be petitioned in writing in Spanish and the aforementioned documents must be attached. In principle, the attached documents must be written in Spanish but if they are written in a foreign language, a free translation into Spanish must be attached. However, tribunals sometimes accept part of the documents written in foreign languages and/or specify that only the most relevant aspects be translated.

Thus, for example, if the arrest of a vessel is petitioned on the grounds that salvage services have been rendered, a certificate issued by the Maritime Authority giving an account of the rendering of these services, may be considered a sufficient document; if the arrest is petitioned in respect of alleged damage to the cargo carried, it is necessary to attach the documents supporting the carriage (bill of lading or equivalent document) and any other document which may serve as proof of the damage sustained by the cargo, such as a receipt certificate issued by Customs, evidencing that the cargo is damaged. In general, especially when the arrest is petitioned in accordance with the special legal system of the Code of Commerce, our tribunals are quite liberal regarding the documents that should be attached.

(b) Which documents must be notarised or otherwise authenticated?

It is not necessary that the documents be authorised by a notary, or that their authenticity be established in any other way. However, if at all possible, ideally copies of original documents should be certified by a notary.

(4) Is it possible to arrest a ship solely in order to obtain security for a claim which will ultimately be determined in another jurisdiction?

According to what we understand to be a principle of international law and what is to be inferred from Article 1207, theoretically speaking, it is possible to petition the arrest in Chile as per the special legal system of the Code of Commerce, even if the Chilean tribunals are not competent to hear the action itself, for example, if the matter is submitted to arbitration abroad.

However, our experience demonstrates that this is a very difficult route, because by virtue of what is set down in Article 1239 of the Code of Commerce, in accordance with Article 280 of the Code of Civil Procedure, whoever has obtained the arrest is obliged to file his complaint requesting that the decreed arrest remain in force within a time period which, in principle, is 10 days, but which may be extended for up to a total of 30 days, provided there is sound basis to do so. If the Chilean tribunals, be they ordinary or arbitration, are not competent to hear the principal action, the situation is evidently uncertain, because the suit could not be filed in Chile.

In our opinion, if such is the case, the suit (or the equivalent proceedings) must be filed abroad within the time period fixed by the Chilean tribunal and you must establish that it has been filed in the aforementioned manner, at the same time petitioning that the measure be maintained. However, in view of the legislative uncertainty existing here, it is especially risky to petition the arrest of a vessel in Chile when the principal action will not be heard in Chile. Bear in mind that the non-fulfilment of the obligation set down in the aforementioned Article 280 of the Code of Civil Procedure means the cancellation of the arrest and liability for the damages which may have been caused, on the irrebuttable presumption that the proceedings for the arrest were fraudulent, that is, if there is no proof to the contrary.

Without prejudice to the foregoing, it is necessary to highlight the fact that the obligation imposed by Article 280 of the Code of Civil Procedure also produces problems when Chile is competent to hear the principal action, because, since 1988, this principal action must be heard (with exceptions), at first instance, by an arbitrator. The formalities for the appointment of an arbitrator, especially if this appointment is not agreed by both sides, may last longer than the time period in which the demand (petitioning that the arrest be maintained according to the terms of Article 280 of the Code of Civil Procedure) must be filed. Evidently, ideally the arbitrator should be appointed, the demand should be filed, the maintaining of the precautionary measure should be petitioned, and all this should be decreed within the maximum time period fixed as per Article 280 of the Code of Civil Procedure, but it is also possible that not all these requirements can be fulfilled within the aforementioned time period.

The situation has given rise to a number of interpretations, and some commentators have reached the conclusion that the demand has to be filed with the ordinary tribunal which granted the arrest, whilst others have said that the petition for summons to a hearing to appoint an arbitrator must be considered as equivalent to filing the demand mentioned in Article 280 of the Code of Civil Procedure. In view of the high degree of uncertainty arising, it is usual that those who have petitioned and suffered the arrest should reach agreement in respect of these aspects. The present procedural situation in our law prevents us from giving a definite reply.

(5) What kind of security is normally acceptable to enable the ship to be released from arrest?

In court the guarantee usually requested and granted is a bank guarantee, issued to the order of the court, either in US dollars or Chilean pesos. Also acceptable, depending on the amount, is a banker's draft in the name of the court or a cash deposit in the court's account. Out of court, and by agreement with the arresting party, P & I Club letters are also accepted; it is usual, however, for claimants to demand they confer jurisdiction on the competent Chilean courts. The arresting party's agreement is vital, since Chilean courts are unfamiliar with Club letters.

(6) In what circumstances can a claimant be made to give security and what security is acceptable?

Regarding the cases requiring a guarantee, we refer to what we stated in answer to the first question, that is:

(a) when a privileged credit of the Code of Commerce is invoked, the tribunal can only demand that a guarantee be constituted if sufficient antecedents are not attached or if the petitioner states they are not available to him yet; and
(b) when the arrest is petitioned in accordance with the common legal system of the Code of Civil Procedure as a prejudicial precautionary measure, that is, before filing the demand itself, it is essential to render a guarantee.

Regarding the nature of the guarantee, the law contains no specific ruling and, when this exceptional situation arises, each tribunal usually proceeds in a different way. We have seen cases where a specific third party constitutes himself liable for the damages which may arise; we have seen cases where bank guarantees are attached for a specific amount; and we have also seen cases where the petitioner of the arrest (normally when he is a cargo underwriter) attaches a guarantee policy for a specific amount.

(7) In the event that the arrest was ultimately shown to have been wrongful, can a claim be made for wrongful arrest and what must be established in order to successfully maintain such a claim?

The first thing to bear in mind regarding this matter is what we have said regarding Article 280 of the Code of Civil Procedure; that is, when the obligation to file a demand within a specific time period is not fulfilled, the petitioner should petition that the precautionary measure be maintained and the tribunal should in fact do so. It is even more difficult to conclude that an indemnity for damages may be obtained in the event that, although the arrest was decreed by the tribunal, it might subsequently be declared null and void.

Without prejudice to what we have said regarding Article 280 of the Code of Civil Procedure, if whoever petitioned the arrest is ordered to pay costs, it is possible to claim payment of these costs, although the usual practice in Chile is that the tribunal decides that the petitioner of the arrest had plausible reasons for bringing the action and, therefore, each party should bear his own costs.

Regarding the damages which may arise from an arrest subsequently declared null and void, these would have to be claimed in separate ordinary proceedings.

(8) What are the court fees which must be paid in order to make an arrest? Are they recoverable in the event of a successful claim?

There are no court fees payable; the only costs are the fees of the bailiff who informs the Maritime Authority of the arrest and later informs them when it has been lifted. These are a minor item.

(9) How are the lawyers' fees calculated? If possible, please estimate the costs of a typical arrest.

The legal principle is that the fees must be fixed conventionally, and in the absence of agreement, by the competent ordinary court. However, in actual practice, the fee for the arrest is usually fixed at a lump sum, without necessarily considering the time used.

It is difficult to calculate the quantum, but a typical arrest may cost about US$5,000.

(10) Are all or any part of the lawyers' fees recoverable in the event of a successful arrest?

Yes, but costs are usually only granted if the judge rules that there was no reasonable basis to start the proceedings in the first place, which is seldom the case.

(11) How quickly can a ship be arrested after the local lawyer is fully instructed?

If all the necessary antecedents are available and if the written presentation of the case is ready, the arrest may be obtained in a few hours or within a maximum of 24 hours, assuming it is petitioned along the lines of the special legal system of the Code of Commerce, which is the usual practice. On the other hand, an arrest petitioned in accordance with the general legal system of the Code of Civil Procedure, which is unusual, may last several days because the corresponding petition must be filed with the Court of Appeal for distribution to the tribunal that must hear it, and a guarantee must be lodged, and so on.

However, in actual practice, arrests are always petitioned in accordance with the special legal system of the Code of Commerce, in force since 1988.

(12) Is there a minimum amount in dispute for which a ship may be arrested?

There is no minimum amount established by law to petition for and obtain an arrest, but in actual practice the tribunals are not likely to decree it when the amounts are comparatively small because they are aware that the damages arising from the arrest can be much higher. However, legally speaking there is no minimum amount fixed and the tribunal should decree the arrest without taking the quantum into consideration.

The smallest amount for which we have seen a ship arrested is US$6,000.

(13) Is it possible to arrest a sister ship or a ship in "associated ownership"?

Article 1234 establishes that the lien on the ship granted by a privileged credit can be exercised on (a) the actual ship; (b) a ship in the same ownership; or (c) a ship in the same administration or operated by the same person.

However, if the arrest is petitioned in accordance with the system of the Code of Civil Procedure, only a vessel belonging to the debtor can be arrested, be it the one which gave rise to the debt to the creditor or another one.

(14) What is the order of priorities in the event of the distribution by the court of the proceeds of sale of the ship?

The order of priorities for the payment of maritime privileged credits is established in Articles 844 to 846, without prejudice to the fact that Articles 851, 852, 853 and 854 are also relevant (see Annex).

(15) Are the claims in respect of which a ship may be arrested subject to a time bar (or prescription) and, if so, are these different according to the nature of the claim?

The privileged credits which enable the arrest in accordance with the special legal system of the Code of Commerce, independent of the causes determining the extinction of the credit itself, expire for the following reasons:

1. the elapse of the time limit of one year counted from the date upon which the pertinent credits may have originated. This time limit cannot be interrupted or extended in any way, except in favour of a creditor who may have obtained the retention or legal embargo of the assets affected by the privilege, or by a creditor who because of some legal impediment was unable to exercise his privileged credits prior to that date;
2. by the judicial sale of the vessel, whether this is voluntary or forced, as from the date of its inscription in the pertinent register, or after 30 consecutive days counted from the date of the sale, whichever is the lesser; and
3. in the event of voluntary sale of the vessel, 90 consecutive days counted from the date of inscription of the transfer.

What is set down in numbers 2. and 3. above shall be without prejudice to the right of the privileged creditors to exercise their preference over the unpaid balance of the sale price, if any (Article 855).

However, at least as a general rule, the prescription of the credit itself is extinguished in a two-year period (Article 1248 of the Code of Commerce), during which an arrest petitioned in accordance with common law (Code of Civil Procedure) would be in order.

(16) Is it possible to apply for the arrest of a ship outside the normal working hours of the court?

No, it is not. This also applies when trying to lift the arrest.

(17) Please provide any other information which you believe is relevant in deciding whether or not to arrest a ship in your jurisdiction.

(a) It is important to know the lawyers who are likely to arrest since it is possible to avoid arrests or ease the lifting of arrests. Additionally, since Club letters are virtually unknown to Chilean courts, knowing the right lawyers is important.

(b) Fighting arrests: In our experience, Chilean courts are very reluctant to declare arrests wrongful and throw them out of court, leaving the arresting party without any guarantee, particularly if there is a social aspect involved (e.g. in personal injury cases). It is much wiser to grant the guarantee and then fight the arrest deemed to be wrongful: it may take time, but it is less costly to the shipowner and does get results.

We have had experience of one case in which the P & I Club concerned opted for the reverse order and spent nine months fighting unsuccessfully in court: the ship did not sail, the arrest was not declared wrongful (although it clearly was) and the matter was settled out of court.

(c) As expressed above, it is not advisable to petition an arrest in Chile if the principal action must be heard by a foreign tribunal, either ordinary or arbitration.

(d) It is most relevant to bear in mind that the only certain manner to obtain the lifting of the arrest is by supplying, in nature and quantum, precisely the guarantee ordered by the tribunal which, in turn, usually accedes in this sense to what the petitioner of the arrest has requested. However, the tribunal is authorised to qualify the sufficiency of the guarantee offered by the defendant, even if it is not exactly what he was ordered to provide. This must be understood to refer more to its nature than to its quantum. Thus, a tribunal may have ordered that a deposit be made, but, finally, may instead accept a bank guarantee, or otherwise (Article 1236).

(e) Without prejudice to what is stated in (d) above, any petition concerning the amendment, reduction, lifting and objection to the quantum or manner of constituting the guarantee, gives rise to formalities the extent of which is very difficult to specify and which, in fact, may result in maintaining the arrest more or less indefinitely (Articles 1237 and 1238).

(f) Despite the fact that the law expressly states that "the quantum of the guarantee cannot exceed the value of the arrested vessel", we have seen in practice arrests ordered for amounts which exceed the vessel's value. As expressed in (e) above, the petition to reduce the guarantee would give rise to incidental proceedings.

ANNEX

ARTICLES OF BOOK III OF THE CHILEAN CODE OF COMMERCE QUOTED IN THE REPLY TO THE QUESTIONNAIRE

Article 844

The following credits enjoy privilege over the vessel, with preference over the mortgagees and in the order of preference set down hereunder:

1° Legal costs and other disbursements caused by reason of a suit, in the common interest of the creditors, for the preservation of the vessel or for its forced alienation and distribution of the yield;

2° The remunerations and other benefits arising from the contracts of embarkation of the vessel's crew, in accordance with labour norms and civil law which regulate the concurrence of these credits, together with the emoluments paid to the pilots at the service of the vessel.

This privilege shall apply to the indemnities which are due for death or bodily injuries of the servants who survive ashore, on board or in the water, and always provided that they stem from accidents related directly with the trading of the vessel.

3° The charges and rates of ports, channels and navigable waters, together with fiscal charges in respect of signalling and pilotage.

4° The expenses and remunerations due in respect of assistance rendered at sea and general average contributions. This same privilege shall be applied to the reimbursement of expenses and sacrifices incurred by the authority or third parties, in order to prevent or minimize pollution damages or hydrocarbon spills or other contaminating substances to the environment or third party property, when the fund of limitation of liability has not been constituted as established in Title IX of the Law of Navigation, and

5° The indemnities for damages or losses caused to other vessels, to port works, piers or navigable waters or to cargo or luggage, as a consequence of the collision or other accidents during navigation, when the respective action is not susceptible to be founded upon a contract, and the damages in respect of bodily injury to the passengers and crew of these other vessels.

Article 845

Mortgage credits shall be preferred to those detailed in the following article and shall be regulated by the dispositions contained in paragraph 5 of this Title.

This same preference shall be applicable to the secured credits on minor vessels.

Article 846

Moreover, the following shall enjoy privilege over the vessel in the order enumerated, but in subsequent degree to those indicated in article 844:

1° The credits in respect of the sale price, construction, repair and equipping of the vessel;
2° The credits in respect of supply of products or materials, which are indispensable for the trading or conservation of the vessel;
3° The credits arising from contracts of passage money, affreightment or carriage of goods, including the indemnities for damages, slackage and short deliveries in cargo and luggage, and the credits deriving from damages in respect of contamination or the spilling of hydrocarbons or other contaminating substances;
4° The credits in respect of disbursements incurred by the Master, agents or third parties, for account of the owner, for the purpose of trading the vessel, including agency service, and
5° The credits in respect of insurance premiums concerning the vessel, be they hull, machinery or third party liability.

Article 851

The privileged credits of the final voyage have preference over those of preceding voyages even if the latter be of greater degree. However, the credits deriving from a full contract of shipment which comprises several voyages, concur as one single voyage, in the order and place of preference foreseen by article 844, with the other privileged credits originating during the last voyage.

Article 852

The privileged credits arising from one same voyage are preferred in the order set down by articles 844 and 846.

The credits comprised in each of the numbers of the cited articles, shall concur on a pro rata basis in the event of insufficiency of the assets upon which they may fall.

Article 853

In the event of doubt concerning the voyage to which a credit corresponds, the following rules are to apply:

1° For liner vessels which provide regular and pre-established schedules, respect will be given to the numeration or symbol which the owner or carrier may have assigned to the voyage during which the credit was generated.
2° For vessels which conduct full cargo contracts of affreightment it will be understood that the voyage commences from the time the vessel departs to load the cargo and ends upon total discharge at the final place of destination of the vessel;
3° For vessels which conduct tourism cruises, the voyage shall comprise the navigation from the initial port up to the port of termination or until the return of the vessel to the port where the cruise commenced, as indicated in the respective schedule.
4° For fishing vessels or those conducting scientific investigations, it shall be understood that the voyage comprises the duration of the respective expedition.

If it were not possible to apply the preceding rules, the preference to the credits mentioned in articles 844 and 846 shall be determined in each case by the inverse order to the respective dates without distinction of voyages.

Article 854

Credits arising from one same occurrence shall be considered as initiated at the same time.

The credits indicated in No. 4 of article 844 have priority among those in the inverse order to the dates upon which they originated, in the same way as those set down in Nos. 1, 2 and 4 of article 846.

The credits for contribution to general average initiate on the date of the act which brings them into being and the credits for assistance at sea shall be considered as originating on the dates upon which these operations terminated.

CHAPTER 8

CHINA

(1) What are the types of claim for which a ship may be arrested in China?

In China, a ship can be arrested in connection with those claims relating to or resulting from matters concerning a ship's ownership, construction, occupancy right, transport operations, transaction, security and right of mortgage, as well as maritime liens. They are specified as follows:

(1) ship collisions or other accidents;
(2) a result of personal injury or loss of life caused by ships, ship operations or transport undertaking;
(3) damage to sea waters caused by ship pollution;
(4) measures taken to prevent likely pollution or to reduce and eliminate the damaging effect of pollution;
(5) rescue operations undertaken in maritime disasters or salvage and removal of ship wreckage or other sunken or floating objects;
(6) charterparties;
(7) contracts regarding the carriage of goods or passengers;
(8) general average;
(9) towage and pilotage;
(10) supplies to ships or daily essential requirements of food, commodities, materials, fuel, equipment (including containers) and related labour expenses incurred;
(11) payment of port, canal, and channel dues;
(12) the construction, repair, modification and equipping of a ship;
(13) the right to mortgage ships;
(14) marine insurance contracts;
(15) payment of wages of captains and crew members and their social insurance fund expenses;
(16) the payment of ship expenses by captains, owners, bareboat charterers and other charterers or agents;
(17) the payment of ship's commission, service charge and agency fee by the owner, the bareboat charterer or by other representatives on their behalf;
(18) ship ownership or right of occupancy;

(19) issues between common owners of a ship in relation to operations and profit distribution;
(20) ships transaction contracts.

(2) Is there a distinction between claims which give rise to a maritime lien and other types of claim?

The following five items are defined by the Maritime Code of PRC as maritime liens which give the claimant priority in compensation over other claimants:

(1) claims for wages, other remuneration, crew repatriation and social insurance costs made by the master, crew members and other members of the complement in accordance with the relevant labour laws, administrative rules and regulations or labour contracts;
(2) claims in respect of loss of life or personal injury which occur during the operation of the ship;
(3) claims for ship's tonnage dues, pilotage dues, harbour dues and other port charges;
(4) claims for salvage;
(5) claims for loss of or damage to property resulting from a tortious act in the course of the operation of the ship.

Compensation claims for oil pollution damage caused by a ship carrying more than 2,000 tons of oil in bulk as cargo that has a valid certificate attesting that the ship has oil pollution liability insurance coverage or other appropriate financial security are not within the scope of sub-paragraph (5).

In general, the maritime courts make a ruling of arrest of a ship on the basis that if the right of maritime claim is tenable and if the ship can be arrested on the basis of the evidence submitted by the plaintiff, there is no distinction between claims which give rise to a maritime lien and other types of claim.

(3) (a) What pleadings, affidavits and documents must be presented to the court when applying for an arrest and in what language?
(b) Which documents must be notarised or otherwise authenticated?

When a plaintiff is to apply for an arrest before one of the maritime courts in China, he should prepare the following documents in Chinese to present to the court for decision:

(1) the application signed and chopped, which shall contain:
 (i) the plaintiff's name and address, and the legal representative's name
 (ii) the defendant's name and address, and the legal representative's name

(iii) the ship's name (including its name in a foreign language) and nationality;
(iv) the amount of the security and the type of the security currency;
(v) the guarantee clause which indicates that the plaintiff shall be responsible for the losses of the defendant in the case of a wrongful arrest;

(2) all necessary supporting evidence, originals and copies, and if those documents are in a foreign language, a translation version is required;
(3) power of attorney (POA);
(4) certificate of legal representative.

(note: items 3 and 4 shall be duly notarised and shall also be legalised by the local Chinese Consulate Office.)

(5) counter-security shall be submitted to the court so as to guarantee that the plaintiff will be responsible for any losses of the defendant in the event of wrongful arrest.

The claimant may contact Hua Tai to obtain the security issued by PICC against the counter-security provided by their P & I Club or underwriter. A bank guarantee is also acceptable.

(4) Is it possible to arrest a ship solely in order to obtain security for a claim which will ultimately be determined in another jurisdiction?

Yes, a plaintiff can apply to arrest a ship solely in order to obtain security for a claim, even though the competent court is outside China.

(5) What kind of security is normally acceptable to enable the ship to be released from arrest?

The owner of the arrested ship could request their P & I Club or H & M underwriter to contact Hua Tai so as to obtain the security issued by PICC which must be counter-secured by the Club or the underwriter's security. The normal charge is 1 per cent of the security amount.

Security from the China P & I Club and a Chinese bank guarantee is also acceptable.

(6) In what circumstances can a claimant be made to give security and what security is acceptable?

Please refer to the answer to question (3) item (5).

(7) In the event that the arrest was ultimately shown to have been wrongful, can a claim be made for wrongful arrest and what must be established in order to successfully maintain such a claim?

In the event of wrongful arrest, the defendant could raise a claim before the court so as to recover his loss arising from the wrongful arrest, with the necessary supporting evidence. It is not possible to precisely define the grounds for a successful wrongful arrest claim but essentially it must be shown that the arrest was completely misconceived and that the claimant knew and should have known this.

(8) What are the court fees which must be paid in order to make an arrest? Are they recoverable in the event of a successful claim?

The application fee is RMB 5,000, which shall be for the plaintiff's account, and can be recovered from the defendant should the plaintiff's claim prove successful. A deposit may have to be lodged to cover the expenses of guarding the vessel.

(9) How are the lawyers' fees calculated? If possible please estimate the cost of a typical arrest.

Usually, the lawyers' fees for the application are around US$1,000, but this depends on the particular case.

(10) Are all or any part of the lawyers' fees recoverable in the event of a successful arrest?

Even if the plaintiff wins the case through arrest, his lawyers' fees will not be recovered from the defendant.

(11) How quickly can a ship be arrested after the local lawyer is fully instructed?

In urgent cases the arrest can be effected within 24 hours of receipt of instructions.

(12) Is there a minimum amount in dispute for which a ship may be arrested?

No.

(13) Is it possible to arrest a sister ship or a ship in "associated ownership"?

The claimant can also apply to arrest the sister ships currently owned by the owner of the offending vessel. The relevant regulations also allow for the arrest of vessels which are owned, operated or chartered by the responsible operator or charterer.

Although it appears that the claimant is given a wide right of arrest by the regulations in this respect, the ship cannot be sold if the responsible party refuses to present security after the arrest and so a stalemate can arise. The safer view is that the regulations only apply where the operator is a state-owned enterprise or the charterer is a bareboat charterer.

In the case of a maritime claim relating to ownership, mortgage and ship's management or income distribution only the offending vessel can be arrested; there is no right of sister ship arrest.

(14) What is the order of priorities in the event of the distribution by the court of the proceeds of sale of ship?

The order is maritime lien, possessory liens, claims under a mortgage, and then common maritime rights.

The maritime claims set out in answer to question (2) shall be satisfied in the order listed. However, any of the maritime claims set out in item (4) arising later than those under items (1) to (3) shall have priority over those under items (1) to (3). In case there are more than two maritime claims under items (1), (2), (3) or (5), they shall be satisfied at the same time regardless of their respective occurrences; where they could not be paid in full, they shall be paid pro rata. Should there be more than two maritime claims under item (4), those arising later shall be satisfied first.

Furthermore, the legal costs for enforcing the maritime liens, the expenses for preserving and selling the ship, the expenses for distribution of the proceeds of sale and other expenses incurred for the common interests of the claimants, shall be deducted and paid first from the proceeds of the auction sale of the ship.

(15) Are the claims in respect of which a ship may be arrested subject to a time bar (or prescription) and, if so, are these different according to the nature of the claim?

Yes, normal time bars apply, such as one year for a cargo claim and two years for a collision claim. Time extensions are not recognised by the Chinese courts.

(16) Is it possible to apply for the arrest of a ship outside the normal working hours of the court?

The application for arrest of a ship should be made within the normal working hours of the court. A five-day working week now applies in China. However, in urgent cases the court may, at its discretion, execute the arrest outside normal working hours.

CHAPTER 9

DENMARK

(1) What are the types of claim for which a ship may be arrested in Denmark?

Denmark is a party to the International Convention for the Unification of Certain Rules Relating to the Arrest of Sea-Going Ships, Brussels, 10 May 1952 and a similar set of rules relating to the arrest of ships has been incorporated into chapter 4 of the Danish Merchant Shipping Act of 16 March 1994, sections 91 to 96.

The claim must fall within the listed maritime claims in Article 1 of the Brussels Convention.

(2) Is there a distinction between claims which give rise to a maritime lien and other types of claim?

In addition to being a claim for which a ship may be arrested in Danish law the following claims are secured by maritime liens on a ship:

(a) wages and other payment due to the master and other members of the crew in respect of their service on board the ship;
(b) port, canal and other waterway dues and pilotage dues;
(c) claims for damages in respect of personal injury occurring in direct connection with the operation of the ship;
(d) claims for damages in respect of damage to property occurring in direct connection with the operation of the ship provided that such claim is not founded in contract;
(e) claims in respect of salvage, removal of wreck and general average contributions.

A maritime lien on a ship is only extinguished after a period of one year from the time when the lien arose. In order to make the limitation cease to run, the ship must be arrested before the expiry of the time limit and the arrest must be followed by a forced sale if not solved amicably. The time limit shall not run if the lien holder is prevented by law from arresting the ship, but otherwise it is not possible to suspend or interrupt the time limit.

(3) (a) What pleadings, affidavits and documents must be presented to the court when applying for an arrest and in what language?

The court will exercise its discretion as to whether or not a claim exists. There are no special requirements in connection with documents which must be presented to the courts. The application to the court must be in the Danish language and in practice a photocopy, a telefax or a telex will be sufficient to evidence the claim. In principle, the documents in support of the claim must be translated into Danish as the legal language in Denmark is Danish. Documents in the English language may, however, be accepted.

(b) Which documents must be notarised or otherwise authenticated?

The documents need not be notarised nor otherwise authenticated.

A notarised power of attorney from the claimant to the lawyer is not necessary in the Danish legal system.

(4) Is it possible to arrest a ship solely in order to obtain security for a claim which will ultimately be determined in another jurisdiction?

Yes, Danish courts will permit arrest solely for the acquisition of appropriate security, but only for maritime claims and with respect to Article 3, subsection 3 of the Brussels Convention.

The Danish courts will respect any agreed venue, but will always have the right to decide on the lawfulness of the arrest.

(5) What kind of security is normally acceptable to enable the ship to be released from arrest?

An arrest may be staved off or lifted if the debtor provides security for the claim with the addition of outstanding and estimated interest plus likely costs of the arrest proceedings, the subsequent case to validate the claim and arrest, and the case concerning the claim. It is at the discretion of the court to determine whether the security is sufficient.

Last, but not least, jurisdictions will accept a P & I Club letter of guarantee. A bank guarantee must be from a Danish bank. Invariably, the parties agree between themselves the security to be deposited.

(6) In what circumstances can a claimant be made to give security and what security is acceptable?

The bailiff court may ask for counter-security from the claimant and in practice they always do. When the application is filed with the bailiff, the bailiff is entitled to demand security for the damage or inconvenience that the debtor may suffer in connection with the arrest. As a point of departure such an amount shall not exceed an amount equivalent to five days loss of hire for the ship. In case of uncertainty about the hire the claimant may substantiate the loss of hire by means of a declaration from a shipbroker or the like about the daily hire that the ship must be presumed to earn if it had been chartered out on a time charter. The bailiff court may, however, fix the security at an amount higher than that of five days loss of hire in the event that the debtor is capable of substantiating that the loss is considerably higher.

(7) In the event that the arrest was ultimately shown to have been wrongful, can a claim be made for wrongful arrest and what must be established in order to successfully maintain such a claim?

If the court has found the arrest to be wrongful a claim for damages will only succeed if all other conditions for liability to pay damages have been proven.

(8) What are the court fees which must be paid in order to make an arrest? Are they recoverable in the event of a successful claim?

The court fees are DKK 300 plus one half a per cent of the claimed amount in excess of DKK 3,000 and they are recoverable. (Hence the fact that the fees are normally added to the claim and included in the security given to enable the ship to be released from arrest.)

(9) How are the lawyers' fees calculated? If possible please estimate the cost of a typical arrest.

The lawyers' fees are normally calculated at the prevailing hourly rate.

In addition to court fees and lawyers' fees there are the fees to the bailiff who boards the vessel. These are DKK 400 plus taxi expenses which will also be charged to the debtor. Other expenses might be technical assistance to remove a vital part of the machinery in order to prevent the vessel from escaping arrest. The costs of a typical arrest excluding negotiations with the debtor are approximately DKK 30,000.

(10) Are all or any part of the lawyers' fees recoverable in the event of a successful arrest?

The lawyers' fees are recoverable, however, it remains in the discretion of the court to decide thereon.

(11) How quickly can a ship be arrested after the local lawyer is fully instructed?

The speed with which a ship may be arrested depends on the discretion of the bailiff who may sometimes claim insufficient capacity to expedite the arrest.

In the major maritime jurisdictions and provided the bailiff is put on alert, the arrest may take place the same day the application is filed or the following day.

(12) Is there a minimum amount in dispute for which a ship may be arrested?

There is no minimum amount in dispute for which a ship may be arrested.

(13) Is it possible to arrest a sister ship or a ship in "associated ownership"?

Yes, arrest of ships can be made on any other ship owned by the party owning the ship with which the claim is concerned at the time of the occurrence of the claim. Ships will have the same owner when all parts in the ship belong to the same person or persons notwithstanding any difference in the amount or the distribution of the parts.

Arrest may not be made on ships upon which execution cannot be levied to satisfy a claim; thus, where the owner of the ship is not liable for the claim, arrest will be possible only where the claim is guaranteed by maritime lien.

(14) What is the order of priorities in the event of the distribution by the court of the proceeds of sale of the ship?

The order of priorities when the court distributes the proceeds of sale of the ship in public auction are:

(1) costs related to the auction.
(2) maritime liens.
(3) registered mortgages.
(4) registered executions.
(5) ordinary creditors.

(15) Are the claims in respect of which a ship may be arrested subject to a time bar (or prescription) and if so are these different according to the nature of the claim?

Yes, claims are subject to time bar according to their nature. The general time bar in Danish law is five years. The Danish Merchant Shipping Act has a set of rules of time bar for maritime claims: cargo claims one year, collision and salvage claims two years, personal injury claims two years to mention the most relevant types of maritime claims.

(16) Is it possible to apply for the arrest of a ship outside the normal working hours of the court?

If the bailiff receives the request within office hours the ship may be arrested after normal working hours including weekends.

(17) Please provide any other information which you believe is relevant in deciding whether or not to arrest a ship in your jurisdiction

The rules relating to the arrest of ships require that the vessel is physicallypresent and physically banned from sailing. Pursuant to the rules of the Administration of Justice Act a claimant may issue an interim injunction on a vessel in order to provide security for a maritime claim, without the ship being banned from sailing. This is relevant if what the claimant wishes is a bailiff's decree that may be registered in the Ships Register and will thus obtain protection against *bona fide* agreements, transferees and creditors.

If the parties do not agree to waive the action to justify the arrest it follows from the Danish Administration of Justice Act that proceedings concerning the claim must be instituted within two weeks of the arrest at the accepted venue, and action to justify the arrest must be brought in Denmark within the same time limit. The Danish court is under obligation to stay the case until the decision of a foreign court is available, apart from the issue of the lawfulness of the arrest, which may be decided immediately.

CHAPTER 10

EGYPT

(1) What are the types of claim for which a ship may be arrested in Egypt?

Pursuant to the Egyptian Maritime Code (promulgated by Act No. 8 of 1990) there are two types of arrest of vessels:

1. Conservatory arrest (Sections 59–66 of the Code). This aims at obtaining security from the shipowner to safeguard the claimant's interests in a maritime claim. A ship may be arrested under this procedure only in respect of any maritime claim (Section 60). Maritime claims are the same as determined in Article 1 of the International Convention for the Unification of Certain Rules Relating to the Arrest of Sea-Going Ships 1952 plus claims for expenses in the removal of wrecks.
2. Executory arrest (Sections 67–77 of the Code). This is done in order to obtain satisfaction of a court order or judgment ending in the sale of the vessel at public auction.

(2) Is there a distinction between claims which give rise to a maritime lien and other types of claim?

Sections 29–40 of the Code deal with rules relating to maritime liens. The claims which give rise to liens are almost identical to those enumerated in the 1926 Brussels Convention on Maritime Liens and Mortgages. The claims enjoying maritime liens rank in priority to other types of claim and are also secured by a lien that follows the subject vessel into whatever hands it may pass.

(3) (a) What pleadings, affidavits and documents must be presented to the court when applying for an arrest and in what language?
(b) Which documents must be notarised or otherwise authenticated?

An order of the court must be obtained from the president of the competent court having appropriate jurisdiction. This will be the court in the port where the subject vessel is anchored.

The legal proceedings consist of an application for the conservatory arrest explaining the subject matter of the maritime claim and justifying the urgency of adequate security being placed by the vessel. Supporting documents substantiating the claim must be annexed and the application must be in Arabic. If the documentation is in another language a certified Arabic translation must also be filed.

Documents notarised or otherwise authenticated abroad should also be counter-signed at the nearest Egyptian Consulate.

The judge acts on the application for the conservatory arrest *ex parte* and at his own discretion, fixing the amount of the subject claim in respect of which the arrest order has been granted. In order to receive the executory copy of the order from the Court Registry, the applicant's lawyer has to present a fully legalised power of attorney duly given by his principal/claimant.

(4) Is it possible to arrest a ship solely in order to obtain security for a claim which will ultimately be determined in another jurisdiction?

This is a controversial question and Section 65 of the Code requires that the claimant, within eight days of enforcing the order of arrest, must file a case giving details of the substantive claim and validity of the arrest. The claimant may then commence legal proceedings before the competent Egyptian court. On the first hearing of the case he may then request suspension of such proceedings pending the eventual conclusion of the dispute in the jurisdiction already agreed by the parties. The above procedure is unnecessary where the shipowner provides adequate security for lifting the arrest.

(5) What kind of security is normally acceptable to enable the ship to be released from arrest?
(6) In which circumstances can a claimant be made to give security and what security is acceptable?

To enable the ship to be released from arrest, security is normally acceptable in the form of an irrevocable bank guarantee covering the total amount of the claim or in the form of a P & I undertaking if agreed by the claimant.

(7) In the event that the arrest was ultimately shown to have been wrongful, can a claim be made for wrongful arrest and what must be established in order to successfully maintain such a claim?

In the event that the arrest was eventually found to have been wrongful, a claim for damages can be made by the shipowner, either by way of a counter-claim in the substantive proceedings before the Egyptian court or by separate legal proceedings.

In such a case the shipowner must establish that the arrest was entirely unjustified, done in bad faith and/or based on false documents. Damages claimed will comprise the loss of the use of the vessel during the period of arrest, direct losses *vis-à-vis* a third party as a consequence of the arrest, bank charges for the security provided in order to lift the arrest, etc.

(8) What are the court fees which must be paid in order to make an arrest? Are they recoverable in the event of a successful claim?

The court fees that must be paid in order to make an arrest will not exceed 100 Egyptian pounds. Consequently it is unnecessary to make a recovery in the event of a successful claim. However, once the court makes a decision on the substantive claim in favour of the claimant, court fees will be charged to the shipowner at the rate of 7.5 per cent on the amount awarded by the court to the claimant.

(9) How are the lawyers' fees calculated? If possible please estimate the costs of a typical arrest.

According to Egyptian law and practice the following factors are taken into consideration in calculating the lawyers' fees:

1. the lawyers' services rendered from commencement until conclusion.
2. the amount claimed.
3. the amount ultimately awarded.
4. the time spent in attending legal proceedings, trial hearings and attendance in court.
5. the standard and prestige of the law office instructed.

A payment on account of fees is made when instructions are first given to the lawyer. Further interim payments are made during the proceedings both at first instance and on appeal. Any further proceedings to the Supreme Court of Egypt ("Cassation") will be charged separately in advance, due to the fact that such proceedings are very protracted.

(10) Are all or any part of the lawyers' fees recoverable in the event of a successful arrest?

Lawyers' fees are not recoverable from the defendant in the event of a successful arrest enforced in Egypt.

(11) How quickly can a ship be arrested after the local lawyer is fully instructed?

Arrest proceedings are expeditious by nature, and are dealt with promptly.

Once a local lawyer is fully instructed, and the relevant documents are received from the claimant and duly translated, and in view of the natural urgency to act as soon as possible before the vessel sails from Egyptian waters, a diligent lawyer may well be ready to apply for the arrest within two days.

The application having been properly presented to the competent court and in accordance with the Egyptian Code of Procedure, the president/judge of the court will decide whether to grant the arrest order (or reject the application) within 24 hours.

(12) Is there a minimum amount in dispute for which a ship may be arrested?

There is no minimum amount in dispute for which a ship may be arrested, but such amount must be reasonably substantial to justify the arrest.

However, in cases of claims by crewmen, the amount(s) of wages or injury compensation, albeit small, will allow the arrest of the vessel.

(13) Is it possible to arrest a sister ship or a ship in "associated ownership"?

According to Section 61 of the Code, a claimant (in respect of a maritime claim) may arrest a sister ship owned by the same debtor provided she has been in his ownership at the time when the claim arose. Exceptions to this are claims arising out of disputes relating to the ownership of a ship, disputes between co-owners as to the ownership or possession of a ship and the mortgage of a ship.

(14) What is the order of priorities in the event of the distribution by the court of the proceeds of sale of the ship?

In accordance with Section 76 of the Code the "executory judge" will order the distribution of the sale proceeds of the ship, applying the pertinent Arts. in the Egyptian Code of Procedure (473–480). The priority of lien claims over the "general creditors" will then be complied with.

(15) Are the claims in respect of which a ship may be arrested subject to a time bar (or prescription) and, if so, are these different according to the nature of the claim?

The maritime claims in respect of which a ship may be arrested are subject to time bar(s) or prescriptions according to the particular case and the applicable law.

Under Egyptian law, the prescription period, as applicable to the particular case, is interrupted by making the arrest and/or filing the substantive claim; a new period equal to the initial one will then run.

(16) Is it possible to apply for the arrest of a ship outside the normal working hours of the court?

It is quite rare, albeit feasible, to apply for the arrest of a ship outside the normal working hours of the court, provided the court fees have already been paid.

CHAPTER 11

ENGLAND AND WALES

(1) What are the types of claim for which a ship may be arrested in England and Wales?

A ship may be arrested in England and Wales for any claim for which Admiralty proceedings *in rem* may be commenced. The Admiralty jurisdiction of the English High Court is set out in section 20 of the Supreme Court Act 1981 and the mode of exercise of that jurisdiction is set out in section 21 of that Act; see below:

20(2).(a) any claim to the possession or ownership of a ship or to the ownership of any share therein;

(b) any question arising between the co-owners of a ship as to possession, employment or earnings of that ship;

(c) any claim in respect of a mortgage of or charge on a ship or any share therein;

(d) any claim for damage done by a ship;

(e) any claim for loss of life or personal injury sustained in consequence of any defect in a ship or in her apparel or equipment, or in consequence of the wrongful act, neglect or default of:

(i) the owners, charterers or persons in possession or control of a ship; or

(ii) the master or crew of a ship, or any other person for whose wrongful acts, neglects or defaults the owners, charterers or persons in possession or control of a ship are responsible;

being an act, neglect or default in the navigation or management of the ship, in the loading, carriage or discharge of goods on, in or from the ship, or in the embarkation, carriage disembarkation of persons on, in or from the ship;

(f) any claim for loss of or damage to goods carried in a ship;

(g) any claim arising out of any agreement relating to the carriage of goods in a ship or to the use or hire of a ship;

(h) any claim in the nature of salvage (including any claim arising by virtue of the application, by or under [section 87 of the Civil Aviation Act 1982], of the law relating to salvage of aircraft and their apparel and cargo);

(j) any claim in the nature of towage in respect of a ship or an aircraft;

(k) any claim in the nature of pilotage in respect of a ship or an aircraft;

(l) any claim in respect of goods or materials supplied to a ship for her operation or maintenance;

(m) any claim in respect of the construction, repair or equipment of a ship or in respect of dock charges or dues;

(n) any claim by a master or member of the crew of a ship for wages (including any sum allotted out of wages or adjudged by a superintendent to be due by way of wages);
(o) any claim by a master, shipper, charterer or agent in respect of disbursements made on account of a ship;
(p) any claim arising out of an act which is or is claimed to be a general average act;
(q) any claim arising out of bottomry;
(r) any claim for the forfeiture or condemnation of ship or of goods which are being or have been carried, or have been attempted to be carried, in a ship, or for the restoration of a ship or any such goods after seizure, or for droits of Admiralty.

(2) Is there a distinction between claims which give rise to a maritime lien and other types of claim?

Claims which give rise to a maritime lien, i.e. for damage done by a ship, salvage, master's wages and disbursements, and seamen's wages, together with any claim to the possession or ownership of a ship or a share in the ship, any question arising between the co-owners of a ship as to possession, employment or earnings of that ship, any claim in respect of a mortgage or charge on a ship or any share therein, and any claim for the forfeiture or condemnation of a ship or for the restoration of a ship are the only claims which can be considered to be truly *in rem*. In such cases an arrest is available against the ship concerned irrespective of who may be liable on the claim *in personam* and irrespective of ownership of the vessel at the time the action is commenced, so that the action remains against the ship even if there has been a change or changes of ownership since the cause of action arose.

Theoretically a claim for bottomry carries a maritime lien but in practice is more or less obsolete.

The remainder of the claims for which a vessel can be arrested are limited by considerations of ownership. In such cases it is necessary to show that the person who would be liable on the claim if sued personally was the owner or the charterer or in possession or control of the ship when the cause of action arose, *and* at the time the writ is issued is the beneficial owner of all the shares in the ship against which the action is brought, or is the demise charterer of it.

Therefore if there has been a change of ownership since the cause of action arose this would defeat the claim. Similarly in situations where, although there has been no change in ownership, the person liable for the claim would in fact have been the charterer of the vessel, if that charter has come to an end before proceedings are commenced then that too would mean that an action *in rem* could not be brought against the ship and therefore she could not be arrested. In such cases the only remedy for the claimant is to bring his action *in personam* against the person responsible.

(3)(a) What pleadings, affidavits and documents must be presented to the court when applying for an arrest and in what language?

The pleadings, etc., which need to be presented to either the Admiralty Registry or the Admiralty District Registry outside London, together with necessary copies, are as follows:

(i) Writ of Summons;
(ii) Acknowledgement of Service of Writ;
(iii) Warrant of Arrest;
(iv) Request for Service of the Writ by the Admiralty Marshal;
(v) Request that the Marshal executes the Warrant of Arrest incorporating the personal undertaking to pay the fees of the Admiralty Marshal in respect of the arrest and care of the ship whilst under arrest;
(vi) An affidavit in support of the arrest, which will vary to some extent depending upon the type of claim being brought, e.g. whether it gives rise to a maritime lien or not and whether the ship to be arrested is the ship in connection with which the claim arose or whether it is a sister ship. This affidavit can be and usually is sworn by the solicitor representing the arresting party. All the documentation presented to the court should be in English.

(b) Which documents must be notarised or otherwise authenticated?

It is not necessary for any documentation to be notarised or otherwise authenticated.

(4) Is it possible to arrest a ship solely in order to obtain security for a claim which will ultimately be determined in another jurisdiction?

Yes it is possible to arrest the ship solely in order to obtain security for a claim which will ultimately be determined in another jurisdiction, provided that the claim gives rise to a right of action *in rem* as in the answer to question (1) above, so that if for some reason the claim is not progressed in another jurisdiction it can be progressed through to a final hearing in the English courts. If the matter is taken up elsewhere then the English proceedings can be stayed.

(5) What kind of security is normally acceptable to enable the ship to be released from arrest?

The only method of security provided by the rules of the English High Court is by way of bail bond, but in practice, and subject of course to the agreement of the arresting party, a suitably worded letter of guarantee by a bank, P & I Club or insurance company is the normal method of giving security to effect release. It should be borne in mind that the amount of the security should be sufficient to cover not only the claim but also interest and costs, which would have to be estimated, but which would be based on the matter progressing to a contested hearing.

(6) In what circumstances can a claimant be made to give security and what security is acceptable?

It is not necessary for a claimant to give security.

(7) In the event that the arrest was ultimately shown to have been wrongful, can a claim be made for wrongful arrest and what must be established in order to successfully maintain such a claim?

Even if the arrest is ultimately shown to have been wrongful, a counter-claim for damages for wrongful arrest can only be successful if the counter-claimant can establish *mala fides* on the part of the arresting party.

(8) What are the court fees which must be paid in order to make an arrest? Are they recoverable in the event of a successful claim?

At present the court fees are £120 for the issue of the writ and £100 for the warrant of arrest. There will also be a fee for swearing the affidavit in support of the arrest which presently stands at £5 for the affidavit plus £3.50 for each exhibit. Where ownership needs to be established this is usually done by means of a fax from either Lloyd's Maritime Information Services or the RSS at Cardiff in relation to a fishing vessel and there is a fee to be paid for such a search, which fee currently stands at £117 plus VAT by Lloyd's, rather less from the RSS. A personal undertaking has to be given by the solicitor for the above fees and expenses, which together with solicitors' costs, are added to the amount claimed and should be recoverable in the event of a successful claim.

(9) How are the lawyers' fees calculated? If possible please estimate the costs of a typical arrest.

Lawyers' fees are on a time basis with an uplift for care and control which varies according to the nature of the claim. As it is often the case that instructions to arrest need to be dealt with as a matter of extreme urgency, and taking into account the fact that the solicitors give a personal undertaking in relation to the Admiralty Marshal's charges, etc., a premium rate often has to be charged. Typical costs for a relatively straightforward arrest of a ship in a provincial District Registry would be some £700 to £800 plus disbursements, and VAT if applicable. However, if there are any

complicating factors which involve a greater than normal amount of time, higher charges can be expected. It is likely that the costs will be considerably more if the matter is dealt with in London.

(10) Are all or any part of the lawyers' fees recoverable in the event of a successful arrest?

Lawyers' fees are not necessarily recoverable in the event of a successful arrest *per se*. If a judgment is obtained then it is normal to also receive an order for costs which are then claimed against the owner of the vessel or the guarantor. If the vessel is sold by the court and there is an application for payment out of the funds in court, the costs of arrest have a high priority. If costs cannot be agreed between the parties they have to be taxed by the court.

(11) How quickly can a ship be arrested after the local lawyer is fully instructed?

Usually, the documentation can be presented to the court within a couple of hours or so of receiving full instructions, but it should be borne in mind that the court offices are only open between 10 a.m. and 4 p.m. Monday to Friday. Although an Admiralty writ *in rem* can be issued and served outside those hours, arrest proceedings cannot.

(12) Is there a minimum amount in dispute for which a ship may be arrested?

Whilst there is technically no minimum amount for which a ship may be arrested small claims would proceed in one of the county courts. See later.

(13) Is it possible to arrest a sister ship or a ship in "associated ownership"?

It is possible in certain cases to arrest a sister ship but a number of conditions have to be satisfied, namely that the claim must have arisen in connection with a ship; that the person who would be liable on the claim in an action *in personam*, must have been the owner or the charterer or in possession or control of that ship when the cause of action arose; and at the time the writ is issued that person must be the beneficial owner of all the shares in the ship against which the action is brought, i.e. the sister ship.

(14) What is the order of priorities in the event of the distribution by the court of the proceeds of sale of the ship?

First charge on the proceeds of sale of the ship when sold by the court are the Admiralty Marshal's costs and expenses of effecting and maintaining the arrest and of arranging for the ship to be sold. Priority is then granted to the original arrestor in respect of his costs of the arrest and then the costs of the party who obtained the order for appraisement and sale (if different to the arrestor).

As far as the competing claims are concerned, a maritime lien takes first priority followed by possessory liens, e.g. repairers who have surrendered their lien to the Admiralty Marshal, then mortgages or other charges, then finally claims which give rise to statutory liens only. Claims in this latter category rank *pari passu.*

(15) Are the claims in respect of which a ship may be arrested subject to a time bar (or prescription) and, if so, are these different according to the nature of the claim?

There are differing time limits according to the nature of the claim, e.g. there is a one-year time limit in respect of cargo claims under the Hague-Visby Rules, a two-year time limit for cargo claims under the Hamburg Rules and claims by passengers for loss of life, injury or baggage damage against the carrying ship, and claims under the Maritime Convention Act 1911 also have a two-year time limit. Most claims which carry a statutory lien such as repairs and goods supplied, etc., carry the normal six-year time limit but of course since these are subject to the ownership requirements as already indicated, the longer such a claim is left the more chance there is of ownership having changed or the charter having come to an end.

(16) Is it possible to apply for the arrest of a ship outside the normal working hours of the court?

Although it is possible to issue and serve an Admiralty writ *in rem* outside the normal working hours, it is not possible to apply for the arrest of the vessel outside normal court hours.

(17) Please provide any other information which you believe is relevant in deciding whether or not to arrest a ship in your jurisdiction.

Most claims can be brought in the Admiralty division of the High Court in which case the proceedings can be commenced in the Admiralty Court in London or in any District Registry having Admiralty jurisdiction, irrespective of where the vessel is situated in England and Wales; for example, the action and arrest proceedings can be commenced in the Kingston upon Hull District Registry even if the ship is berthed in Liverpool, Southampton, King's Lynn, etc. However, small claims may have to be commenced in the county court and in such cases those proceedings have to be commenced in the county court which has Admiralty jurisdiction for the district in which the vessel is lying. The procedure and cost is similar to that of the High Court, and the county courts have jurisdiction over most of the matters but not claims relating to the ship itself such as ownership disputes, disputes regarding possession, earnings or employment of a ship, mortgages, general average, bottomry, or claims for forfeiture or condemnation of a ship or goods.

One of the major considerations in deciding whether or not to arrest a ship is, of course, whether the judgment is likely to be satisfied. This is particularly relevant for claimants with only statutory liens, i.e. repairers, suppliers, etc., as very often vessels are subject to mortgages or other charges which equal or even exceed the actual value of the vessel. Therefore even if a judgment is obtained and the vessel is sold by the court the repayment of the mortgage and other priority claims may well extinguish the funds in court.

CHAPTER 12

FRANCE

(1) What are the types of claim for which a ship may be arrested in France?

Since France has ratified the Brussels Convention dated 10 May 1952 on arrest of sea-going ships, the types of claims for which a ship may be arrested will depend on whether or not the ship flies the flag of a country which has ratified the above-mentioned Brussels Convention.

(a) Ship flying the flag of a state which has ratified the Brussels Convention of 10 May 1952

According to Article 2 of the Convention the ship can be arrested *only* for a maritime claim as defined in Article 1 of the Convention.

(b) Ship not flying the flag of a state which has ratified the Brussels Convention of 10 May 1952

According to Article 8 of the Brussels Convention, the ship may be arrested for claims for which it can be arrested under French domestic legislation.

French domestic legislation considers a ship like any other moveable asset and therefore entitles a claimant to arrest a ship for *any type of claim* (maritime or non-maritime).

(2) Is there a distinction between claims which give rise to a maritime lien and other types of claims?

The distinction between claims which give rise to a maritime lien and ordinary claims is that the claims secured by a maritime lien are paid on the ship proceeds in priority to the mortgage and to ordinary claims when the ship is sold by court auction.

Also when the ship is sold by its owners where the claim secured by a maritime lien has not been paid, the claimant can still arrest the ship to get payment of his secured claim, since "the claims secured by a maritime lien follow the vessel into whatever hands it may pass" (*cf.* Article 8 of the Brussels Convention dated 10 April 1926, Art. 39 of a French law dated 3 January 1967).

The claims secured by a maritime lien are those listed in Article 2 of the

Brussels Convention dated 10 April 1926 on Maritime Liens and Mortgages which has been ratified by France.

According to its Article 14, this International Convention applies in each Contracting State when the ship flies the flag of a state which has ratified it.

The provisions of this International Convention have been incorporated into French domestic law (Articles 31 to 41 of the law dated 3 January 1967).

The claims which give rise to a maritime lien are:

1. law costs due to the State, and expenses incurred in the common interest of the creditors in order to preserve the vessel or procure its sale and the distribution of the proceeds of sale; tonnage dues, lights or harbour dues, and other public taxes and charges of the same character; pilotage dues, the cost of watching and preservation from the time of entry of the vessel into the last port;
2. claims arising out of the contract of engagement of the master, crew, and other persons hired on board;
3. remuneration for assistance and salvage, and the contribution of the vessel in general average;
4. indemnities for collision or other accident of navigation, as also for damage caused to works forming part of harbours, docks, and navigable ways; indemnities for personal injuries to passengers or crew; indemnities for loss of or for damage to cargo or baggage;
5. claims resulting from contracts entered into or acts done by the master, acting within the scope of his authority, away from the vessel's home port, where such contracts or acts are necessary for the preservation of the vessel or the continuation of its voyage, whether the master is or is not at the same time owner of the vessel and whether the claim is his own or that of ship chandlers, repairers, lenders, or other contractual creditors.

There is also under French law a lien, which does not exist in the International Convention of 10 April 1926. This lien is provided by Art. 12 of French law dated 3 January 1969.

It secures the ship agent's claim for disbursements paid outside the port of registry of the vessel.

This claim is secured by the same lien as is provided at Art. 31-6 of the law dated 3 January 1967, which secures the claims arising from contracts entered into by the master outside the vessel's home port for the continuation of the voyage or for the preservation of the vessel.

(3) (a) What pleadings, affidavits and documents must be presented to the court when applying for an arrest and in what language?

A petition to arrest the ship must be made to the President of the Commercial Court of the vessel's port of call.

The petition is presented *ex parte* by the claimant's lawyer, who explains why the arrest is sought and also the meaning of the documents supporting the arrest petition.

The arrest is authorised when the claim is sufficiently proven by the documents disclosed by the petitioner.

The documents needed to arrest a ship are those evidencing the claim (such as contracts, invoices, letters requesting payment, etc.).

Most Presidents of French Commercial Courts (who are not professional magistrates but businessmen and, for that reason, often conversant in English) will not request a translation of these documents when they are in English.

However, when the supporting documents are in other languages a translation may be requested. In that case, an office translation will suffice.

(b) Which documents must be notarised or otherwise authenticated?

Documents need not be notarised or otherwise authenticated in France.

(4) Is it possible to arrest a ship solely in order to obtain security for a claim which will ultimately be determined in another jurisdiction?

The answer is yes.

(5) What kind of security is normally acceptable to enable the ship to be released from arrest?

Normally a bank guarantee given by a French bank is requested to release the ship from arrest.

However, if the lawyer acting for the arresting party is familiar with maritime practices, he will accept a guarantee given by the major P & I Clubs.

(6) In what circumstances can a claimant be made to give security and what security is acceptable?

Though French domestic law provides the possibility to request a claimant to give security, this possibility is very rarely used in France.

(7) In the event that the arrest was ultimately shown to have been wrongful, can a claim be made for wrongful arrest and what must be established in order to successfully maintain such a claim?

The rule prevailing under French law is that the right to sue or to arrest property can amount to a wrongful act which entitles the party who has been sued or whose property has been arrested to claim compensation, but only in cases of malice, bad faith, or gross error equivalent to wilful misrepresentation.

On account of that rule, it is extremely rare that French courts grant damages for wrongful arrest.

(8) What are the court fees which must be paid in order to make an arrest? Are they recoverable in the event of a successful claim?

The court fees are minimal, in the region of FF 500.

The claimant must however pay the costs and fees of the bailiff who will serve the arrest upon the vessel's master or the ship agent and also upon the Port Authorities and Customs, since the notification of the arrest to the above-mentioned persons and public bodies is a requirement of French law.

The costs and fees of the bailiff are proportional to the amount for which the ship is arrested.

The court costs and costs and fees of the bailiff are recoverable if and when the substantive proceedings are instituted in France, which is the only time when the claimant can request the French court to order the shipowner to pay these costs.

(9) How are the lawyers' fees calculated? If possible please estimate the costs of a typical arrest.

Usually the lawyers' fees are calculated on an hourly basis. It must be said that when a lawyer is instructed to arrest a ship he must usually act with the utmost urgency and thus temporarily abandon any other work.

A typical ship arrest will last at least two days since the lawyer must confer with the client in order to decide which documents are needed for the arrest, study the documents supporting the claim, draft the arrest petition, present the arrest petition, and once the arrest is served upon the vessel, discuss with the lawyer acting for the shipowner the terms and conditions of the letter of guarantee to be posted to release the ship from arrest.

If the shipowner resists the arrest and enters summary proceedings to have the arrest lifted, the time spent will be increased since defence pleadings will have to be filed to fight such an application and oral argument will take place before the President of the Commercial Court who authorised the arrest.

If the application fails, more time will be spent on negotiating the wording of the bank guarantee substituting the arrest of the ship.

We would estimate the costs of a typical arrest to be in the region of FF 20,000/25,000 to which should be added the above-mentioned costs and fees of the bailiff.

(10) Are all or any part of the lawyers' fees recoverable in the event of a successful arrest?

If the arrest alone leads to a payment the lawyer could be entitled to a success fee which would depend on the amount at stake; this success fee should be discussed and agreed with the client.

(11) How quickly can a ship be arrested after the local lawyer is fully instructed?

Usually the ship is arrested within two or three hours after the local lawyer has been fully instructed. It can take less time in a case of extreme urgency depending on the availability of the President of the Commercial Court who rules on the arrest.

(12) Is there a minimum amount in dispute for which a ship may be arrested?

Legally speaking there is no minimum amount for which a vessel can be arrested. In practice, however, the President of the Commercial Court concerned will hesitate to authorise the arrest if the claim is for less than FF 20,000.

In that case, the judge may request the claimant to contact the local ship agent in order to persuade him to give security or pay the claim, failing which the arrest could be granted.

In such cases the simple threat to arrest usually produces a positive reaction from the shipowner.

(13) Is it possible to arrest a sister ship or a ship in "associated ownership"?

It is of course possible to arrest another ship belonging to the same owner to secure a claim against the common owner of the ships.

Moreover, French jurisprudence has developed the possibility to arrest a ship, even if the claim does not relate to that ship, if it belongs to the same "beneficial" or "associated" owner.

To illustrate this possibility, a typical example is where a Panamanian company describes itself in the Lloyd's Register of Ships or Lloyd's Confidential Index or other similar publications as the "manager" of several ships, listed under its name; each ship belongs to different Panamanian companies, whose shareholders are also the shareholders of the company managing the ships.

In such a case, French courts have decided that the Panamanian companies have no real autonomy and that in reality all the shipowning companies belong to the same persons with the consequence that any ship belonging to these "associated companies" can be arrested to secure the debt incurred by any of the "associated companies".

In such a case, if substantive proceedings have been instituted in France to claim payment, the court will order the "associated" company to pay the claim severally with the company owning the ship on which the claim arose.

This was decided by the Court of Appeal of Aix en Provence in a case concerning the vessel *Irini M* by judgment dated 19 February 1988. This judgment was approved by the Cour de Cassation (French Supreme Court) by judgment dated 28 November 1989.

(14) What is the order of priorities in the event of the distribution by the court of the proceeds of sale of the ship?

The law of 3 January 1967 or the Brussels Convention of 10 April 1926 on

Maritime Liens and Mortgages when applicable gives the order of priorities in the event of the distribution by the court of the proceeds of sale of the ship.

The order of priorities is mentioned in the answer to question (2) above.

The mortgage ranks *after* the claims secured by a maritime lien, but *before* the claims secured by an ordinary lien (non-maritime) and the ordinary claims.

(15) Are the claims in respect of which a ship may be arrested subject to time bars (or prescription) and, if so, are these different according to the nature of the claim?

The claims for which a ship may be arrested are subject to the time limitation prevailing under the law of the contract.

However, one must make the distinction between the time bar of the *claim* and the time bar of the *lien* securing the claim.

The time bar (or prescription) of the maritime lien is governed by the provisions of the International Convention of Brussels dated 10 April 1926 on Maritime Liens and Mortgages (Article 9) when applicable or by Art. 39 of the French law dated 3 January 1967.

The time limitation is *one year* for the claims listed in Arts. 2.1 to 2.4 of the Brussels Convention of 10 April 1926 as well as for those listed in Arts. 31-1 to 31-5 of the French law.

The time limitation for claims listed under Art. 2.5 of the Brussels Convention of 10 April 1926, or Art. 31-6 of the French law dated 3 January 1967, is *six months* running from the date of the supply.

(16) Is it possible to apply for the arrest of the ship outside the normal working hours of the court?

It is possible to apply for the arrest of the ship outside the normal working hours of the court, since French law provides that in cases of emergency the arrest petition may be presented at the place where the President of the Commercial Court concerned lives.

In such a case, there is always the possibility that the President is absent from his residence. In that case the claimant will have to wait until his return with the possibility that the ship has left port in the meantime.

Also when the arrest must be effected outside legal days and hours, the claimant must ask the court to specify in the order of arrest that the bailiff is entitled to proceed accordingly.

CHAPTER 13

GERMANY

(1) What are the types of claim for which a ship may be arrested in Germany?

Under German procedural law a vessel may be arrested for any monetary claim or claim which may become a monetary claim which is directed against the shipowner *in personam*.

In the case of an arrest of a vessel flying the flag of a member state of the International Convention for the Unification of Certain Rules Relating to the Arrest of Sea-Going Ships of 10 May 1952, the claim must further be a maritime claim as set out in Article 1(1) sub-paragraphs (a) to (o) of that Convention.

(2) Is there a distinction between claims which give rise to a maritime lien and other types of claim?

Under German law the shipowner must only submit to an arrest of his vessel if he is also the debtor of the claim to be secured.

The only exemptions from this principle are the cases in which the debt of a third party is secured by a maritime lien on the vessel. This is possible in two ways:

(a) the ownership of the vessel has changed and there is a claim against the previous shipowner which is secured by a maritime lien not yet time-barred.

The new shipowner has to suffer the arrest of the vessel for this claim. Only the following claims are secured by a maritime lien under German law (Sec. 754(1) HGB—German Commercial Code):

- claims for the wages of the master and other crew members
- navigation, port and pilotage dues levied by state authorities
- claims for damages for loss of life or personal injury and for loss of or damage to property if such claims have arisen from the use of the vessel (save for claims for loss of or damage to property which are or may be based on contract)

- salvage costs; general average contributions by the vessel and cargo; claims for wreck removal
- claims by the social security authorities, including claims for unemployment insurance contributions against the shipowner.

If the claim is subject to a foreign law and secured by a maritime lien under such foreign law, even if this is not contained in the list above, such claim and maritime lien can also serve as a basis for an arrest in Germany;

(b) the vessel is or was bareboat-chartered or chartered by demise and the claim against the bareboat-charterer or charterer by demise is secured by a maritime lien from the list above (it is assumed that the bareboat-charterer or charterer by demise either navigates the vessel himself or entrusts her navigation to a master employed by him).

Again the (registered) shipowner has to suffer the arrest of the vessel to secure the claim against such bareboat-charterer or demise charterer as a third party if the claim is secured by a maritime lien.

There have been two decisions by the Hamburg Court of Appeal in 1987 holding in effect that in the case of a bareboat-charterer the arrest proceedings are not available to secure the claim, but only proceedings for an injunction. This view has unanimously been rejected by the German legislature and it is assumed that the Hamburg Court of Appeal will not uphold it any longer. In these cases also, arrest proceedings should be the proceedings available.

(3) (a) What pleadings, affidavits and documents must be presented to the court when applying for an arrest and in what language?

It is necessary to submit to the court a written application for the arrest order, which has to set out the relevant facts justifying the request for an arrest. The application must be accompanied by an affidavit confirming the facts. The affidavit should be given by somebody having first-hand knowledge of the facts (e.g. surveyor, employee of the claimant, etc.), not normally by the lawyer acting for the applicant.

It is in the discretion of the claimant whether any documents are attached to the application: this depends on whether the judge can be persuaded of the correctness of the stated facts by the affidavit alone. A power of attorney for the lawyer should be attached.

(b) Which documents must be notarised or otherwise authenticated?

Documents need not be notarised or authenticated.

(4) Is it possible to arrest a ship solely in order to obtain security for a claim which will ultimately be determined in another jurisdiction?

(a) The arrest proceedings according to the German law of civil procedure serve to procure security for the enforcement of a judgment against the debtor at a later time. Generally, the judgment against the debtor must be a judgment from a German court rendered in the main proceedings—the relevant claim therefore being subject to German jurisdiction—or a foreign judgment enforceable in Germany which requires guaranteed reciprocity on this point between Germany and the foreign judgment state.

(b) A further precondition for the arrest order—Sec. 917(1) ZPO (German Code of Civil Procedure)—is that the claimant must show that without the arrest order being granted the enforcement of the judgment at a later time would be frustrated for lack of assets, or substantially endangered. Such a risk exists, for example, if the debtor is about to dispose of essential parts of his assets, especially transferring them abroad, or to encumber his property in a collusive way. The judge will decide this point on the basis of objective facts which the applicant must submit. A generally bad financial position of the debtor is as such not sufficient.

(If the debtor has continuously or regularly sufficient assets within Germany—e.g. a shipowner running a liner service to German ports with his own vessels or having regular freight amounts with his German agent—the precondition that a later enforcement of the judgment must be frustrated or endangered without the arrest order being granted is, of course, not met.)

(c) According to Sec. 917(2) ZPO the precondition for the arrest order as set out under (b) above is deemed to be fulfilled if the judgment for the monetary claim will have to be enforced abroad. No specific facts showing that the enforcement will become impossible or endangered need be submitted.

However, the scope of this provision has materially been reduced by recent court decisions:

— the judgment in the main proceedings whose later enforcement is to be secured must be a judgment from a German court; thus this court must have jurisdiction for the claim as such (claims subject to the jurisdiction of a foreign court or subject to an arbitration clause are therefore outside the scope of this provision; the same applies to a German judgment recognising a foreign judgment in the main proceedings and granting enforcement of it in Germany); and

— even if the claim is subject to German court jurisdiction but the debtor is domiciled in a member state of the European

Union, this provision is not applicable since its application in such a case would amount to a discrimination according to Arts. 7 and 220 of the EEC Treaty (see European Court of Justice, Ruling of 10.2.1994, Case C–398/92, in the matter *Mund & Fester* v. *Hatrex Internationaale Transport*).

Sec. 917(2) ZPO is therefore of importance only if the main claim is subject to German court jurisdiction and directed against a debtor domiciled outside the European Union.

Unsettled is the further question whether instead of the jurisdiction of a German court for the main claim the jurisdiction of a court in a member state of the European Union is sufficient to apply this provision. It is rather assumed that the answer must be given in the negative.

(5) What kind of security is normally acceptable to enable the ship to be released from arrest?

In the arrest order the court fixes the amount of security which the shipowner must furnish in order to have the arrest order lifted. The amount is the aggregate of the amount of the main claim, an amount for interest (for about two years) and the estimated costs (arrest proceedings, attachment of the vessel, main proceedings). The claimant normally in his application gives an estimate of these amounts.

Unless the parties agree on a certain other kind of security (e.g. a letter of undertaking from a P & I Club), the amount fixed in the arrest order must be paid into court or may, under a court order issued upon the application of the shipowner, be given in the form of a guarantee from a leading German bank.

(6) In what circumstances can a claimant be made to give security and what security is acceptable?

It is in the discretion of the court whether or not to order that the claimant put up a counter-security before he may enforce the arrest order by attaching a vessel or other assets of the shipowner. German courts nowadays normally request such security, the amount of which varies and should be assessed with a view to the possible damage incurred by the shipowner if in the end the arrest and attachment prove to be unjustified. Upon application of the claimant the counter-security normally may be put up in the form of a guarantee from a leading German bank.

(7) In the event that the arrest was ultimately shown to have been wrongful, can a claim be made for wrongful arrest and what must be established in order to successfully maintain such a claim?

If the arrest was unjustified (which must be shown by the shipowner in proceedings by lodging an opposition against the arrest order of the court, ending with a judgment by the court lifting the arrest order and dismissing the initial application of the claimant), the claimant is liable to pay damages to the shipowner regardless of any fault on his part. The damages extend to all losses, including loss of profit, suffered by the shipowner.

The shipowner must show in his opposition to the arrest order that either the claim which was to be secured by the arrest proceedings does not exist or is not enforceable, or that there is no justification for an arrest since there is no danger that the main judgment will not be enforced later or for want of any other precondition as mentioned above.

(8) What are the court fees which must be paid in order to make an arrest? Are they recoverable in the event of a successful claim?

The court fees are calculated according to a tariff which is based on the money interest at stake for the claimant. The court will fix this interest at an amount between 50 per cent and 100 per cent of the claim amount to be secured. Example (present tariff): claim for DM 1.0 million; claimant's interest fixed by the court at DM 500,000; the court fees would amount to DM 3,545. In addition there are the costs of the court bailiff actually attaching the vessel and for the custody of the vessel under arrest.

These fees and costs are recoverable from the shipowner if the arrest order remains unopposed or is upheld in opposition proceedings.

(9) How are the lawyers' fees calculated? If possible please estimate the costs of a typical arrest.

The lawyers' fees are calculated according to the German lawyers' legal tariff, which again is based on the amounts at stake (here also the amount fixed by the court is material). For the example in reply to question (8) the lawyers' fees for applying for the arrest order and instructing the court bailiff to attach the vessel would amount to DM 5,572.50 (there may be due additional fees if the lawyer negotiates and obtains the security from the shipowner or his P & I Club; and of course further fees arise if the shipowner initiates opposition proceedings against the arrest order).

(10) Are all or any part of the lawyers' fees recoverable in the event of a successful arrest?

The lawyers' fees are recoverable in full as regards the fees for the application for the arrest order and for instructing the court bailiff.

(11) How quickly can a ship be arrested after the local lawyer is fully instructed?

An arrest order can be obtained from the court within about two to three hours from the lodging of the application with the court. This depends a bit on the availability of a judge. To obtain an arrest order during the weekend is much harder as usually only judges of the criminal court are on duty and only during certain hours.

If the court orders that the claimant has to put up security, this must be furnished before a court bailiff attaches the vessel. It is therefore imperative to prepare everything in advance with a local bank for the immediate issue of the bank guarantee for the security amount requested by the court.

(12) Is there a minimum amount in dispute for which a ship may be arrested?

There is no minimum amount fixed in law for which a ship may be arrested. It could be that a court declines to grant an arrest order for a very small amount if thereby the proceedings would be used *contra bonam fidem*. But arrest applications for claims of say DM 5,000 or DM 10,000 are possible.

(13) Is it possible to arrest a sister ship or a ship in "associated ownership"?

The basis for arrest proceedings in Germany is a personal claim against the shipowner (with the exception of claims secured by a maritime lien). Security for the claim can therefore be sought by arrest and attachment of all assets of the shipowner; the claim need not have arisen in connection with the operation of the vessel to be arrested. Sister ships, if fully owned by the debtor of the claim, may therefore be arrested.

Ships in "associated ownership" do not belong fully to the debtor (the shipowner of the other ship) and the debtor will only have a financial interest in them. Arrest proceedings for such vessels not directly the property of the debtor are not possible under German law.

(14) What is the order of priorities in the event of the distribution by the court of the proceeds of sale of the ship?

The court acting in the arrest proceedings will only very rarely order a forced sale of the vessel. This will be done only if there is a real danger of a very considerable decrease in value of the vessel if the arrest continues, or if the costs of custody of the vessel are out of proportion to her value. If the vessel is sold at public auction by order of the court, the proceeds are to be placed on deposit with the court.

The proceeds plus accrued interest are distributed in accordance with subsequent court orders. The claimant first needs to obtain a judgment in the main proceedings against the debtor. As of the time he attached the vessel under the arrest order his claim is secured by a sort of statutory lien if it is a foreign vessel, or an encumbrance if it is a vessel registered in Germany, and ranks prior to arrests/attachments effected later by other creditors.

The order in which the proceeds are finally distributed is as follows:

(a) costs of the arrest and the custody of the vessel up to her auction and the costs of the auction itself;
(b) maritime liens;
(c) mortgages;
(d) liens on the vessel by arrest of the vessel (as far as they do not arise under the execution of a maritime lien or mortgage); several such liens rank in the order of time they were effected;
(e) any other unsecured claim against the shipowner.

Any creditor of such a claim must notify the court of it in order to take part in the distribution.

(15) Are the claims in respect of which a ship may be arrested subject to a time bar (or prescription) and, if so, are these different according to the nature of the claim?

The basis of any arrest order by the court is a valid payment claim against the shipowner which is not time-barred or for other reasons unenforceable. There are no special time bars for bringing the arrest proceedings as such.

If the claim is secured by a maritime lien, the time bar for enforcing a maritime lien is to be observed.

(16) Is it possible to apply for the arrest of a ship outside the normal working hours of the court?

As arrest proceedings are deemed to be matters of urgency, one can obtain the order also from a substitute judge on duty. During weekdays one should lodge the application with the court at the latest by about 3.00 p.m. (with prior notice by a telephone call to the judge). On Saturdays and Sundays there is normally only a judge of the criminal court on duty for about two hours (during the weekend there is also the difficulty of putting up the counter-security by a bank guarantee or the like if ordered by the judge).

CHAPTER 14

GREECE

(1) What are the types of claim for which a ship may be arrested in Greece?

A ship flying the flag of any of the contracting states to the 1952 Convention countries is subject to arrest in Greece only in respect of the maritime claims of Article 1 of the Convention.

Nevertheless, it is maintained that the above applies when the arresting party is also domiciled or established in one of the contracting countries.

A ship flying the flag of a non-contracting state is subject to arrest in Greece in respect of any claim whatsoever, whether maritime as per the Convention or not, the right to arrest such a ship being conferred upon any claimant.

A ship flying the Greek flag may be arrested for any claim whatsoever. However, it is also maintained that this applies only if the arresting party is domiciled or established in Greece.

(2) Is there a distinction between claims which give rise to a maritime lien and other types of claim?

There is no distinction between claims which give rise to a maritime lien and other types of claim under Greek law.

(3) (a) What pleadings, affidavits and documents must be presented to the court when applying for an arrest and in what language?

When applying for an arrest, an application drawn up in Greek is submitted to the court's clerk. Such an application must contain:

(i) the full names, or in the case of bodies corporate the full titles and styles, of the plaintiff and the registered owner of the ship to be arrested, their permanent or registered address or, if such is unknown, their principal place of business;

(ii) an accurate description—in a brief but comprehensive manner—of the facts which give rise to the claim;

(iii) the name, flag, port and number of registry of the ship, and its net and gross tonnage and international call-sign, if known;

(iv) the cause, as a matter of urgency, for which the "security measure" of the arrest should be ordered by the court;
(v) the amount for which the arrest should be ordered by the court;
(vi) a request for a provisional order of arrest pending decision on the arrest, to be granted upon the lodging of the application with the court.

After the submission of the application to the court's clerk the "judge on duty" fixes the hearing date as well as the date upon which the plaintiff must summon the defendant for the hearing.

The judge on duty considers the application supported by any available documents, and those parts crucial to the case must, at least, be translated into Greek, if such documents are drafted in a foreign language; and by the evidence of any witness produced by the plaintiff, the judge may grant a provisional order for the detention of the ship—if it is flying a foreign flag—or prohibiting a change of the legal status of the ship—if it is flying a Greek flag—up to the hearing of the application, where the hearing judge shall decide whether the order should be further maintained until his decision on the arrest is handed down.

(b) Which documents must be notarised or otherwise authenticated?

Since, most commonly, no original documents are lodged with the court, copies are certified by lawyers to be true and exact photocopies of the originals either in their hands or presented to them.

Both parties may lodge with the court affidavits, signed before notaries, of witnesses who either could not appear at the hearing or were not allowed to testify due to lack of time.

(4) Is it possible to arrest a ship solely in order to obtain security for a claim which will ultimately be determined in another jurisdiction?

It is common to arrest a ship in order to obtain security for a claim which will ultimately be determined in another jurisdiction.

According to Greek law the arresting plaintiff within 30 days, starting from the day after the arrest decision has been served on the defendant, has to file a writ with the competent court, in the competent jurisdiction, to decide the case on the merits and further, within the same period, has to effect service of summons on the defendant.

If the case is to be decided by arbitration, action initiating the arbitration proceedings, in accordance with the applicable law, must be taken within the same 30-day period.

The above regarding the 30-day period applies, provided that no legal action has already been taken by the arresting plaintiff.

Where the arresting plaintiff fails to take the appropriate legal action in time, the arrest decision is rendered ineffective, and upon a motion by the defendants the court shall order the arrest to be lifted.

(5) What kind of security is normally acceptable to enable the ship to be released from arrest?

A bank guarantee.

(6) In what circumstances can a claimant be made to give security and what security is acceptable?

A hearing judge would be most reluctant, upon a motion by the defendant, to order the plaintiff to provide security—in the form of a bank guarantee—to the defendant for possible damage or loss suffered by the defendant as a result of the arrest if the claim against him eventually failed.

Such a counter-security measure is extremely rare in practice.

(7) In the event that the arrest was ultimately shown to have been wrongful, can a claim be made for wrongful arrest and what must be established in order to successfully maintain such a claim?

In order to successfully maintain a claim for wrongful arrest it must be established that the arresting party was aware (a case of "fraud") or, due to gross negligence, was unaware of the fact that he had no valid claim. This is most difficult to establish and for that reason claims made in Greece for wrongful arrest are bound to fail.

(8) What are the court fees which must be paid in order to make an arrest? Are they recoverable in the event of a successful claim?

Court fees, such as fees for filing an application, obtaining exact copies of the application certified by the court's clerk, hearing fees and process server fees, are minimal, and are estimated to be £100 to £200 sterling. Such fees are not recoverable.

(9) How are the lawyers' fees calculated? If possible please estimate the costs of a typical arrest.

A standard basis upon which lawyers' fees are calculated does not apply (although the legal profession's code of conduct provides for a percentage of the amount of the claim or a lump sum per court appearance), and there seems to be no way of discovering how much an individual lawyer will charge, except by questioning such lawyer. Furthermore, it is evident that fees charged by a certain lawyer may vary according to the nature of the case, the work involved and the time spent, as well as the amount at stake.

(10) Are all or any part of the lawyers' fees recoverable in the event of a successful arrest?

Lawyers' fees, just like court fees as above, under (8), are not recoverable since no costs are awarded to a successful plaintiff. The legislature considered that the defendant in arrest proceedings should not bear the costs of a litigation which was initiated by the plaintiff as a security measure for his own benefit.

(11) How quickly can a ship be arrested after the local lawyer is fully instructed?

It depends upon the nature and the complexity of the case, since an accurate description of the facts which give rise to the claim needs to be contained in the arrest application. Further, it depends upon the number of the supporting documents, since at least the parts crucial to the case must be translated into Greek if such documents are drawn up in a foreign language. Translations made and certified by lawyers are admissible according to Greek law, consequently the provisional order prohibiting the vessel's sailing from a Greek port can be obtained within hours of filing the application with the court.

(12) Is there a minimum amount in dispute for which a ship may be arrested?

There is no minimum amount in dispute for which a ship may be arrested.

(13) Is it possible to arrest a sister ship or a ship in "associated ownership"?

It is not possible to arrest a sister ship or a ship in "associated ownership" under Greek law.

(14) What is the order of priorities in the event of the distribution by the court of the proceeds of sale of the ship?

Art. 205 of the Greek Maritime Code provides for a number of liens attaching to the ship and the freight, which rank in priority over all other claims, including the mortgage. That article reads as follows:

Only the following claims in the following order constitute liens on the ship and the freight:

(a) legal costs incurred in the common interest of the creditors, the dues and charges to which the ship is subject, the taxes relevant to the navigation, as well as the ship's custody and maintenance expenses from the time of its arrival at the last port (port of arrest);
(b) claims of the master and crew arising out of the employment contract, as well as the contributions to the Seamen's Pension Fund in respect of the crew's employment;
(c) expenses and rewards on account of assistance and rescue at sea and of salvage;

(d) indemnities due to ships, passengers and cargo on acccount of collision of ships.

The liens rank in priority over the mortgage.

The Brussels Convention on Maritime Liens and Mortgages, 1926, has not been ratified by Greece, in an attempt to make financing easier for Greek shipowners by limiting the claims which may rank in priority over the mortgage. However, Greek courts apply the Convention in determining the maritime liens, for ships which are registered under the Greek flag as foreign capital, and accordingly claims provided for in the Convention rank in priority over the mortgage.

Greek courts considering the question of maritime liens attaching to ships under foreign flags, as in the case of public sale of such ships in Greece, have ruled that the law of the flag state applies only as to which claims constitute maritime liens attaching to the ship, while as to their order of priority Greek law is applicable as a matter of procedure.

(15) Are the claims in respect of which a ship may be arrested subject to a time bar (or prescription) and, if so, are these different according to the nature of the claim?

Greek law provides for different time bars with regard to different categories of claims in respect of which a ship may be arrested; for instance:

Art. 289 of the Greek Maritime Code provides for a *one-year* time bar for the following claims:

(a) of the master and the crew for the payment of their wages and allowances arising out of the contract of employment;
(b) of the shipowner against the master or the crew for their actions in tort in the performance of their duty;
(c) arising out of the provision of the ship with equipment or food supplies, or out of the performance of shipbuilding works and repairs, or out of the offer of equipment or supply services to the ship;
(d) arising out of a charterparty, a passenger or goods transport contract, as well as out of the non-performance, or the performance not in accordance with the contractual terms, of the above contracts;
(e) arising out of a general average contribution;
(f) arising out of the collision of ships, for damage to persons or goods.

Art. 290 of the Greek Maritime Code provides for a *two-year* time bar for the following claims:

(a) of the co-owners of the ship against each other or against the manager of the co-ownership arising out of the exploitation or the management of the ship;

(b) arising out of maritime insurance;
(c) arising out of assistance and rescue at sea, for the payment of the relevant fees and expenses;
(d) against the shipbuilder for defects of the ship.

According to Art. 291 of the Code the above one-year and two-year periods *commence at the end of the year during which the claim arose.*

All other claims fall within the general provisions of the Greek Civil Code providing either for a five-year or a 20-year time bar.

(16) Is it possible to apply for the arrest of a ship outside the normal working hours of the court?

It is possible to apply for the arrest of a ship on Saturdays, Sundays, and bank holidays as the interested party may always be informed of the name of the respective judge on duty and contact him during those periods.

CHAPTER 15

HONG KONG

(1) What are the types of claim for which a ship may be arrested in Hong Kong?

The types of claim in respect of which the Supreme Court of Hong Kong exercises its admiralty jurisdiction are set out in section 12A(2) of the Supreme Court Ordinance Cap 4 Laws of Hong Kong ("SCO"). A copy of the relevant extract is in the Annex to this chapter.

Section 12B of the SCO provides that an action *in personam* lies in respect of *all* cases within the admiralty jurisdiction (s.12B(1)). With one exception, these claims also give rise to an action *in rem*, in connection with which a right to arrest arises. The claim singled out is "any claim for damage received by a ship" (s.12A(2)(d)) which is omitted from s.12B(2) and (4) of the SCO.

(2) Is there a distinction between claims which give rise to a maritime lien and other types of claim?

A distinction still exists and can be of importance.

Section 12B(3) expressly provides for an action *in rem* in "any case in which there is a maritime lien or other charge . . .".

Some of the claims included under s.12A(2) are in fact maritime liens under the common law (e.g. salvage, claim for wages, master's disbursements, etc.).

A maritime lien arises simultaneously with the cause of action and "runs" with the *res* to which it is attached. The claim *in rem*, and thus the right to arrest, survives a change of ownership, regardless of whether the purchasers have notice of the claim. A maritime lien can only be defeated by a sale under the order of a competent court.

A claim which by virtue of the SCO is given a statutory right to proceed *in rem* is enforced by the issue of a writ. It does not travel with the *res* unless the writ is issued before the change of ownership. If the writ *in rem* is not issued before the change of ownership, the claim can no longer be enforced against the *res* and the right to arrest is lost. The claim can still be enforced by an action *in personam*, unless time-barred.

(3) (a) What pleadings, affidavits and documents must be presented to the court when applying for an arrest and in what language?

The right to arrest arises only in an action *in rem*, which shall have been commenced when the application for an arrest is made. A warrant to arrest is sought at the same time the writ is issued if the vessel to be arrested is in port. The following documents are required:

(a) Writ *in rem* (issued before or at the time of the application to arrest);
(b) Praecipe for service of the writ *in rem*;
(c) Affidavit to lead to Warrant to Arrest;
(d) Warrant to Arrest;
(e) Praecipe for Warrant to Arrest;
(f) Solicitors' Undertaking to pay the Bailiff's Costs and Expenses.

The above documents should be in English. By a practice direction issued on 19 August 1991, a statement of claim proposed to be served on a party or intended party who is likely to be Chinese speaking and may not be proficient in English is required to be translated into Chinese. A warrant to arrest had initially been made subject to the practice direction, but was exempted by a subsequent practice direction.

Documents in support of the claim intended for use in court should be translated into English, if not already in English. They should support a *prima facie* claim against the *res*. Evidence on ownership of the vessel to be arrested must also be included.

(b) Which documents must be notarised or otherwise authenticated?

The affidavit to lead to a warrant of arrest is required to be sworn by the solicitors acting for the arresting party; it should verify the facts and matters in support of the issue of a warrant of arrest, exhibiting relevant documents where necessary. There is, however, no requirement for any particular document to be notarised or otherwise authenticated.

(4) Is it possible to arrest a ship solely in order to obtain security for a claim which will ultimately be determined in another jurisdiction?

Whilst the Hong Kong court has jurisdiction to arrest or maintain an arrest, the court should not arrest a ship solely in order to give security in aid of foreign proceedings whether judicial or arbitral. The purpose of an arrest is to obtain security in respect of a judgment of the court or a sum due under a settlement in the action *in rem* to which the arrest relates, and not some other proceedings.

Where a plaintiff has already commenced action in a foreign jurisdiction for the claim, any duplicate action commenced locally solely to obtain security will be liable to be set aside.

As regards arbitration, there is currently no legislation equivalent to section 26 of the Civil Jurisdiction and Judgments Act 1982 in England, which would permit the arrest of a ship as security for an arbitration award. Although *in rem* proceedings may be commenced, the existence of a foreign arbitration clause obliges the court to grant a stay. However, whilst the court is obliged to grant a stay of the proceedings, the court retains a discretion whether to order the release of the vessel if the plaintiffs can bring themselves within the exception established in *The Rena K* [1978] 1 Lloyd's Rep 545. If the plaintiffs are able to show that the arbitration award is unlikely to be satisfied, the court may allow the arrest to stand, or order a release subject to the provision of adequate security. The purpose of this is that if the action *in rem* has to be pursued at a later stage to enforce the award, security is available.

The jurisdiction to issue a warrant to arrest under the Hong Kong Rules of the Supreme Court is still a discretionary one. There has not been a rule change as in England of RSC Order 75, rule 5. Material non-disclosure is relevant. Where the claim is subject to a foreign arbitration clause or a foreign jurisdiction clause, the plaintiff must disclose that fact to the court prior to arresting. Otherwise, the court may discharge any security obtained as a result of the arrest.

(5) What kind of security is normally acceptable to enable the ship to be released from arrest?

(a) Contractual security in the form of a letter of undertaking provided by a P & I Club (normally within the international group) or a bank guarantee would normally be accepted.
(b) Alternatively, owners may post formal bail in the form of a "bail bond" under Order 75, rule 16. This is unpopular as the requirements are cumbersome and the procedure time consuming, and is only used where contractual security cannot be agreed.

(6) In what circumstances can a claimant be made to give security and what security is acceptable?

(a) Apart from his solicitors' undertaking to pay the bailiffs' costs on demand, the plaintiff's solicitors may be required to pay a cash deposit against the bailiffs' expenses incurred in the arrest and maintenance of the vessel. There is no procedure available whereby an arresting party may be made to provide security for an *arrest.*
(b) As far as security for the defendant's *legal costs* are concerned, this is provided for under Order 23 of the Rules of the Supreme Court. The ordering of security is a matter of discretion of the court.
(c) There is otherwise no security required from a claimant in arresting a vessel.

(7) In the event that the arrest was ultimately shown to have been wrongful, can a claim be made for wrongful arrest and what must be established in order to successfully maintain such a claim?

A claim can be made but is not easy to prove. The owners would need to establish gross negligence or bad faith on the part of the arresting party.

(8) What are the court fees which must be paid in order to make an arrest?

Current court fees

HK$1,045 for issue of writ *in rem*;
HK$1,045 for praecipe for warrant to arrest;
HK$110 for service of the writ.

(Current exchange rate: US$1 = HK$7.8)

Are they recoverable in the event of a successful claim?

Yes, all these are recoverable as disbursements in the event of a final judgment in favour of the plaintiff.

(9) How are the lawyers' fees calculated? If possible please estimate the costs of a typical arrest.

Lawyers' fees in Hong Kong are generally calculated on a time spent basis. In our experience the costs of a typical arrest are likely to be in the region of HK$25,000. (These costs will obviously be higher if there are subsequent and protracted negotiations regarding security.)

(10) Are all or any part of the lawyers' fees recoverable in the event of a successful arrest?

Legal fees incurred for effecting an arrest can usually be recovered if the *claim* is eventually successful. However, a successful party would usually be able to recover only on a "party and party" basis. This is approximately two-thirds of his costs.

(11) How quickly can a ship be arrested after the local lawyer is fully instructed?

Execution of an arrest warrant is relatively swift, owing much to the proximity of the locations where ships are stationed within Hong Kong waters, and to the co-operation of the Marine Department and the Bailiffs' Office. Normally it takes no more than a few hours from the filing of papers in court.

(12) Is there a minimum amount in dispute for which a ship may be arrested?

No.

(13) Is it possible to arrest a sister ship or a ship in "associated ownership"?

A sister ship can be arrested in respect of claims set out in section 12A(2)(e) to (q) of the SCO, but not in respect of the rest of the claims included under that section. The requirements for a sister ship arrest are set out in section 12B(4)(b)(ii) of the SCO. A copy of the relevant extract is in the Annex to this chapter.

(14) What is the order of priorities in the event of the distribution by the court of the proceeds of sale of the ship?

The order is as follows:

(a) the bailiffs' expenses and costs of arrest (plus one per cent of the sale price as commission);
(b) recoverable legal costs incurred by the plaintiff from commencement of the action up to and including the time of the sale, including the arrest, preservation and sale of the vessel;
(c) maritime liens (e.g. salvage, claim for wages, etc.);
(d) mortgages;
(e) other claims;
(f) owners to have surplus, if any.

(15) Are the claims in respect of which a ship may be arrested subject to a time bar (or prescription) and if so are these different according to the nature of the claim?

The right to arrest hinges upon an action *in rem*. If the right to proceed *in rem* is lost by reason of a time bar, so is the right to arrest.

The relevant limitation varies according to the nature of the claims.

General limitation under the Limitation Ordinance Cap. 347 Laws of Hong Kong:

(i) claim for loss of life and personal injuries, three years;
(ii) claim in contract or in tort, six years

from the date of accrual of the cause of action; unless other Statutory Convention or contractual time limits are applicable.

(16) Is it possible to apply for the arrest of a ship outside the normal working hours of the court?

Yes it is, but for good measure as much advance notice as possible should be given to the relevant officers of the court and of the Bailiffs' Office.

In case of urgency, an arrest may even be applied for and effected during public holdays. A "duty judge" will be available after office hours or during public holidays to hear applications for the issue of the writ and of the warrant of arrest.

(17) Please provide any other information which you believe is relevant in deciding whether or not to arrest a ship in your jurisdiction.

Substantial expenses, such as crew wages, water, bunkers and port dues, may be incurred by the bailiff. The arresting party should, as a prudent measure, consider the possible proceeds of sale of the vessel and whether there is a market for the vessel.

ANNEX

SUPREME COURT ORDINANCE CAP 4

12A Admiralty jurisdiction of High Court

(1) The Admiralty jurisdiction of the High Court shall consist of—

(a) jurisdiction to hear and determine any of the questions and claims mentioned in subsection (2);

(b) jurisdiction in relation to any of the proceedings mentioned in subsection (3);

(c) any other Admiralty jurisdiction which it had immediately before the commencement of the Supreme Court (Amendment) Ordinance 1989 (3 of 1989).

(2) The questions and claims referred to in subsection (1)(a) are—

(a) any claim to the possession or ownership of a ship or to the ownership of any share therein;

(b) any question arising between the co-owners of a ship as to possession, employment or earnings of that ship;

(c) any claim in respect of a mortgage of or charge on a ship or any share therein;

(d) any claim for damage received by a ship;

(e) any claim for damage done by a ship;

(f) any claim for loss of life or personal injury sustained in consequence of any defect in a ship or in her apparel or equipment, or in consequence of the wrongful act, neglect or default of—

(i) the owners, charterers or persons in possession or control of a ship; or

(ii) the master or crew of a ship, or any other person for whose wrongful acts, neglects or defaults the owners, charterers or persons in possession or control of a ship are responsible,

being an act, neglect or default in the navigation or management of the ship, in the loading, carriage or discharge of goods on, in or from the ship, or in the embarkation, carriage or disembarkation of persons on, in or from the ship;

(g) any claim for loss of or damage to goods carried in a ship;

(h) any claim arising out of any agreement relating to the carriage of goods in a ship or to the use or hire of a ship;

(i) any claim in the nature of salvage (including any claim arising by virtue of the application, by or under section 51 of the Civil Aviation Act 1949 (1949 c. 67 U.K.) in its application to Hong Kong, of the law relating to salvage to aircraft and their apparel and cargo);

(j) any claim in the nature of towage in respect of a ship or an aircraft;

(k) any claim in the nature of pilotage in respect of a ship or an aircraft;

(l) any claim in respect of goods or materials supplied to a ship for her operation or maintenance;
(m) any claim in respect of the construction, repair or equipment of a ship or in respect of dock charges or dues;
(n) any claim by a master or member of the crew of a ship for wages (including any sum allotted out of wages or adjudged by a superintendent to be due by way of wages);
(o) any claim by a master, shipper, charterer or agent in respect of disbursements made on account of a ship;
(p) any claim arising out of an act which is or is claimed to be a general average act;
(q) any claim arising out of bottomry;
(r) any claim for the forfeiture or condemnation of a ship or of goods which are being or have been carried, or have been attempted to be carried, in a ship, or for the restoration of a ship or any such goods after seizure, or for droits of Admiralty;
(s) any claim arising under section 7 of the Merchant Shipping (Prevention and Control of Pollution) Ordinance (Cap. 413). (*Replaced 37 of 1990 s.12(2)*)

(3) The proceedings referred to in subsection (1)(b) are—

(a) any application to the High Court under—
(i) the Merchant Shipping Acts 1894 to 1979 in their application to Hong Kong;
(ii) the Merchant Shipping Ordinance (Cap. 281);
(iii) the Merchant Shipping (Safety) Ordinance (Cap. 369);
(iv) the Merchant Shipping (Liability and Compensation for Oil Pollution) Ordinance (Cap. 414); (*Amendment 55 of 1993 s.30*)
(v) the Merchant Shipping (Registration) Ordinance (Cap. 415); or (*Replaced 74 of 1990 s.104(3). Amended 55 of 1993 s.30*)
(vi) the Merchant Shipping (Limitation of Shipowners Liability) Ordinance (Cap. 434); (*Added 55 of 1993 s.30*)
(b) any action to enforce a claim for damage, loss of life or personal injury arising out of—
(i) a collision between ships;
(ii) the carrying out of or omission to carry out a manoeuvre in the case of 1 or more of 2 or more ships; or
(iii) non-compliance, on the part of 1 or more of 2 or more ships, with the collision regulations;
(c) any action by shipowners or other persons under—
(i) the Merchant Shipping Acts 1894 to 1979 in their application to Hong Kong;
(ii) the Merchant Shipping Ordinance (Cap. 281);
(iii) the Merchant Shipping (Safety) Ordinance (Cap. 369); (*Amended 55 of 1993 s.30*)
(iv) the Merchant Shipping (Liability and Compensation for Oil Pollution) Ordinance (Cap. 414); or (*Amended 55 of 1993 s.30*)
(v) the Merchant Shipping (Limitation of Shipowners Liability) Ordinance (Cap. 434), (*Added 55 of 1993 s.30*)

for the limitation of the amount of their liability in connection with a ship or other property. (*Replaced 38 of 1990 Sch. 2*)

(4) The jurisdiction of the High Court under subsection (2)(b) includes power to

settle any account outstanding and unsettled between the parties in relation to the ship, and to direct that the ship, or any share thereof, shall be sold, and to make such other order as the court thinks fit.

(5) Subsection (2)(e) extends to—

(a) any claim in respect of a liability incurred under Part II of the Merchant Shipping (Liability and Compensation for Oil Pollution) Ordinance (Cap. 414); and

(b) any claim in respect of a liability incurred by the International Oil Pollution Compensation Fund under Part III of that Ordinance. (*Replaced 38 of 1990 Sch. 2*)

(6) The reference in subsection (2)(i) to claims in the nature of salvage includes a reference to such claims for services rendered in saving life from a ship or an aircraft or in preserving cargo, apparel or wreck as, under sections 544 to 546 of the Merchant Shipping Act 1894 (1894 c. 60 U.K.) in their application to Hong Kong, or any Order in Council made under section 51 of the Civil Aviation Act 1949 (1949 c. 67 U.K.) in its application to Hong Kong, are authorised to be made in connection with a ship or an aircraft.

(7) Subsections (1) to (6) apply—

(a) in relation to all ships or aircraft, whether British or not and whether registered or not and wherever the residence or domicile of their owners may be;

(b) in relation to all claims, wherever arising (including, in the case of cargo or wreck salvage, claims in respect of cargo or wreck found on land); and

(c) so far as they relate to mortgages and charges, to all mortgages or charges, whether registered or not and whether legal or equitable, including mortgages and charges created under foreign law.

(8) Nothing in subsection (7) shall be construed as extending the cases in which money or property is recoverable under any of the provisions of—

(a) the Merchant Shipping Acts 1894 to 1979 in their application to Hong Kong;

(b) the Merchant Shipping Ordinance (Cap. 281);

(c) the Merchant Shipping (Safety) Ordinance (Cap. 369);

(d) the Merchant Shipping (Liability and Compensation for Oil Pollution) Ordinance (Cap. 414); (*Replaced 38 of 1990 Sch. 2. Amended 55 of 1993 s.30*)

(e) the Merchant Shipping (Registration) Ordinance (Cap. 415); or (*Added 74 of 1990 s.104(3). Amended 55 of 1993 s.30*)

(f) the Merchant Shipping (Limitation of Shipowners Liability) Ordinance (Cap. 434). (*Added 55 of 1993 s.30*)

(*Added 3 of 1989 s.2*)

12B Mode of exercise of Admiralty jurisdiction

(1) Subject to section 12C an action in personam may be brought in the High Court in all cases within the Admiralty jurisdiction of that court.

(2) In the case of any such claim as is mentioned in section 12A(2)(a), (c) or (r) or any such question as is mentioned in section 12A(2)(b), an action in rem may be brought in the High Court against the ship or property in connection with which the claim or question arises and such action shall be deemed to be brought by and upon the issue of the writ in rem.

(3) In any case in which there is a maritime lien or other charge on any ship, aircraft or other property for the amount claimed, an action in rem may be brought in the High Court against that ship, aircraft or property.

(4) In the case of any such claim as is mentioned in section 12A(2)(e) to (q), where—

(a) the claim arises in connection with a ship; and
(b) the person who would be liable on the claim in an action in personam ("the relevant person") was, when the cause of action arose, the owner or charterer of, or in possession or in control of, the ship,

an action in rem may (whether or not the claim gives rise to a maritime lien on that ship) be brought in the High Court against—

(i) that ship, if at the time when the action is brought the relevant person is either the beneficial owner of that ship as respects all the shares in it or the charterer of it under a charter by demise; or
(ii) any other ship of which, at the time when the action is brought, the relevant person is the beneficial owner as respects all the shares in it.

(5) In the case of a claim in the nature of towage or pilotage in respect of an aircraft, an action in rem may be brought in the High Court against that aircraft if, at the time when the action is brought, it is beneficially owned by the person who would be liable on the claim in an action in personam.

(6) Where, in the exercise of its Admiralty jurisdiction, the High Court orders any ship, aircraft or other property to be sold, the court shall have jurisdiction to hear and determine any question arising as to the title to the proceeds of sale.

(7) In determining for the purposes of subsections (4) and (5) whether a person would be liable on a claim in an action in personam it shall be assumed that he has his habitual residence or a place of business within Hong Kong.

(8) Where, as regards any such claim as is mentioned in section 12A(2)(e) to (q), a ship has been served with a writ or arrested in an action in rem brought to enforce that claim, no other ship may be served with a writ or arrested in that or any other action in rem brought to enforce that claim; but this subsection does not prevent the issue, in respect of any one such claim, of a writ naming more than 1 ship or of 2 or more writs each naming a different ship.

(*Added 3 of 1989 s.2*)
[*cf. 1981 c. 54 s.21 U.K.*]

CHAPTER 16

IRELAND

(1) What are the types of claim for which a ship may be arrested in Ireland?

The types of claims are the classes of claims which apply in relation to vessels registered in countries which are parties to the 1952 Brussels Arrest Convention.[1]

In respect of vessels which are registered in non-Convention countries, the types of claims giving rise to a right of arrest are identical, subject to the qualification that disbursements made by shippers, charterers or agents on behalf of a ship or her owner be classifiable as necessaries.

It is important to note that sister ship arrest is only permitted where the vessels are registered in countries which are parties to the 1952 Brussels Arrest Convention. This means that vessels from CIS countries are not amenable to sister ship arrest.

(2) Is there a distinction between claims which give rise to a maritime lien and other types of claim?

Where a maritime lien exists, a claim can be brought against the vessel irrespective of a change of ownership. Other claims, e.g. those for necessaries, agents' fees, do not give rise to a maritime lien and therefore claims of this nature can only be brought while the vessel remains in the same ownership.

(3) (a) What pleadings, affidavits and documents must be presented to the court when applying for an arrest and in what language?

All that is needed to arrest a vessel in this jurisdiction is:

(i) a writ;
(ii) an affidavit which will exhibit the relevant invoices, charterparty, bill of lading or whatever document is relevant to the particular claim;
(iii) where the claim is prospectively a sister ship one would normally exhibit an extract from the register to establish the same ownership.

1 For the full text of the 1952 Brussels Convention please see Appendix 1.

(b) Which documents must be notarised or otherwise authenticated?

It is not necessary to have any documents notarised or authenticated for a straightforward arrest. The affidavit which forms the basis for the court application is normally sworn by the solicitor who represents the claimant seeking the arrest and the affidavit is sworn before another solicitor or commissioner for oaths. If, for any reason, a claimant resident abroad wishes to swear the affidavit, the affidavit would need to be notarised before a notary public or the local Irish Consul.

All documents submitted to the court must be in the English language. Where a document is self-evident, e.g. an invoice, no translation would be required.

(4) Is it possible to arrest a ship solely in order to obtain security for a claim which will ultimately be determined in another jurisdiction?

Yes, it is possible to arrest a ship in order to obtain security for a claim which will ultimately be determined in another jurisdiction, provided that the claim itself is one which gives an entitlement to arrest in this jurisdiction. It presupposes that:

(i) either there is a jurisdiction clause in the contract documentation; or
(ii) that both parties wish to have the matter determined in another jurisdiction.

Jurisdiction is normally agreed upon at the time when security is being obtained and the letter of guarantee/security documentation will contain a clause specifying that the dispute is to be resolved in another jurisdiction (by litigation or arbitration) and will ideally contain a clause nominating lawyers in the agreed jurisdiction to represent the owners.

(5) What kind of security is normally acceptable to enable the ship to be released from arrest?

The following types of security are normally acceptable in this jurisdiction:

(i) a bond/guarantee from a bank, insurance or P & I Club;
(ii) a guarantee (called a bail bond) entered into by an individual or body on behalf of the owners of the vessel. The arresting party can object to the identity of the proposed surety and require proof of assets;
(iii) payment into court of the amount claimed together with the sum for costs.

(6) In what circumstances can a claimant be made to give security and what security is acceptable?

An arresting party is never required to give security in respect of an arrest.

(7) In the event that the arrest was ultimately shown to have been wrongful, can a claim be made for wrongful arrest and what must be established in order to successfully maintain such a claim?

It is possible to bring a claim for wrongful arrest under Irish law. To succeed, however, an owner would have to prove that the arresting party was guilty of bad faith and/or gross negligence in having the arrest carried out.

(8) What are the court fees which must be paid in order to make an arrest? Are they recoverable in the event of a successful claim?

The court fees payable in order to make an arrest consist of stamp duty on the warrant of arrest (currently £50) and a similar amount of stamp duty on the warrant for release.

In addition the arresting party is responsible for the payment of shipkeepers' fees, i.e. cost of maintaining a watch on board the vessel for the duration of the arrest. When applying for an arrest warrant a solicitor must give an undertaking to the court to be responsible for the shipkeepers' fees. Court fees and shipkeepers' fees are recovered from the owners and normally one would require payment (or an undertaking to do so) as a precondition to releasing the vessel.

(9) How are the lawyers' fees calculated? If possible please estimate the costs of a typical arrest.

There is no fixed guideline as to how lawyers' fees for an arrest should be calculated. Some would charge an hourly rate—others would base their charges on a fee agreed in advance with the client. The fees would also depend on whether a barrister is used.

The cost of a typical arrest and release is £1,700. If a barrister is used to draft the summons and affidavit and to make the court application, the solicitor's professional fee will be somewhat lower and the fee allowed for the barrister would be £400. In addition, stamp duty (on the writ, affidavit, warrant and release) amounts to approximately £250.

(10) Are all or any part of the lawyers' fees recoverable in the event of a successful arrest?

Approximately two thirds of the lawyers' fees are recoverable in the event of a successful arrest. Normally, one would agree a figure as a precondition to having the vessel released.

(11) How quickly can a ship be arrested after the local lawyer is fully instructed?

If the local lawyer is fully instructed with the correct documents and information and is prepared to draft the summons and affidavit (without using a barrister), a ship can be arrested within a matter of one and a half to two hours subject to the availability of a judge (or the Master of the High Court) to deal with the case. Arrests are given priority and usually there is no difficulty in having a judge (or the Master) made available.

(12) Is there a minimum amount in dispute for which a ship may be arrested?

There is no minimum amount in respect of which a ship may be arrested. In practical terms, one would not recommend a client to arrest a vessel for a small debt.

(13) Is it possible to arrest a sister ship or a ship in "associated ownership"?

In certain circumstances it is possible to arrest a sister ship, provided that ship is in the same ownership. The concept of "associated" ownership does not apply under Irish law. Ships are regarded as being in the same ownership when "all the shares ... are owned by the same person or persons". This excludes any concept of "associated ownership".

Sister ship arrest is only available where the vessels concerned are registered in Convention countries (i.e. countries which have ratified and implemented the 1952 Brussels Arrest Convention). Sister ship arrest is not available in respect of vessels registered in non-Convention countries. This results from the decision of the Supreme Court in the case of the *Kapitain Labunetz*.

(14) What is the order of priorities in the event of the distribution by the court of the proceeds of sale of the ship?

The following is the order of priorities in the event of the distribution by the court of the process of sale of a ship:

(i) admiralty marshal's expenses. These include the shipkeepers' fees, i.e. the cost of maintaining a watch on board from the date of arrest to the date of sale and stamp duty on the sale of the vessel at 10 per cent of the sale price;
(ii) the plaintiff's costs of arrest or the claimant's costs of arrest;
(iii) the cost of appraisement on sale. This would include advertising expenses and the costs of the fees of the auctioneer appointed to conduct the sale. These are charged at two and one half per cent of the sale price;
(iv) maritime liens in the nature of crew wages (including arrears of pension contributions);
(v) salvor's lien where the salvage consists of the salvage of a sunken vessel;

(vi) maritime lien in respect of collision damage;
(vii) maritime lien for salvage;
(viii) registered mortgages;
(ix) unregistered mortgages;
(x) possessory liens.

(15) Are the claims in respect of which a ship may be arrested subject to a time bar (or prescription) and if so are these different according to the nature of the claim?

There is a two-year time bar period in respect of salvage and collision claims although the court has discretion to extend that period in the event that there has been no opportunity to effect an arrest because the vessel has been outside the jurisdiction. In such cases, however, one would be advised to issue the writ within the two-year period and if necessary renew it. All writs (summonses) are valid for a period of one year from the date of issue but can be renewed if the court is satisfied that there are reasonable grounds for so doing.

The time bar period in respect of claims brought for breach of contract is six years unless the contract specifically provides for a different time bar period or a different limitation period. Likewise claims for outstanding monies due and claims for tort have a six-year time bar period with the exception of personal injury claims where the time bar period is three years.

(16) Is it possible to apply for the arrest of a ship outside the normal working hours of the court?

Arresting a vessel outside the normal working hours of the court is possible. In theory one must issue a writ in order to apply for an arrest. If therefore a vessel is scheduled to come in over a weekend, it is advisable to have the writ issued in advance during normal working hours of the court and to have given notice to the judge/Master of the High Court of the likelihood that an arrest outside working hours will be necessary.

(17) Please provide any other information which you believe is relevant in deciding whether or not to arrest a ship in your jurisdiction.

The procedure for arrest in Ireland is straightforward and requires no security from the arresting party. Both the law and practice are broadly similar to the position in the UK. Where we differ is in relation to:

(i) the requirement to pay for shipkeepers' fees, i.e. for a watchkeeper to remain on board the vessel for the duration of the arrest (although as mentioned above, those costs can be recovered from the owners as a precondition to releasing the vessel);

(ii) the time lag in obtaining an order for sale and disposing of an arrested vessel can be in the order of three months and one obviously has to weigh up whether the sale price will be sufficient to cover all the costs, including the shipkeepers' fees and the priority claims;

(iii) the stamp duty levy of ten per cent on the sale price of a vessel under a forced sale (only).

CHAPTER 17

ISRAEL

(1) What are the types of claim for which a ship may be arrested in Israel?

The arrest of ship is a remedy available only in Admiralty proceedings and in the framework of an *in rem* claim.

Admiralty jurisdiction in which an *in rem* claim can be brought is limited to those causes of action which are included in the English Admiralty Court Acts of 1840 and 1861, which are still in force in Israel (by virtue of their indirect application through the Admiralty Court Act of 1952).

The causes of action which will be dealt with under the above enactment are: foreclosure of mortgage (subject to certain conditions), salvage, necessaries, damage to imported cargo, wages, damage caused to ship, damage caused by a ship, Master's disbursements, shipbuilders and repairers claim (subject to certain conditions).

In addition, it has been held that where there is a claim to enforce a maritime lien (even if not one of the causes enumerated above) the Admiralty jurisdiction shall apply.

(2) Is there a distinction between claims which give rise to a maritime lien and other types of claim?

The Admiralty Court may exercise its *in rem* jurisdiction either to enforce a maritime lien or where the claim involves a statutory right *in rem*.

There are claims that can both give rise to a maritime lien and also by themselves be eligible to be *in rem* claims (e.g. wages, damage caused by ship). On the other hand, a claim to foreclose a mortgage may invoke *in rem* jurisdiction without its being in itself a maritime lien. A charterparty dispute is not within the Admiralty jurisdiction, nor will it be recognised as a maritime lien and, therefore, will not entitle an arrest.

(3) (a) What pleadings, affidavits and documents must be presented to the court when applying for an arrest and in what language?

Arrest of a ship requires a writ *in rem* endorsed by the Court Secretariat as well as an application to arrest the ship supported by an affidavit to which all relevant documents should be attached. The writ and application will always be in Hebrew while the affidavit and supporting documents may be in a foreign language. For practical reasons, if the affidavit/documents are in a language other than English, it is likely that at least a free translation shall be required.

(b) Which documents must be notarised or otherwise authenticated?

As a general rule the affidavit must be sworn before a lawyer in Israel or before a consular representative of Israel abroad. In urgent cases the authentication may be substituted by a written statement which later will have to be duly authenticated.

(4) Is it possible to arrest a ship solely in order to obtain security for a claim which will ultimately be determined in another jurisdiction?

The relevant rule provides that a warrant of arrest may be issued "... in an action *in rem* ...". This would lead one to assume that a claim will be required in Israel in order to establish jurisdiction and obtain an arrest. It will, however, be legitimate for the claimant to use the proceedings (claim and arrest) in Israel as only ancillary to proceedings commenced abroad.

(5) What kind of security is normally acceptable to enable the ship to be released from arrest?

Letters of guarantee of P & I Clubs are usually acceptable. In the absence of such documents a bank guarantee or a cash deposit would be required.

(6) In what circumstances can a claimant be made to give security and what security is acceptable?

The statutes dealing with Admiralty jurisdiction do not provide for such security and for many years the practice was that such security was not required.

In a very recent case the Supreme Court held that the matter is entirely within the discretion of the Admiralty Court and the matter must be considered on the merits of each case. In a more recent case a receiver of cargo was required by the Admiralty Court to give security of some US$100,000 by way of a self letter of undertaking.

(7) In the event that the arrest was ultimately shown to have been wrongful, can a claim be made for wrongful arrest and what must be established in order to successfully maintain such a claim?

On the assumption that damages arising from a wrongful arrest may be proved, there would lie a claim for such damages. The extent of damages and the shipowner's diligent attempt to minimise the damage will have to be proved.

(8) What are the court fees which must be paid in order to make an arrest? Are they recoverable in the event of a successful claim?

There are no court fees for the arrest as such. However, court fees must be paid in connection with the claim. The court fees are two and one half per cent of the amount claimed payable in two equal instalments, the first at the commencement of the proceedings and the second at the commencement of the hearings. The court fees are recoverable in the event of a favourable judgment.

(9) How are the lawyers' fees calculated? If possible please estimate the costs of a typical arrest.

Lawyers' fees would depend on the agreements in each particular case. There are no restrictions in Israel on any particular manner of charging and, accordingly, there are charges based on an hourly basis, contingency or otherwise—in each case according to the agreement between lawyer and client. Based on an hourly basis the arrest (without further proceedings) may involve costs of up to US$5,000.

(10) Are all or any part of the lawyers' fees recoverable in the event of a successful arrest?

Lawyers' fees are recoverable (at least in part) in the case of a favourable judgment. A successful arrest is only an intermediate stage of the litigation.

(11) How quickly can a ship be arrested after the local lawyer is fully instructed?

In normal circumstances, and with all documentation received from the client, it would be a matter of several hours to prepare the documents required for the arrest. The proceedings in court would require an additional two to three hours, if application is brought to the court during working hours. If it is after working hours it may require some four to six hours.

(12) Is there a minimum amount in dispute for which a ship may be arrested?

No.

(13) Is it possible to arrest a sister ship or a ship in "associated ownership"?

Inasmuch as an arrest within *in rem* proceedings is applied for, no remedy can be sought against a sister ship or against a ship in "associated ownership". Attachment within the rules of civil procedure (see (17) hereunder) may be sought against any property of the defendant/owner (including a sister ship).

(14) What is the order of priorities in the event of the distribution by the court of the proceeds of sale of the ship?

(a) The order of priorities is provided for by section 41 of the Shipping Law (Vessels) of 1960. This section provides for the creation of maritime liens and their priority as follows:
  (1) the expenses incurred in order to bring about the sale of the vessel and the distribution of the proceeds of the sale, and taxes and other compulsory charges due to the State or to another authority in respect of the sale or distribution;
  (2) wharfage, anchorage, pilotage and lighthouse fees, port fees, etc;
  (3) expenses of guarding and maintenance of the vessel;
  (4) payments claimed by the master, the members of the crew, etc;
  (5) payments due for the saving of the lives of persons in the vessel, for aid to the vessel while stranded or in distress or for the salvage of the vessel or of cargo, and in respect of the contribution of the vessel to general average;
  (6) compensation for the death or bodily injury of passengers;
  (7) compensation for damage resulting from collision at sea or from some other navigational accident;
  (8) payments claimed for or in connection with supplies or services provided to the vessel under agreements or transactions entered into by the master of the vessel.

(b) Section 57 of the said Shipping Law provides that a registered mortgage shall have priority over all claims except those specified in sub-paras (1)–(7) of section 41. This means, in effect, that a mortgage ranks prior to a claim for necessaries, etc.

(15) Are the claims in respect of which a ship may be arrested subject to a time bar (or prescription) and, if so, are these different according to the nature of the claim?

In general, the prescription period under Israeli law is seven years from the date of the creation of the cause of action. There are exceptions to this general principle (e.g. one-year period for cargo claims or extension of the period in certain cases of bodily injury up to 10 years). The security afforded by the maritime lien expires after one year with certain circumstances which extend the expiry date, but always to not more than three years.

(16) Is it possible to apply for the arrest of a ship outside the normal working hours of the court?

Yes. However, an application to arrest which will be brought very late in the evening or during the night time is not likely to be dealt with, except in cases of extreme urgency.

(17) Please provide any other information which you believe is relevant in deciding whether or not to arrest a ship in your jurisdiction.

Apart from the arrest of the ship within Admiralty jurisdiction there is an alternative remedy which has been used from time to time by plaintiffs against vessels.

(a) Rules of civil procedure provided for in the interlocutory remedy of attachment of property of the defendant.

(b) In spite of doubts as to the applicability of this remedy to foreign vessels, practice has developed to use this remedy, whenever the plaintiff cannot bring his claim within Admiralty jurisdiction.

(c) The effect of such attachment is similar to the Mareva injunction, i.e. the vessel is prevented from departing from Israel.

(d) The rules of civil procedure require that the application for attachment shall be related to a claim for a certain amount of money (as distinct from a claim for a declaration, injunction, etc.) and that the application shall be supported by a sworn affidavit showing a *prima facie* case of the plaintiff. The application is heard *ex parte* and attachment is usually granted if the affidavit shows a *prima facie* case, as aforesaid.

The rules require that counter-security shall be provided by the plaintiff; the nature and amount of security are matters within the discretion of the court.

(e) The attachment, if granted *ex parte,* is subject to an application to set aside, which the defendant may apply for within 30 days. The defendant may also apply to substitute the attached property by offering alternative suitable security.

CHAPTER 18

ITALY

(1) What are the types of claim for which a ship may be arrested in Italy?

Italy has ratified the International Convention for the Unification of Certain Rules Relating to the Arrest of Sea-Going Ships, signed at Brussels on 10 May 1952.

The provisions of such Convention are applicable in Italy in respect of vessels flying the flag of a contracting state. Italian law contemplates different rules which may be applicable to vessels flying the flag of a non-contracting state or to Italian vessels.

Briefly, the position is as follows:

(a) Vessel flying the flag of a state party to the 1952 Brussels Convention

Article 1 of the Convention lists the maritime claims for which a ship can be arrested, namely:

- (a) damage caused by any ship either in collision or otherwise;
- (b) loss of life or personal injury caused by any ship or occurring in connection with the operation of any ship;
- (c) salvage;
- (d) agreement relating to the use or hire of any ship whether by charterparty or otherwise;
- (e) agreement relating to the carriage of goods in any ship whether by charterparty or otherwise;
- (f) loss of or damage to goods including baggage carried in any ship;
- (g) general average;
- (h) bottomry;
- (i) towage;
- (j) pilotage;
- (k) goods or materials wherever supplied to a ship for her operation or maintenance;
- (l) construction, repair or equipment of any ship or dock charges and dues;
- (m) wages of masters, officers, or crew;

(n) master's disbursements, including disbursements made by shippers, charterers or agents on behalf of a ship or her owner;
(o) disputes as to the title to or ownership of any ship;
(p) disputes between co-owners of any ship as to the ownership, possession, employment or earnings of that ship;
(q) the mortgage or hypothecation of any ship.

The vessel flying the flag of a contracting state, therefore, can be arrested by an Italian court pursuant to the application of the party having a maritime claim, upon condition that the party produces evidence satisfying the court of the good grounds of the claim. No other evidence is required.

(b) Vessel flying the flag of a non-contracting state

Article 8(2) of the 1952 Brussels Convention provides that a ship flying the flag of a non-contracting state may be arrested (in the jurisdiction of any contracting state) in respect of any of the maritime claims enumerated in Article 1 or of any other claim for which the law of the contracting state permits the arrest. Italian law does not contain any provision limiting the type of claims for which a ship can be arrested. Therefore ships flying the flag of a non-contracting state can be arrested for any claim whatsoever, including those listed at Article 1 of the 1952 Brussels Convention.

(c) Vessels flying the Italian flag

The provisions of the 1952 Brussels Convention would apply to an Italian vessel in the event the application for arrest with the Italian courts is filed by a foreign claimant. In such a case, the Italian vessel can be arrested only for the types of claim listed under heading (a) above.

(2) Is there a distinction between claims which give rise to a maritime lien and other types of claim?

Under Italian law, the distinction between claims giving rise to a maritime lien and other claims is that the former attach to the ship (whoever is her owner), whilst other claims can be enforced exclusively on the assets (including ships) belonging to the debtor. In other words, a claimant who has a maritime lien may arrest the ship to which the claim refers even though the person liable for the claim is a party other than the registered owner, whilst this would not be possible in the absence of a maritime lien.

In the case of arrest of a ship flying the flag of a non-contracting state, the general principles of Italian law would apply so that the arrest of the ship belonging to a party other than the one responsible for the claim can be arrested only where the claim gives rise to a maritime lien.

It has to be noted that the existence of a maritime lien on a ship is determined by the Italian courts on the basis of the provisions of the law of her flag.

(3) (a) What pleadings, affidavits and documents must be presented to the court when applying for an arrest and in what language?

In order to apply for arrest the arrestors must deposit with the competent court pleadings describing the basis and the reasons for the arrest. The pleadings should be accompanied by all necessary supporting documentation, translated into Italian (normally, for the purpose of an arrest application, a free translation is sufficient). Photocopies or fax copies of the documents are generally accepted.

(b) Which documents must be notarised or otherwise authenticated?

The party applying for an arrest must be represented by a lawyer acting on the basis of a power of attorney. The power of attorney can be contained and executed by the party in the application for arrest when its execution is effected in Italy. In such case, the Italian lawyer has the power to authenticate the signature.

When the power of attorney is issued abroad, it must be notarised by a local notary public. The notarisation should then be legalised either by the Italian Consul or by means of the Apostille provided by The Hague Convention of 5 October 1961.

There may be other bilateral or multilateral international conventions, such as the Convention signed at Brussels on 25 May 1987, under which legalisation is not required.

(4) Is it possible to arrest a ship solely in order to obtain security for a claim which will ultimately be determined in another jurisdiction?

It is possible to arrest a ship for the purpose of obtaining security even if the Italian courts have no jurisdiction on the merits of the claim.

Arrestors must commence proceedings on the merits of the dispute in the proper jurisdiction within 30 days of the order of arrest or within the term fixed by the court.

Under Article 7 of the 1952 Brussels Convention, if an arrest of a ship is made in Italy, the Italian courts have jurisdiction on the merits of the dispute in the following cases:

(a) if the claimant has his habitual residence or principal place of business in Italy;
(b) if the claim arose in Italy;
(c) if the claim concerns the voyage of the ship during which the arrest is made;
(d) if the claim arose out of a collision or in circumstances covered by Article 13 of the International Convention for the Unification of Certain Rules of Law with respect to Collisions between Vessels, signed at Brussels on 23 September 1910;

(e) if the claim is for salvage;
(f) if the claim is upon a mortgage or hypothecation of the ship arrested.

(5) What kind of security is normally acceptable to enable the ship to be released from arrest?

For liquidated claims the order of arrest contains an indication of the amount for which the arrest is granted (normally covering principal amount, interest and costs). The shipowner can release the vessel from arrest by providing security for such amount in the form of a cash deposit.

The court, however, may authorise the release of the ship against other forms of security and generally a bank guarantee is accepted. Of course, the parties may agree upon different forms of security, for instance a ship's P & I Club letter of undertaking.

For unliquidated claims (i.e. for instance, for claims relating to ownership or possession of the ship), it is not possible for the shipowner to release the vessel from arrest by providing security. However, the court may authorise the employment of the ship under arrest.

(6) In what circumstances can a claimant be made to give security and what security is acceptable?

The judge (at the moment of the issue of the order of arrest or subsequently during the course of proceedings) may, but is not bound to, order the claimants to put up a counter-security covering the legal costs and the damages which the shipowner may suffer in case of wrongful arrest.

The amount of such counter-security is left to the discretion of the judge. According to Italian law, security should be given in the form of a cash deposit but the court may authorise different forms of counter-security. Normally, a bank guarantee is accepted.

(7) In the event that the arrest was ultimately shown to have been wrongful, can a claim be made for wrongful arrest and what must be established in order to successfully maintain such a claim?

Under Italian law, there is a wrongful arrest if:

(a) the claim for which the arrest has been granted does not exist, and
(b) the claimant did not act with normal diligence.

(8) What are the court fees which must be paid in order to make an arrest?

There are no court fees to be paid in order to make an arrest; however, for each application there are duties to be paid in the amount of, roughly, 50 dollars.

Are they recoverable in the event of a successful claim?

Yes, but subject to conditions mentioned under question (10).

(9) How are the lawyers' fees calculated? If possible please estimate the costs of a typical arrest

The fees of Italian lawyers are calculated on the basis of tariffs provided for by the professional law. Such tariffs indicate a minimum or a maximum amount of fees for each procedure and for each single act of each procedure, to be applied by taking into account the amount of the claim.

The professional law provides also for the payment of the services rendered by the lawyer himself or by a different lawyer in respect of the activity performed as "proctor" ("*procuratore*"). Such services consist of the accomplishment of formalities in the court, such as the deposit and the registration of pleadings, exhibits, applications.

It is very difficult, therefore, to provide an estimate of the lawyers' fees which can be incurred in arrest proceedings in Italy since the amount of such fees would exclusively depend upon the value at stake and the services rendered which, in their turn, may vary from case to case.

Very roughly, we may indicate that, normally, the lawyers' fees for an arrest of a ship in respect of a claim not exceeding US$100,000 would not exceed US$3,000/5,000.

(10) Are all or any part of the lawyers' fees recoverable in the event of a successful arrest?

The lawyers' fees and all other legal costs are, in principle, recoverable in the event of the successful arrest. The decision depends on the judge having jurisdiction on the merits of the dispute who may or may not be an Italian judge.

The Italian courts, by means of the judgment on the merits of the dispute, acknowledging the claim for which the arrest was granted, normally order the arrested party to reimburse the lawyers' fees connected to the arrest proceedings. The court, however, in assessing the recoverable fees, takes into account strictly the tariffs fixed by the professional law for the services rendered in court (therefore, no recovery is granted for the extra court services like correspondence with clients, meetings, written advice, etc.) and generally the amount assessed is lower than the one actually payable by the successful party.

(11) How quickly can a ship be arrested after the local lawyer is fully instructed?

Briefly, the procedure to be followed in order to arrest a ship is as follows:

(a) an application supported by pleadings, evidence and power of attorney is deposited with the Clerk of the competent court;

(b) the President of the court appoints a judge who immediately examines the application;

(c) before taking any decision on the application, the judge entrusted with the case must immediately fix a hearing for the parties' appearance and cannot take any decision before such hearing is held;

(d) in an urgent case, the judge can issue the order of arrest on the basis of the application only, without first hearing the two parties. In such a case, however, he must fix a hearing for the parties' attendance within the next 15 days, on which occasion the order of arrest can be confirmed, revoked or modified.

Applications for the arrest of a ship are normally considered by the Italian courts as urgent so that, in most of the cases, it is possible to obtain an arrest on the basis of the urgent matters procedure mentioned at paragraph (d) above.

It would take a few hours, from the moment a local lawyer is fully instructed, to obtain an arrest, and one should take into account the fact that the Italian courts are open only from 8.30 a.m. until 1.30 p.m.

Of course there might be cases in which the competent judge refuses to grant the arrest on the *ex parte* application only, so that getting an order of arrest may take some days and the vessel may sail in the meantime. However, the judge may order the ship not to sail before a decision on the application for arrest is issued.

(12) Is there a minimum amount in dispute for which a ship may be arrested?

Under Italian law, there is in principle no minimum amount for which a ship may be arrested.

(13) Is it possible to arrest a sister ship or a ship in "associated ownership"?

It is a general principle of Italian law that a claimant may obtain a guarantee for its claim only by arresting or attaching the assets belonging to the debtor. Such principle, applied to shipping matters, means that a claimant can normally arrest only those ships whose registered owner is the debtor.

The strictness of this rule, with reference to the arrest of ships subject to the 1952 Brussels Convention, has been mitigated as a consequence of the implementation under Italian law of the Convention. Article 3 of the Convention provides for the possibility of arresting either the particular ship to which the claim refers or any other ship in the same ownership. Paragraph 2 of Article 3 clarifies that "ships shall be deemed to be in the same ownership when all the shares therein are owned by the same person or persons". It has been held by the Italian courts that, by virtue of the provisions contained in Article 3(1)(2) of the 1952 Brussels Convention, it is possible to arrest a ship when the shares of the owning company are owned by the same companies or persons or person owning the ship in respect of which a maritime claim arose. The burden of proof regarding the ownership is on the arrestor.

(14) What is the order of priorities in the event of the distribution by the court of the proceeds of sale of the ship?

Under Italian law, the order of priorities amongst preferred claims is to be determined on the basis of the provisions of the law of the flag of the ship.

The order of priorities under Italian law, which however applies to the sale of Italian ships only, is the following:

(a) maritime liens as provided by the Code of Navigation;
(b) mortgages;
(c) liens provided by the Civil Code;
(d) ordinary creditors.

The list of maritime liens on ships is provided by Art. 552 of the Code of Navigation and is as follows:

(a) law costs due to the state, and expenses incurred in the common interest of the creditors in order to preserve the vessel or to procure its sale and the distribution of the proceeds of sale; tonnage dues, light or harbour dues, and other public taxes and charges of the same character; pilotage dues; the cost of watching and preservation from the time of the entry of the vessel into the last port;
(b) claims arising out of the contract of engagement of the master, crew, and other persons hired on board;
(c) claims resulting from expenses anticipated by the Administration of the Mercantile Marine or of the Inland Navigation or by the Consular Authority for the maintenance and repatriation of crew members; the credits for mandatory contributions due to institutions of social providence and assistance for the seamen and for the personnel of the inland navigation;
(d) remuneration for assistance and salvage, and the contribution of the vessel in general average;
(e) indemnities for collision or other accident of navigation, as also for damage caused to works forming part of harbours, docks, and navigable ways; indemnities for personal injury to passengers or crew; indemnities for loss of or damage to cargo or baggage;
(f) claims resulting from contracts entered into or acts done by the master, acting within the scope of his authority, away from the vessel's home port, where such contracts or acts are necessary for the preservation of the vessel or the continuation of its voyage, whether the master is or is not at the same time owner of the vessel.

(15) Are the claims in respect of which a ship may be arrested subject to a time bar (or prescription) and, if so, are these different according to the nature of the claim?

Normally, the claims in respect of which a ship may be arrested are subject to a time bar or a prescription and these are different according to the nature of the claim. However, the time bar or prescription is to be determined on the basis of the provisions of the substantive law applicable to the claim.

(16) Is it possible to apply for the arrest of a ship outside the normal working hours of the court?

It is not possible to file an application for the arrest of a ship outside the normal working hours of the Italian courts, which are from 8.30 a.m. until 1.30 p.m. from Monday to Saturday, public holidays excluded.

CHAPTER 19

JAPAN

For the better understanding of readers, we should like to state the following:

Japan is a Civil Law country. Japan has neither ratified the 1952 Arrest Convention nor has a concept similar to "maritime claim" under the Convention and Lisbon draft Convention. Nor does the concept of an action *in rem* exist. However, to provide for the arrest of a ship that would stay in port only for a short period and quickly move on, there is a new device for a preliminary and tentative arrest, which can be used before an application for official auction is filed.

(1) What are the types of claim for which a ship may be arrested in Japan?

In Japan there are three types of claim for which a ship may be arrested:

(i) the first type of claim is the monetary claim with a maritime lien or mortgage;

(ii) the second type of claim is the ordinary monetary claim (without a maritime lien) by which a ship may be arrested to obtain security for the future enforcement of the claim awarded in a court judgment or arbitration award (Art. 13 of the Civil Enforcement Preservation Law) (provisional attachment); and

(iii) the third type of claim is the claim to demand delivery of the ship or the cargo, etc. if there is the specific necessity to do so provided for in paragraphs 1 and 2 of Art. 23 of the Civil Enforcement Preservation Law (provisional disposition or injunction).

With regard to the above (ii) and (iii) type claims, there is also an arrest by a final court judgment after both parties have disputed such claims at the proper court or place of arbitration and a favourable award has been rendered to the claimant.

There are two methods of arrest for the first type of claim (with maritime lien/mortgage) (claim (i) in the above: (1) one is a tentative arrest for five days before filing an application for an official auction with the court, details of which are explained below; and (2) another is an arrest by an official auction order.

If there is a risk that an official auction would be extremely difficult unless the ship's nationality certificate, etc. was lifted[1] prior to filing an application for an official auction, an application for tentative arrest of the ship for five days may be filed with the court and such a tentative arrest is enforced under Art. 189 and Art. 115 of the Civil Enforcement Law (the "Law"). When filing an application for an official auction an applicant must deposit moneys on account of the cost of the official auction procedures, but when filing application for a tentative arrest the applicant is not required to make such deposit. Another advantage of the tentative arrest is that an applicant for arrest may file such an application with a court which has jurisdiction over the ship's registered port, and if she is a foreign flag ship, with the Tokyo District Court and 11 other district courts (Civil Enforcement Regulation Art. 77) regardless of the location of the prospective port of call in Japan. After obtaining a court order for such arrest, the court order remains valid for two weeks (Art. 115(7) of the Law). The applicant may wait for the ship to arrive at a port in Japan, with an arrest order in hand, and may arrest her within such period.

Therefore, it is usual that the tentative arrest method is chosen for arrest of an ocean-going ship. But in order to obtain a tentative arrest order, it is necessary to produce a reasonable explanation that unless the ship's nationality certificate etc. is removed from the ship before applying for an official auction, official auction of the ship would be extremely difficult (Art. 115 of the Law).

Contrary to the tentative arrest application, in an application for an official auction the applicant must file such application with a district court which has proper jurisdiction over the particular port where the ship is docked (Arts. 189, 113 of the Law).

Except for the above differences, the documentation for an application for a tentative arrest and that for an official auction are virtually the same.

(2) Is there a distinction between claims which give rise to a maritime lien and other types of claim?

There is a clear distinction between the first type, monetary claims with maritime lien, and the second type, ordinary monetary claim by which arrest can be made (provisional attachment). The distinction is as follows: with regard to the claim with maritime lien, a ship must be the same ship for which the claim with maritime lien has arisen against the shipowner, the bareboat charterer or the time charterer,[2] in principle within one year from the occurrence of the maritime lien; whereas the second type ordinary money claim must be a claim against the shipowner of a ship who is the same one as the obligor. Where the claimant intends to arrest the ship (just like attaching

1 This arrest will be effected when the nationality certificate etc. is lifted from the ship.
2 It is a kind of quasi-action *in rem*.

the assets of the shipowner) for future enforcement of such claim, the limitation period for making such provisional attachment (arrest) depends upon the prescription period (limitation period) of such claims. Under provisional attachment, the claim need not be due, but under the arrest by maritime lien, the claim must be due.

The third type of claim is the claim to demand delivery of the ship or the cargo. Arrest of the ship can be made in order to enforce delivery of the ship or the cargo, etc. where there is a strong necessity to do so.

The first type of claims which give rise to a maritime lien under Japanese law are as follows:

(i) maritime lien under the Commercial Code Art. 842.

1. expenses relating to the sale of the ship and its appurtenances by official auction, and the expenses of preservation after the commencement of the proceedings for the sale by official auction;
2. expenses of preservation of the ship and its appurtenances at the last port;
3. all public dues levied on the ship in respect of the voyage;
4. pilotage dues and towage dues;
5. salvage remuneration and the ship's contribution to general average;
6. claims which have arisen from the necessity for the continuance of the voyage[3];
7. claims of the master and other mariners which have arisen from their contracts of employment;
8. claims which have arisen from the sale or construction and the equipment of the ship, in cases where the ship has not yet made any voyage after her sale or construction; and claims in respect of the equipment, food and fuel of the ship for her last voyage[4];

(ii) maritime lien under Art. 19 of the Japanese COGSA. Where a part or whole of a ship has been the object of a contract of carriage for the goods, and the charterer in turn has made a contract of carriage with a third party, those who may claim the compensation for damage to the goods arising within the scope of the master's duties may exercise a preferential right for his claim against the ship and her accessories.

(iii) maritime lien under Arts. 3 and 95 of the Shipowners etc. Liability Limitation Law. The following listing of the respective claims is made in accordance with Art. 2 of the Convention on Limitation of

3 In this regard, a stevedore company's claim for stevedore work in a port does not give rise to a maritime lien since it is not necessary for continuation of the voyage.

4 When the voyage commenced, such a maritime lien will be extinguished under the Commercial Code Art. 847.

Liability for Maritime Claims, 1976 which Japan ratified in 1986. The listing of the claims in Article 3 of the Japanese Shipowners etc. Liability Limitation Law is virtually the same as the above Convention.

1. Claims in respect of loss of life or personal injury or loss of or damage to property occurring on board or in direct connection with the operation of the ship or with salvage operations, and consequential loss resulting therefrom[5];
2. claims in respect of loss resulting from delay in the carriage by sea of cargo, passengers or their luggage;
3. claims in respect of other loss resulting from infringement of rights other than contractual rights, occurring in direct connection with the operation of the ship or salvage operations;
4. claims in respect of the raising, removal, destruction or the rendering harmless of a ship which is sunk, wrecked, stranded or abandoned, including anything that is or has been on board such ship;
5. claims in respect of the removal, destruction or the rendering harmless of the cargo of the ship;
6. claims of a person other than the person liable in respect of measures taken in order to avert or minimise loss for which the person liable may limit his liability and further loss caused by such measures.

(iv) maritime lien under Art. 5 and para. 1 of Art. 40 of the Oil Pollution Damage Compensation Law with regard to oil pollution damage (see CLC Art. 3 para. 1).

(v) lien by ship's registered mortgage by Art. 848 of the Commercial Code.[6]

Choice of laws question in arrest by maritime lien

In order to enforce a maritime lien and arrest a ship, both the governing law of the claim and the law of the ship's flag must allow such a maritime lien for the purpose of fair and equitable treatment of the many interested persons under choice of laws. Recently, the Tokyo District Court admitted enforcement of a maritime lien based only on Japanese law (*Manila Transporter* case by Tokyo District Court on 19 August 1991, *Hanrei Jiho* No. 1402 page 91 and *Nagasaki Spirit* case by Tokyo District Court on 15 December 1992, *Hanrei Times* No. 811 page 229); however, these cases

5 In cases of a cargo damage claim or a collision claim, a claimant can usually claim a maritime lien under this category of the Shipowners etc. Liability Limitation Law.

6 Possessory lien. A possessory lien holder such as a ship repairer who possesses a ship may file an application for official auction (Art. 195 of the Law) and may practically enjoy the first priority in distribution over a maritime lien and mortgage (see page 387 of Annotated Civil Enforcement Law Vol. 5).

were garnishment cases on the hull insurance money by the maritime lien holder and they were not cases of arrest of a ship. After the decisions, other judges of the Tokyo District Court have required proof for maritime liens admitted by the flag law in a different case.

Therefore, it is considered that in order to arrest a ship by maritime lien, both the governing law of the claim and the law of the ship's flag must allow the particular maritime lien. However, in view of the above two court cases, there is a risk that a foreign flag ship may be arrested by a Japanese maritime lien alone.

(3)(a) What pleadings, affidavits and documents must be presented to the court when applying for an arrest and in what language?

(i) In general

Unlike the countries where an arrest order is given upon production of a lawyer's affidavit or a complaint to a court, in Japan it is necessary to produce supporting evidence to reasonably prove the claim (in respect of provisional attachment or injunction) or to fully prove the maritime lien.

(ii) Language

Application must be made in Japanese. The relevant parts of the supporting documents in a foreign language have to be translated into Japanese under the Law, and the supporting documents together with the Japanese translation thereof have to be produced when an application is filed with the court.

(iii) Necessary pleadings and documents for tentative arrest application

1. An application for a delivery order for the ship's nationality certificate, etc. is required before filing an application for the ship's official auction when the claim is by virtue of a mortgage or a maritime lien (Arts. 189, 115 of the Law).

2-1. *Mortgage.* A certified copy of the public registration record of mortgage or a certified copy of a notarised mortgage deed executed by a notary public (Arts. 189 and 181, para. 1, items 2 and 3 of the Law).

2-2. *Maritime Lien.* Copies of claim documents which show the existence of a maritime lien; for example, documents which show that the originals are on board the ship or services were made to the ship. For example, for a bunker claim, a chief engineer's receipt would be good evidence in addition to an invoice (Arts. 189 and 181, para. 1, item 4 of the Law).

3. An explanation of relevant provisions of the foreign flag law regarding the foreign mortgage/maritime lien, and the granting of arrest by such foreign mortgage/maritime lien, and a legal opinion of a qualified foreign lawyer thereto are required.

4. Sometimes, the court requires the production of the relevant provisions of the foreign law which qualifies the master of such foreign ship to receive service of court documents. But, we consider that it is not a mandatory requirement (see Tokyo District Court judgment of 20 December 1968, *Chase Manhattan Bank* v. *Tokyo-To District Labour Committee*, *Hanrei Jiho* No. 563 page 54).
5. Statement explaining the risk that the ship's arrest by an official auction would be extremely difficult unless the ship's nationality certificate, etc. is removed before applying for an official auction.
6. Copies of the record of the ship in the Lloyd's Register of Ships.
7. Two affidavits certifying the corporate existence and the representative of the corporation of the claimant.
8. Two affidavits of the powers of attorney to the lawyer for the claimant.

(iv) Necessary pleadings and documents for arrest by official auction

1. An application for official auction.
2. Documents listed in (iii) above except for the documents of 1. and 5.

(v) Necessary documents for application for provisional attachment order or provisional disposition order

1. An application with a court for provisional attachment or provisional disposition (Art. 13 of Civil Enforcement Preservation Law and Art. 13 of Civil Security Regulation).
2. A copy of the record of the ship in the Lloyd's Register of Ships (to prove the ship itself and the name of the owner of the ship) (Art. 20, item 2 sub-item c of Civil Enforcement Preservation Regulation).
3. Three affidavits certifying the corporate existence and the name of the representative of the corporation of the claimant.
4. Three powers of attorney notarised in favour of the lawyer from the claimant's representative.
5. Documents to prove the monetary claim or the claim for delivery of the ship, the cargo or the bunker (Art. 13, para. 2 of Civil Enforcement Preservation Law).
6. Documents to prove the necessity to make provisional attachment (invoices, reminders, request to postpone payment by debtor and documents to prove financial difficulty, etc.).
7. Explanation Statement as to why the provisional attachment or the provisional disposition is required (Art. 13, para. 2 of Civil Enforcement Preservation Law).

8. Document to prove the value of the ship (Art. 20, item 2 sub-item d of Civil Enforcement Preservation Regulation).
9. Document to prove that the ship remains in a port to prove the proper jurisdiction of the court (Art. 12 of Civil Enforcement Preservation Law).

(b) Which documents must be notarised or otherwise authenticated?

A mortgage deed needs to be notarised. A corporate certificate of an applicant for arrest and that of a shipowner and a power of attorney are usually authenticated or notarised. At the time of application for arrest, fax copies of the corporate certificate and power of attorney would be acceptable, but the originals should be submitted in due course.

(4) Is it possible to arrest a ship solely in order to obtain security for a claim which will ultimately be determined in another jurisdiction?

Yes, it is possible to arrest a ship solely in order to obtain security for a claim which will ultimately be determined in another jurisdiction by virtue of a foreign court jurisdiction clause or a foreign arbitration clause.

(5) What kind of security is normally acceptable to enable the ship to be released from arrest?

(i) Release from arrest by maritime lien

The shipowner shall, in addition to depositing the security fund, be required to assert that the shipowner has an objection to the arrest for lack of cause. There are two requirements to release a ship from arrest:

(1) the shipowner must file an objection against the court's official auction order because there is no valid claim or no maritime lien (Arts. 189, 183, 182, 11 and 10 item 6 of the Law or Art. 23 of the Civil Enforcement Preservation Law); and
(2) the shipowner must post a security bond for all claims and enforcement costs as instructed by the court (Arts. 189, 39, 117 of the Law).

A provisional disposition may be available to release the ship from arrest, too.

(ii) Kind of security required for release from arrest by maritime lien

Cash, negotiable instruments allowed by the court, or a security bond from a Japanese bank, etc. or Japan Ship Owners' Mutual Protection & Indemnity Association or Japanese underwriters (Arts. 117 and 15 of the Law, and Art. 78 of the Civil Enforcement Rule), but no foreign P & I Clubs, or foreign underwriters, etc.

(iii) Kind of security required for release from arrest by provisional attachment or provisional disposition (injunction)

Release of the ship from arrest by provisional attachment or provisional disposition (based on Civil Enforcement Preservation Law) can be effected by depositing *cash* to cover the full claim amount. No security other than cash is accepted.

(6) In what circumstances can a claimant be made to give security and what security is acceptable?

(i) Arrest by provisional attachment or provisional disposition

If it is an arrest by way of provisional attachment or provisional disposition (injunction) under the Civil Enforcement Preservation Law, a claimant (applicant) must deposit security for possible damages to the shipowner for wrongful arrest (Art. 14 of Civil Enforcement Preservation Law). Such security can be made by cash, negotiable instruments or a guaranty letter from a Japanese bank or other Japanese financial institution (Arts. 14 and 4 of Civil Enforcement Preservation Law and Art. 2 of its Regulation). However, in view of the matter of urgency, the security should be deposited in cash. Later, the security may be changed from cash to another kind of security upon application of the claimant (Art. 4, para. 2 of the Civil Enforcement Preservation Law and Art. 116 of the Civil Procedure Law).

The security amount shall be decided by a judge after considering the validity of the claim, the possible loss of earnings (daily detention losses of the ship), the value of the ship and the claim amount, etc. If the claim amount is large compared with the value of the ship, then approximately one third of such claim amount may be allowed as a security amount by the court.

(ii) Arrest by maritime lien

In a case of tentative arrest or official arrest by maritime lien, a claimant is not required to give security for a wrongful arrest.

(7) In the event that the arrest was ultimately shown to have been wrongful, can a claim be made for wrongful arrest and what must be established in order to successfully maintain such a claim?

Yes, a claim can be made for a wrongful arrest. Such a claim is one in tort and the illegal act of the person who arrested a ship must be proved.

Under Japanese law a ship which has completed preparation for commencing a voyage shall not be arrested, with some exceptions (Art. 689 of the Commercial Code). (This restriction is completely different from the 1952 Convention, Article 2, para. 2.)

There is a court case which held that when one arrested a ship violating Art. 543 (currently Art. 689 of the Commercial Code) with knowledge that a third person other than the obligor was in possession of the ship, it was a tortious act intentionally affecting the possessory right (Osaka District Court, judgment date unknown but published by Legal Newspaper No. 827 on 30 November 1911).

Art. 689 of Commercial Code
No exercise of seizure or provisional seizure (excluding the case made according to the method of making registration of provisional seizure) can be levied on a ship which has completed preparations for commencing a voyage. Provided that, this shall not apply in respect of such obligations as may have been incurred for the purpose of making preparations for commencing the voyage.

Note that some courts have allowed the arrest of ships at ports of call after commencement of the voyage.

(8) What are the court fees which must be paid in order to make an arrest? Are they recoverable in the event of a successful claim?

(i) In the case of provisional attachment arrest or provisional disposition arrest

In the case of an application for provisional attachment or provisional disposition, apart from the deposit of the security for possible wrongful arrest, only nominal court fees for the revenue stamp (and the fees to a court sheriff) would be required. Such amounts are not usually recoverable.

(ii) In the case of tentative arrest by maritime lien

In a tentative arrest by maritime lien, an applicant for arrest is required only to pay a small revenue stamp fee and to pay fees for a court sheriff to make service of a court decision and to remove the ship's nationality certificate, etc. from the ship. The fees for a court sheriff for such work would be around 50,000 Yen, which are not usually recoverable.

(iii) In the case of official auction

However, if it is an application for official auction by virtue of a maritime lien or a mortgage, then a court would require the applicant to deposit the full court fees necessary for the official auction procedures until completion thereof (Art. 14 of the Law). Some courts require deposit of the full amount of prospective costs before issuing the commencement decision for official auction, and other courts allow an instalment deposit of such costs, apparently depending upon their past practice and experience.

A ship's arrest under current Japanese law is to order the shipowner to stop the ship from sailing and to remove the ship's important documents such as the ship's nationality certificate, etc. from the ship (Art. 114 of the Law), whereby she will be legally unable to sail. The possession of such an arrested ship still remains in the shipowner's hand. The possession of an arrested ship may be transferred from the shipowner (the master) to a court appointed custodian (usually a court sheriff) only upon an application by the applicant for arrest. Therefore, under the Law, the maintenance cost of the ship shall be borne and paid by the shipowner even after the arrest for official auction has been effected until a custodian is appointed, at a request of the applicant, by the court (Art. 116 of the Law).

Therefore, if the shipowner pays the maintenance cost including the crew's wages, it means that an applicant for arrest is not required to deposit the prospective maintenance cost unless the shipowner and the crew abandon the arrested ship. However, some courts would require an applicant for arrest to deposit such future maintenance cost before issuing the commencement order for official auction.

Apart from the deposit of the maintenance cost (which we do not consider mandatory, theoretically speaking), the costs legally required to be deposited by an applicant for official auction are twofold: (1) court appointed assessor's fees for appraising the value of the arrested ship to determine the minimum price for auction sale of the ship; and (2) the court sheriff's fees for preparation for and presiding over the auction sale of the arrested ship. The court sheriff's fees for official auction are determined by a tariff based on the actual sale proceeds of the ship and, therefore, at the time of deciding the deposit amount, the assessor's fees and the court sheriff's fees are decided by estimate taking into account the kind of ship (gross tonnage, purpose of use of the ship, ship's equipment, etc.), the age of the ship, the maintenance condition, the market, the quotation price for sale, and price determination method to calculate registration tax.

In accordance with the experience and practices of courts, the following courts (which have jurisdiction over ports where many ships call) would require, at their discretion, the following initial deposit. However, such deposit amount may be varied in the future.

Tokyo District Court:	Yen 10,000,000 Tokyo Court, calculated on the basis of previous auction cases wherein wharfages were expensive.
Yokohama District Court:	Yen 1,000,000 for each 1,000 gross tons
Yokohama District Court Kawasaki branch:	Yen 2,000,000
Nagoya District Court:	Yen 500,000
Kobe District Court:	Yen 500,000
Osaka District Court:	Yen 3,000,000 to Yen 5,000,000
Aomori District Court Hachinohe branch:	Yen 1,000,000

The deposit amount may be negotiable if a court requires a high amount of deposit. The necessary amount would be ordered to be added by the court later.

The above court costs come under the expenses of the maritime lien under the Commercial Code, Art. 842, item 1 (see question (2)), and they are recoverable as a top priority from the proceeds of the ship's sale.

(9) How are the lawyers' fees calculated? If possible please estimate the costs of a typical arrest.

Legal fees are calculated in accordance with the Japanese Bar Association's Tariff. An English translation of the fees tariff is available. However, it may be handled on a time basis taking into account the difficulty of the arrest and the merit of the arrest, etc.

As a very rough example, if for a claim of 10,000,000 Yen a ship is arrested and the matter is successfully settled quite quickly, the lawyer's fees would be around 1,000,000 Yen. However, it would vary depending on the location of the port at which the ship is arrested. If it is far from Tokyo, the cost would increase.

(10) Are all or any part of the lawyers' fees recoverable in the event of a successful arrest?

Generally, the lawyers' fees are not recoverable. However, if a claim is in tort, such as a collision case (especially involving a death or injury claim), 10 per cent of the claim amount may be allowed.

(11) How quickly can a ship be arrested after the local lawyer is fully instructed?

It would much depend on the volume of necessary documents to prove the claim, etc. (see question (3)(a)(iii) and (iv) hereof) because the lawyer has to prepare Japanese translations of the relevant supporting documents, which is usually time-consuming work.

If the claim amount, breakdown of the claim and research of the maritime lien under the flag law and the lawyer's opinion thereof, preparation of the supporting documents and the corporate certificates and the power of attorney from the claimant have been completed and the translations of them are available, then a lawyer can prepare the application for arrest. Another important problem is to find out when and at which port the ship in question will call. In Japan there is no agency to detect the whereabouts of a ship. Once such preparation is completed, arrest can be made fairly quickly. Of course, time for meeting with a judge and arrangement with a court sheriff is necessary. In an arrest by provisional attachment or provisional disposition, unlike arrest by maritime lien, there must be time for depositing security with an office of the Judicial Bureau (the governmental agency), which will accept an application for deposit from 9.00 a.m. to 4.00 p.m.

(12) Is there a minimum amount in dispute for which a ship may be arrested?

Provisional attachment arrest

If the claim amount in an application for provisional attachment arrest is a small amount compared with the possible damages for the shipowner (detention loss in case of wrongful arrest), a court may allow arrest of a ship but the security deposit amount may well be much larger than the claim amount considering the ship's detention loss. If the claim amount is small, it is necessary to consider the lawyer's fees (on a time basis) and expenses. It is a matter of sound business judgement. Under the Japanese legal system a ship cannot be arrested by the lawyer's (solicitor's) affidavit only, without security. A lawyer must spend considerable time in preparation.

For your information, a court internal manual states that if the claim amount is very small compared with the value of the ship, a court may consider that it is not necessary to arrest the ship for such a small claim amount to preserve the right for future enforcement of the claim (Art. 13 of Civil Enforcement Preservation Law).

Arrest by maritime lien

If arrest is based on a maritime lien, a court may allow arrest of a ship even if the claim amount is small but the court would require a deposit for official auction costs, which may be larger than the claim amount. The matter will be a business judgement of the claimant. See question (8), opinion in (iii).

(13) Is it possible to arrest a sister ship or a ship in "associated ownership"?

If a ship A and a sister Ship B are 100 per cent owned by the same shipowner and the shipowner is obligor of the monetary claim, ship A or B can be arrested by the claimant by virtue of provisional attachment. A sister ship co-owned by the obligor of the monetary claim and by another person cannot be arrested.

A parent company owns 100 per cent of the shares of a (FOC) paper company which owns a (FOC) ship A and the same parent company also has 100 per cent shares of another (FOC) paper company which owns a (FOC) ship B; such FOC companies do not have an individual business operation but are just paper companies in the accounting book of the parent company. In such a case if the claimant can claim and prove such facts by piercing the corporate veil, the claimant can arrest ship B by the claim against the owner of ship A or the parent company by way of provisional attachment. It is a matter of evidence.

(14) What is the order of priorities in the event of the distribution by the court of the proceeds of sale of the ship?

In the case of the maritime lien listed in Art. 842 of the Commercial Code, priority is in accordance with the order of the item number (Art. 844 of the Commercial Code).

With regard to the maritime lien under Art. 19 of the Japanese COGSA, the maritime lien under the Ship Owner's Liability Limitation Law and the maritime lien under the Oil Pollution Damage Compensation Law, the claims with such maritime liens are subordinate to the item 8 claim of Art. 842 of the Commercial Code. The claim secured by mortgage comes after the claim with maritime lien (Art. 849 of Commercial Code).

In the case of a foreign flag ship, it is the general tendency of Japanese courts that the priority or ranking of claims in distribution shall be determined in accordance with the flag law under the Japanese law regarding the choice of laws. However, some district courts have applied Japanese law for determining the priority.

(15) Are the claims in respect of which a ship may be arrested subject to a time bar (or prescription) and, if so, are these different according to the nature of the claim?

A maritime lien under Japanese law will be extinguished by lapse of one year from the time the lien arose. The maritime lien under item 8 of Art. 842 of the Commercial Code will be extinguished by the sailing of the ship (Art. 847, para. 2 of the Commercial Code). A possessory lien is effective as long as the claim is effective. Arrest by virtue of provisional attachment or provisional disposition can be made as long as the claim itself is valid and not extinguished by an extinctive prescription period (e.g. a time bar).

(16) Is it possible to apply for the arrest of a ship outside the normal working hours of the court?

No, it is not generally possible to apply for arrest of a ship outside the normal working hours of the court.

In an application for tentative arrest for five days based on maritime lien, it is possible to make application before the ship arrives at a port in Japan.

But, in an application for provisional attachment or an application for provisional disposition of the ship, the court will obtain its jurisdiction to accept such application when the ship has arrived at a port within the court's jurisdiction.

There was rather a rare case where a court tentatively accepted a *de facto* or a preliminary application without a docket number, a few days before the ship's arrival, for examination of an application and supporting documents and the judge's preliminary findings. The court allowed a formal examination of an application with a docket number at an early morning time (8.30 a.m.) outside ordinary working hours, as the ship's stay was very brief in the port.

(17) Please provide any other information which you believe is relevant in deciding whether or not to arrest a ship in your jurisdiction.

In view of the foregoing, it is most important that the claimant supply and forward all the necessary supporting documents and other certificates to a lawyer in Japan for preparation well in advance.

Another important point in deciding whether or not to arrest a ship is the market value of the ship. In many cases, the shipowner of a ship which is the target of arrest is usually placed in financial difficulties. Therefore, if the ship is an old ship and if she does not have a commercial market value, then it may well be that no one would be a buyer (bidder) and the master and the crew may leave the ship and the ship may be abandoned.

Then the claimant who has applied for an arrest would receive strong pressure from the court and the Maritime Safety Agency (the Japanese coast guard) for the maintenance and safety of the ship and to prevent possible oil pollution to the coast, or any other marine casualty expecially in a typhoon season.

Therefore, if the ship is old and valueless, the lawyer would be rather reluctant to arrest her. If the ship has a good value in the market, then the mortgagee or financiers (leasing company) may pay the claim amount on behalf of or in place of the owner and the arrest claimant may expect to recover the claim in full or in part from such financiers.

Also, another element to consider is other maritime lien holders' claim amounts and the priority of the claim under the law of the ship's flag and Japanese law.

CHAPTER 20

KOREA

(1) What are the types of claim for which a ship may be arrested in Korea?

In Korea, an arrest of a vessel is possible for any type of claim. Korea has not ratified the International Convention for the Unification of Certain Rules Relating to the Arrest of Sea-Going Ships (1952). Therefore, in Korea, an arrest of a vessel is not limited to maritime claims such as claims arising out of damage caused by any ship, loss of life or personal injury caused by any ship or occurring in connection with the operation of any ship, salvage, agreement relating to the use or hire of any ship, agreement relating to the carriage of goods in any ship, loss of or damage to goods, general average, bottomry, towage, pilotage, etc. which are listed in Article 1 of the Convention.

Under Korean law, a vessel may be arrested under (1) provisional attachment, (2) maritime lien, (3) judgment order, or (4) ship mortgage. Please note that the purpose of arrest under provisional attachment is to obtain security for a claim against the shipowner while the purpose of arrest under maritime lien, judgment order, and ship mortgage is to obtain final satisfaction of the claim.

(2) Is there a distinction between claims which give rise to a maritime lien and other types of claim?

Yes, there are at least five distinctions between claims which give rise to maritime liens and other types of claims.

(a) Under Korean law, only those claims which are legally recognised as maritime liens are maritime liens. They are:
   (i) costs of lawsuit for common interest of the creditors, expenses in respect of public auction of the ship and its appurtenances, all public dues levied on the ship in respect of the voyage, pilotage and tugboat dues, expenses of preservation and inspection of the ship and its appurtenances at the last port;
   (ii) claims arising from contract of employment of the mariners and any other employee of the ship;

(iii) salvage remuneration and claims regarding the contribution to general average; and

(iv) claims for damages caused by a collision of ships, claims for damage to navigation facilities and sea routes caused by other accidents inquired into, and claims for death or personal injury of crew or passengers.

For foreign vessels, the types of claims which give rise to maritime liens are determined by the law of the ship's flag.

(b) Maritime liens have first priority in the event of a court distribution of the sale proceeds of the vessel. They rank higher than ship mortgages and judgment orders. For foreign vessels, the priority of claims is determined according to the law of the ship's flag.

(c) Provisions relating to mortgage apply to maritime liens *mutatis mutandis*. Therefore, execution of vessels proceeds in a way that is similar to the compulsory auction procedure of immovable property. However, unlike ship mortgages, maritime liens are not registered.

(d) Exercise of a maritime lien is an action against the vessel itself rather than against the debtor or the property of the debtor as in the case of provisional arrest of a vessel.

(e) Since maritime liens attach to the vessel itself, even a transfer of title of the vessel will not affect maritime liens.

(3) (a) What pleadings, affidavits and documents must be presented to the court when applying for an arrest and in what language?
(b) Which documents must be notarised or otherwise authenticated?

To arrest a vessel, the claimant's legal representative must submit a notarised power of attorney, a notarised certificate of the corporate nationality of the claimant's company, documents supporting the claim, and the vessel's certificate of registry. These documents must be translated into Korean.

In order to provisionally arrest a vessel for security purposes, the claimant's legal representative must file an application for provisional arrest of the vessel on behalf of the claimant. In order to arrest a vessel under exercise of maritime lien, ship mortgage or court judgment order, the claimant's legal representative must file an application to commence auction sale of the vessel, which includes arrest of the vessel.

Please note that supporting documents do not need to be authenticated in order to arrest a vessel, but they must be authenticated during a formal action on the merits by having the issuer or the preparer of the documents testify in court as to their authenticity or by having the documents notarised by a notary public and confirmed by a Korean Consulate when an opposing party denies authenticity of the evidence.

(4) Is it possible to arrest a ship solely in order to obtain security for a claim which will ultimately be determined in another jurisdiction?

Yes, it is possible to arrest a ship solely in order to obtain security for a claim which will ultimately be determined in another jurisdiction under provisional arrest of a vessel for security purposes.

(5) What kind of security is normally acceptable to enable the ship to be released from arrest?

To release a vessel from provisional arrest, a shipowner may deposit either the full amount of the claim in cash with the court or a letter of guarantee that is acceptable to the claimant. Please note that in Korea, aside from a cash deposit, there is no legal basis for depositing any other forms of security. Therefore, unless the claimant agrees to accept some other forms of security such as a letter of guarantee in exchange for the withdrawal of the arrest application, the shipowner must deposit the full claim amount in cash in order to release the vessel, even if the alleged claim amount is exaggerated. This of course leaves much room for abuse by the claimant, i.e. by stating an excessive claim amount and refusing to accept other forms of security.

To release a vessel arrested for final satisfaction of a claim under maritime lien, mortgage or court judgment order, the shipowner should:

- (i) raise an objection against the decision to commence the auction proceedings or bring a lawsuit for confirmation or declaration of non-existence of maritime liens;
- (ii) apply for the suspension of the auction proceedings;
- (iii) deposit the full claim amount as well as the auction expenses in cash; and
- (iv) apply for cancellation of all procedures for auction sale of the vessel, except for the procedure on distribution of auction proceeds.

The vessel is then released and the court distributes the funds deposited by the shipowner to the claimants when the case at issue is finalised.

(6) In what circumstances can a claimant be made to give security and what security is acceptable?

In order to obtain a court decision for provisional arrest of a vessel, a claimant must deposit about one-tenth to one-eighth of the claim amount in cash or a performance bond issued by the Korean Surety and Fidelity Insurance Co. Ltd. ("KSFI"), which requires collateral such as a personal guarantee of a Korean lawyer, as security against the possible damage to the shipowner of wrongful arrest. Please note that KSFI requires a premium of one per cent of the security deposit.

In order to obtain a court decision for arrest of a vessel under maritime lien, mortgage and court judgment orders, there is no requirement of security other than auction expenses.

(7) In the event that the arrest was ultimately shown to have been wrongful, can a claim be made for wrongful arrest and what must be established in order to successfully maintain such a claim?

Yes, if a court reviews the claim on the merits and does not acknowledge the claim, then the shipowner may sue for wrongful arrest of the vessel.

In Korea, for wrongful arrest, general principles of tort apply and the shipowner has to prove bad faith or negligence of the claimant. Some Supreme Court cases even presume wrongful arrest if a claim is proven to be without merit in the main suit.

In Korea, when a court issues a final judgment on the merits in favour of the shipowner, the claimant may apply to the court for the release of the deposit which was lodged as security against wrongful arrest. The court will issue a notice to the shipowner with respect to the claimant's application for the release and the shipowner would have 14 days to file a lawsuit for wrongful arrest of the vessel.

(8) What are the court fees which must be paid in order to make an arrest? Are they recoverable in the event of a successful claim?

To provisionally arrest a vessel, the claimant has to pay for the cost of having a bailiff exercise the arrest, which is relatively inexpensive. This amount is very difficult to recover because provisional arrest is an optional procedure to secure a claim and is not essential or necessary to the main legal proceedings.

To arrest a vessel under maritime lien, court judgment order or ship mortgage, the claimant must deposit the auction expenses in cash with the court. Such expenses will have first priority at the time of distribution of the sales proceeds of the vessel.

(9) How are the lawyers' fees calculated? If possible please estimate the costs of a typical arrest.

Lawyers' fees are calculated on an hourly basis, which varies depending on the experience of the lawyer, or on a lump sum basis.

The costs of a typical arrest are about US$5,000–6,000 since every document submitted to the court must be translated into Korean and a lawyer would have to go to court to file an application for the arrest and to expedite enforcement of the court order.

(10) Are all or part of the lawyers' fees recoverable in the event of a successful arrest?

In theory, lawyers' fees for provisional arrest are recoverable if provisional arrest has been obtained after a hearing. (The recoverable amount is limited to one-half of the recoverable legal fees provided under Supreme Court Regulations, which is provided hereunder.) However, courts almost always order provisional arrest without holding a hearing. Thus, in practice, lawyers' fees for provisional arrest are not recoverable.

As for the amount of recoverable legal fees for arrest under a maritime lien, mortgage or court order, there is currently no provision on this issue although there are arguments that lawyers' fees for maritime liens which arise from costs of a lawsuit for the common interest of the creditors should be recoverable.

For main actions on the merit, the following is a schedule of recoverable legal fees under the Supreme Court Regulations:

Recovery up to 1 million Won:	10% of the recovery amount
Recovery up to 2 million Won:	100,000 Won plus 9% of the amount exceeding 1 million Won
Recovery up to 3 million Won:	190,000 Won plus 8% of the amount exceeding 2 million Won
Recovery up to 4 million Won:	270,000 Won plus 7% of the amount exceeding 3 million Won
Recovery up to 5 million Won:	340,000 Won plus 6% of the amount exceeding 4 million Won
Recovery up to 10 million Won:	400,000 Won plus 5% of the amount exceeding 5 million Won
Recovery up to 30 million Won:	650,000 Won plus 4% of the amount exceeding 10 million Won
Recovery up to 50 million Won:	1,450,000 Won plus 3% of the amount exceeding 30 million Won
Recovery up to 100 million Won:	2,050,000 Won plus 1% of the amount exceeding 50 million Won
Recovery over 100 million Won:	2,550,000 Won plus 0.5% of the amount exceeding 100 million Won.

(11) How quickly can a ship be arrested after the local lawyer is fully instructed?

After a local lawyer is fully instructed to have a vessel arrested, it will take at least one day to prepare an application for the arrest and to translate the documents, which are to be submitted to the court, into Korean. Once the application is submitted to the court, it will take about one to two days to have the vessel actually arrested.

(12) Is there a minimum amount in dispute for which a ship may be arrested?

There is no regulation on the minimum amount in dispute necessary to have a ship arrested. However, there is a possibility that a court may exercise its discretion and refuse to arrest a vessel if the vessel is large and the claim amount is very small.

(13) Is it possible to arrest a sister ship or a ship in "associated ownership"?

A claimant may arrest either the vessel in question or any other vessel registered by the same shipowner if the arrest is effected under provisional attachment because arrest under provisional attachment is an action *in personam* against the shipowner. Since we understand that a registered owner of a sister ship is different from the registered owner of the vessel in question, it is difficult to arrest a sister ship unless the corporate veil is pierced and the claimant proves that the sister ship actually belongs to the same owner as the vessel in question.

(14) What is the order of priorities in the event of the distribution by the court of the proceeds of sale of the ship?

The order of priorities in the event of a distribution by the court of the proceeds of the auction sale of a ship is as follows:

(a) maritime liens;
(b) ship mortgage claims;
(c) all other claims.

Under the Korean Conflicts of Laws Act, the types of claims which give rise to a maritime lien and the priorities among such claims are determined by the law of the ship's flag. In Korea, the priority among maritime liens is as follows:

(a) costs of the lawsuit for the common interest of the creditors, expenses in respect of public auction of the ship and its appurtenances, all public dues levied on the ship in respect of the voyage, pilotage and tugboat dues, expenses of preservation and inspection of the ship and its appurtenances at the last port;
(b) claims arising from contract of employment of the mariners and any other employee of the ship;
(c) salvage remuneration and claims regarding the contribution to general average;
(d) claims for damages caused by a collision of ships, claims for damage to navigation facilities and sea routes caused by other accidents inquired into, and claims for death or personal injury of crew or passengers.

If various claims giving rise to maritime liens arise out of the same voyage, their priority is determined by the order provided above. However, for salvage or general average contribution liens, later liens have priority over earlier liens and claims arising from the same risk are deemed to have arisen at the same time. If various claims giving rise to maritime liens arise from two or more voyages, claims arising from the later voyage have priority over claims arising from the earlier voyage. However, liens for wages of the master and the crew have the same priority as other liens arising from the first voyage. As for maritime liens which have the same priority, they are paid in proportion to the amounts of their respective claims.

The order of priority among ship mortgage claims is according to the order of the mortgage registration date, with the earlier registered mortgage having a higher priority than a later registered mortgage.

For all other claims, such as those arising out of court judgment or provisional arrest of the vessel, a court distributes the proceeds from the sale of the vessel pro rata among the claimants.

Please note, however, that regardless of the order of priorities, a person with a custody lien will not release the vessel from his custody unless his custody lien is satisfied.

(15) Are the claims in respect of which a ship may be arrested subject to a time bar (or prescription) and, if so, are these different according to the nature of the claim?

Yes, claims for which a ship may be arrested are subject to a time bar and they are different according to the nature of the claim. For example, the time bar for a maritime claim is one year; cargo claim—one year; collision claim—two years; charterparty dispute claim—one year; general commercial claim—five years; general civil claim—10 years; general tort claim—three years; etc.

(16) Is it possible to apply for the arrest of a ship outside the normal working hours of the court?

No, it is not possible to apply for the arrest of a ship outside the normal working hours of the court.

CHAPTER 21

MALAYSIA

(1) What are the types of claim for which a ship may be arrested in Malaysia?

As a general statement, the Malaysian courts enjoy the same jurisdiction and authority in relation to matters of admiralty as is had by the High Court of Justice in England under the United Kingdom Supreme Court Act 1981. Hence, the types of claims for which a ship may be arrested in Malaysia would be as provided in section 20(2) and section 21 of the Supreme Court Act 1981 of England and Wales, which are as follows:

(a) any claim to the possession or ownership of a ship or to the ownership of any share therein;
(b) any question arising between the co-owners of a ship as to possession, employment or earnings of that ship;
(c) any claim in respect of a mortgage of or charge on a ship or any share therein;
(d) any claim for damage done by a ship;
(e) any claim for loss of life or personal injury sustained in consequence of any defect in a ship or in her apparel or equipment, or in consequence of the wrongful act, neglect or default of:
  (i) the owners, charterers or persons in possession or control of a ship; or
  (ii) the master or crew of a ship, or any other person for whose wrongful acts, neglects or defaults the owners, charterers or persons in possession or control of a ship are responsible;

  being an act, neglect or default in the navigation or management of the ship, in the loading, carriage or discharge of goods on, in or from the ship, or in the embarkation, carriage or disembarkation of persons on, in or from the ship;
(f) any claim for loss of or damage to goods carried in a ship;
(g) any claim arising out of any agreement relating to the carriage of goods in a ship or to the use or hire of a ship;
(h) any claim in the nature of salvage (including any claim arising by virtue of the application, by or under [section 87 of the Civil Aviation Act 1982], of the law relating to salvage of aircraft and their apparel and cargo);
(j) any claim in the nature of towage in respect of a ship or an aircraft;
(k) any claim in the nature of pilotage in respect of a ship or an aircraft;
(l) any claim in respect of goods or materials supplied to a ship for her operation or maintenance;
(m) any claim in respect of the construction, repair or equipment of a ship or in respect of dock charges or dues;

(n) any claim by a master or member of the crew of a ship for wages (including any sum allotted out of wages or adjudged by a superintendent to be due by way of wages);
(o) any claim by a master, shipper, charterer or agent in respect of disbursements made on account of a ship;
(p) any claim arising out of an act which is or is claimed to be a general average act;
(q) any claim arising out of bottomry;
(r) any claim for the forfeiture or condemnation of ship or of goods which are being or have been carried, or have been attempted to be carried, in a ship, or for the restoration of a ship or any such goods after seizure, or for droits of Admiralty.

(2) Is there a distinction between claims which give rise to a maritime lien and other types of claim?

In respect of the claims under (a), (c), (r) or any question as is mentioned in (b) above or any case in which there is a maritime lien, an action *in rem* may be brought against the ship and a warrant for her arrest issued pursuant thereto.

For the category of claims mentioned in section 20(d) to (q), the requirements of section 21(4) of the Supreme Court Act 1981 have to be met. Where the claim arises in connection with a ship and the person who would be liable on the claim in an action *in personam* ("the relevant person") was, when the cause of action arose, the owner or charterer of, or in possession or in control of, the ship, an action *in rem* may (whether or not the claim gives rise to a maritime lien on that ship) be brought in the High Court against:

(i) that ship, if at the time when the action is brought the relevant person is either the beneficial owner of that ship as respects all the share in it or the charterer of it under a charter by demise; or
(ii) any other ship of which, at the time when the action is brought, the relevant person is the beneficial owner as respects all the shares in it;

and a warrant of arrest issued in respect of such claim against such ship.

(3) (a) What pleadings, affidavits and documents must be presented to the court when applying for an arrest and in what language?
(b) Which documents must be notarised or otherwise authenticated?

The following documents are filed in court when applying for a warrant of arrest:

(i) a Writ of Summons in an Action *in Rem* with either a special or general endorsement thereon of the claim;
(ii) a Praecipe for Warrant of Arrest for the issue of the Warrant;

(iii) an Affidavit affirmed by the claimant or his agent, before either a Commissioner for Oaths if affirmed in Malaysia, or before a Notary Public if affirmed in a Commonwealth country, or if affirmed in any other country, before a consular officer of a Commonwealth country;
(iv) copies of the Warrant of Arrest to be issued;
(v) Praecipe for the service of the Writ *in Rem* by the Sheriff;
(vi) Memorandum of particulars of the property to be arrested together with an undertaking to pay the costs and expenses of the Sheriff.

The documents are filed in Bahasa Malaysia, the national language of Malaysia, together with an English translation, if necessary. If the affidavit is affirmed in any other language, an unaffirmed Bahasa Malaysia translation thereof is annexed thereto. Of the above documents, only the affidavit is required to be notarised in the manner stipulated in paragraph 3(iii) herein.

(4) Is it possible to arrest a ship solely in order to obtain security for a claim which will ultimately be determined in another jurisdiction?

It is not possible to arrest a ship in Malaysia solely to obtain security for a claim which will ultimately be determined in another jurisdiction.

(5) What kind of security is normally acceptable to enable the ship to be released from arrest?

The Rules of the High Court in Malaysia recognise the filing of a bail bond as security for the release of a ship arrested. The bail bond is executed by two sureties before a Registrar or a Commissioner for Oaths or a notary public or a consular officer of a Commonwealth country. The surety must affirm an affidavit stating that the surety is able to pay the sum for which the bond is given. A corporate surety is to have its director, manager or secretary affirm the affidavit.

However, parties may privately arrange for the provision of a bank guarantee or a P & I Club guarantee as an alternative form of security.

(6) In what circumstances can a claimant be made to give security and what security is acceptable?

The claimant can be made to give security if he is ordinarily resident out of the jurisdiction and does not have assets within the jurisdiction. If an order of court for the payment of security is obtained, a specified sum of money is generally required to be paid by the claimant into court as security.

Parties may, however, negotiate for a bank guarantee or a P & I Club guarantee to be given as an alternative form of security.

(7) In the event that the arrest was ultimately shown to have been wrongful, can a claim be made for wrongful arrest and what must be established in order to successfully maintain such a claim?

In order to successfully maintain a claim for wrongful arrest of a ship, it must be shown that the arrest was *mala fide* or caused by gross negligence.

(8) What are the court fees which must be paid in order to make an arrest? Are they recoverable in the event of a successful claim?

The court fee required to be paid to obtain a warrant of arrest is approximately RM350. However, a deposit towards the Sheriff's costs and expenses will be requested by the court prior to the arrest and the amount of the deposit requested varies from RM5,000 to RM25,000. This deposit is in addition to the unlimited undertaking given to the court to make payment of the Sheriff's expenses on demand.

In the event of a successful claim, the filing fee and Sheriff's expenses are recoverable from the defendant.

(9) How are the lawyers' fees calculated? If possible please estimate the costs of a typical arrest.

The lawyer's fee is usually calculated based on the time spent on the brief, though the urgency of the matter and the complexity of the claim are further factors for consideration. On average the fee charged for an arrest including the taking of instructions, preparation of the documents for the issue of the warrant and the execution of the warrant of arrest, is in the region of RM15,000 to RM20,000.

(10) Are all or any part of the lawyers' fees recoverable in the event of a successful arrest?

In the event of a successful arrest, the lawyer's fee may be recoverable on a party–party basis, as opposed to a solicitor–client basis, from the defendant. The quantum recoverable by the claimant therefore from the defendant may be approximately 65 per cent of the fee charged by his lawyer.

(11) How quickly can a ship be arrested after the local lawyer is fully instructed?

Upon obtaining full instructions, the relevant documents may be prepared in one or two days. Subject to delays involved in the affirmation of the affidavit, whether affirmed locally or abroad, the arrest may be achieved within a day or two after the filing of the relevant papers in court. The speed of the arrest will depend on the port at which the vessel calls, and therefore the travelling distance to the relevant court, and the time of day she comes into port.

(12) Is there a minimum amount in dispute for which a ship may be arrested?

There is no minimum amount required to be in dispute for a ship to be arrested in Malaysia.

(13) Is it possible to arrest a sister ship or a ship in "associated ownership"?

It is possible to arrest a sister ship provided the requirements of section 21(4) of the Supreme Court Act 1981 referred to in answer to question (2) above are satisfied.

(14) What is the order of priorities in the event of the distribution by the court of the proceeds of sale of the ship?

The order of priorities of payment in the event of distribution by the court of the proceeds of sale of the ship is generally as follows:

- (i) Sheriff's charges and expenses;
- (ii) costs of the arresting party;
- (iii) claims with maritime liens including salvage claims, damage claims and claims for wages of crew and master, the priority between them being dependent on the time of accrual of their respective maritime liens;
- (iv) mortgage claims;
- (v) claims for necessaries; and
- (vi) contractual claims.

(15) Are the claims in respect of which a ship may be arrested subject to a time bar (or prescription) and, if so, are these different according to the nature of the claim?

The claims against a ship are subject to the time bar incident upon the particular cause of action and type of claim. Most claims brought in West Malaysia suffer a time bar after the expiry of six years from the date of accrual of the cause of action. However, cargo claims subject to the Hague Rules and collision claims have time limits of one and two years respectively for the commencement of legal action. Claims in East Malaysia are subject to various limitations of time.

(16) Is it possible to apply for the arrest of a ship outside the normal working hours of the court?

It is not the practice in Malaysia to apply for the issue of a warrant of arrest of a ship outside the normal working hours of the court which are between 8.15 a.m. and 4.15 p.m., Mondays to Fridays, and 8.15 a.m. to 12.30 p.m.

on Saturdays. It may, however, be possible to execute the arrest outside these hours subject to the availability of the Court Sheriff.

(17) Please provide any other information which you believe is relevant in deciding whether or not to arrest a ship in your jurisdiction.

On average, a claim in Malaysia will be called for trial between three and six years from the date of issue of the writ *in rem*.

CHAPTER 22

MALTA

(1) What are the types of claim for which a ship may be arrested in Malta?

It is possible to arrest a vessel in Malta either for claims *in rem* (directly against the vessel) or alternatively claims *in personam* (claims against the person owning the vessel).

More often than not, arrests are required when the action is against the ship. In this case, the grounds upon which it is possible to arrest the vessel are limited to those claims over which the Maltese court would exercise jurisdiction *in rem*. These are still regulated by the English Admiralty Court Act of 1840 and the English Admiralty Court Act of 1861 and are limited to the following grounds:

1. claims relating to mortgages;
2. claims relating to title or ownership and possession of a ship arising in actions regarding possession, salvage, damage, wages or bottomry;
3. claims for salvage;
4. claims for damages done by a ship;
5. claims for damages suffered by a ship;
6. claims for towage;
7. claims for necessaries supplied;
8. claims for building, equipping or repairing any ship;
9. claims by the holder of a bill of lading of any goods imported into Malta for any damage done to the goods through negligence or breach of contract on the part of the owner or crew;
10. claims regarding possession, ownership, employment and earnings of a ship registered in Malta as between co-owners;
11. claims by seamen for wages;
12. claims by a master for disbursements made by him for use by the vessel.

It may be possible to arrest a vessel in Malta if the claim is not *in rem* as above but when the claim is *in personam* and therefore against the owning company. Again as in actions *in rem* the court must have jurisdiction over the case *in personam*, and the circumstances which are mainly based on residence and domicile as well as other grounds are set out in section 742 of the Code of Organisation and Civil Procedure.

(2) Is there a distinction between claims which give rise to a maritime lien and other types of claim?

The term "maritime lien" is not a term which is used in Malta. The notion however bears some resemblance to what we call "Special Privileges on Ships". There are a number of circumstances which are listed in section 50 of our Merchant Shipping Act, which section in fact performs two functions. Principally it contains a list of claims used for the purposes of ranking among creditors once the action against the ship has been concluded and either the shipowner has paid his debt or the vessel has been sold by public auction.

The second purpose is that the claims listed in section 50 survive the voluntary sale of the vessel by one year. Consequently if a creditor's claim is one of those listed in the list of privileged claims, the claim against the vessel survives a sale to third parties for up to one year from the sale.

(3) (a) What pleadings, affidavits and documents must be presented to the court when applying for an arrest and in what language?
(b) Which documents must be notarised or otherwise authenticated?

In order to stop a vessel from leaving Malta one needs to file a document called a "Warrant of Impediment of Departure of a Vessel" (as opposed to a Warrant of Impediment of Departure of an Individual). In most jurisdictions the document is referred to as a "Warrant of Arrest". This is a document which for the purposes of the law needs to be drawn up in Maltese; however, for practical purposes and in order that the Captain of the vessel may understand the document when served on him, an English translation is usually also filed. The warrant has to list full vessel particulars, as well as the amount being claimed, and the reason for the arrest. It must also contain a declaration to the effect that the claim would be frustrated by the departure of the vessel. The person filing the application, usually the lawyer, must swear on oath that the contents of the warrant are true to the best of his knowledge.

Once the warrant has been ordered by the court it is first served on the Comptroller of Customs, without whose prior consent the vessel would not be permitted to leave, the Commissioner of Police, and the Master of the vessel.

Apart from issuing a Warrant of Impediment of Departure, it is also normal to issue a Warrant of Seizure simultaneously with a Warrant of Impediment of Departure. The effect of the Warrant of Seizure is to seize from the vessel official documents related to the vessel. This serves a dual purpose. Firstly, should the vessel escape it will be travelling without any documents whatsoever and is therefore likely to get held up at its first port of call, making it easier for a creditor to trace her. The second and more important purpose is that following the arrest should the vessel be sold by auction, the funds obtained from the sale would not be distributed to other creditors without the knowledge of the person obtaining the seizure. One has therefore much more control over what happens to the proceeds.

(4) Is it possible to arrest a ship solely in order to obtain security for a claim which will ultimately be determined in another jurisdiction?

In order to arrest a vessel, as explained above, the courts in Malta must have jurisdiction on the merits. However, as a result of amendments to our law in 1995, once the arrest is effected (having satisfied the criteria of the local courts having jurisdiction on the merits) the law permits a situation where the merits would be resolved by means of arbitration, whether in Malta or abroad. However, if the alternative forum is not an arbitration, then the merits will have to be heard by a court in Malta, and in fact unless a writ on the merits is issued within 10 days of obtaining the Warrant of Impediment of Departure the warrant lapses and may be revoked.

One may add at this point that whereas in England it would first be necessary to issue a writ and then the warrant of arrest, in Malta it is possible to issue a Warrant of Impediment of Departure first, provided that the writ is subsequently issued within 10 days of the granting of the warrant.

(5) What kind of security is normally acceptable to enable the ship to be released from arrest?

The kind of security acceptable very much depends on the person effecting the arrest and therefore it is entirely up to him to accept the kind of guarantee which he deems fit. Our law is vague in this respect in that it does not insist on a cash deposit equivalent to the claim but speaks in generic terms like "if the party against whom it is issued makes such deposit or gives such security as, according to the circumstances of the case, may be sufficient to safeguard the rights or claims stated . . .".

(6) In what circumstances can a claimant be made to give security and what security is acceptable?

The law does not provide for counter-security to be provided as of right, however this must be understood in relation to the answer provided in (7) below.

(7) In the event that the arrest was ultimately shown to have been wrongful, can a claim be made for wrongful arrest and what must be established in order to successfully maintain such a claim?

If the arrest is obtained "maliciously" and is declared so by the court, the party suing out the warrant will be liable to pay a penalty not less than LM3,000. Furthermore in such cases the person suing out the warrant may also be liable for damages and interest.

In view of the above, the law provides that it is possible for the person whose ship is detained to obtain a court order ordering the party suing out the warrant to give within a time fixed by the court sufficient security in an amount not less than LM3,000 for the payment of the penalty, damages and interest and in default to rescind the warrant.

(8) What are the court fees which must be paid in order to make an arrest? Are they recoverable in the event of a successful claim?

(9) How are the lawyers' fees calculated?

(10) Are all or any part of the lawyers' fees recoverable in the event of a successful arrest?

Court fees vary depending on the quantum of the claim. This is a matter normally calculated by the Legal Procurators. As far as legal fees are concerned, it is common to find hourly rates for more complex cases that require careful examination of documents, and general advices and rates established by tariff.

It is also common for lawyers to ask for funds on account prior to an arrest being effected. In those cases where the creditor is not present in Malta and therefore when it is necessary for the lawyer himself to effect the arrest as plaintiff on behalf of a foreign plaintiff, he will be personally liable if it is proved that the arrest was malicious. Consequently and for this reason lawyers would normally ask for money on account.

The court fees paid in order to make the arrest are recoverable in the event of a successful claim, whilst the lawyers' fees are recoverable in part.

(11) How quickly can a ship be arrested after the local lawyer is fully instructed?

This very much depends on the policies and personal work patterns adopted by the lawyer dealing with the case. However having said that, it is possible for local lawyers who specialise in marine litigation and consequently have got the necessary staff in place for that very purpose to effect the arrest of a vessel within hours of being fully instructed.

(12) Is there a minimum amount in dispute for which a ship may be arrested?

There must be a minimum of LM3,000 in dispute for an arrest to be effected.

(13) Is it possible to arrest a sister ship or a ship in "associated ownership"?

Sister ship arrests are not possible, and one can only arrest the vessel with regard to which a claim exists. Malta is not a signatory to the Brussels Arrest Convention of 1952.

(14) What is the order of priorities in the event of the distribution by the courts of the proceeds of the sale of the ship?

As mentioned above, the order of priorities is dealt within section 50 of our Merchant Shipping Act. It is a substantial list which is headed by judicial costs incurred in respect of the sale of the ship and the distribution of the proceeds, and includes wages and expenses for assistance recovery, salvage and pilotage, expenses incurred in the preservation of the ship after her last entry into port, wages of the master and crew, damages due to a seaman for death or personal injury, moneys due to creditors for labour, work, and repairs, agency fees, mortgages, damages due to other vessels or their cargo in the case of collision, etc.

(15) Are the claims in respect of which a ship may be arrested subject to a time bar (or prescription) and, if so, are these different according to the nature of the claim?

Time limits or prescription do apply. Generally speaking, claims in contract have a prescriptive period of five years, whilst claims in tort have a prescriptive period of two years. The Hague Rules are law in Malta, therefore the one-year time bar therein applies.

(16) Is it possible to apply for the arrest of a ship outside the normal working hours of the court?

It is possible to apply for the arrest of a ship outside the normal working hours of court. Normal working hours of the Maltese court in winter is from 8 a.m. to 3 p.m. Should it be necessary to arrest a vessel after 3 p.m., or on Saturdays, Sundays or other public holidays, one has to contact the Registrar on call. He will arrange for the court registry to be opened and the lawyer dealing with the matter will also have to file an urgent application requesting the court to be opened out of official hours. If the duty judge grants the application then the necessary warrants are ordered and served.

(17) Please provide any other information which you believe is relevant in deciding whether or not to arrest a ship in your jurisdiction.

For the very reason that no one case is identical to another, there are always a number of issues that must be considered and taken into account prior to arresting a vessel. One would therefore recommend that the lawyer be requested to give an opinion on the possibility or not of the arrest and on any possible disadvantages before the decision to arrest the vessel is taken. Of course on a number of occasions there simply is no time for any form of detailed correspondence; however, it is still recommended that the client have as complete and clear a picture as possible of the situation before making a calculated decision.

CHAPTER 23

THE NETHERLANDS

(1) What are the types of claim for which a ship may be arrested in The Netherlands?

A distinction should be made between:

(i) ships not flying the flag of a contracting state to the International Convention for the Unification of Certain Rules Relating to the Arrest of Sea-Going Ships (the Brussels Convention of 1952); and
(ii) ships flying the flag of such a contracting state.

Under Dutch law a ship not flying the flag of a contracting state may be arrested for practically any claim on the shipowner.

Under Article 2 of the International Convention it is stipulated that a ship flying the flag of a contracting state may only be arrested for so-called maritime claims.

The maritime claims are described in Article 1. Dutch jurisprudence has broadened the definition of maritime claim somewhat to, for instance, claims for container hire. Container hire is considered to be "goods or materials whatever supplied to a ship for her operation or maintenance" as mentioned under Article 1(k) of the International Convention.

Foreign judgments, foreign notarial deeds and foreign or domestic arbitral awards can be enforced in The Netherlands after an enforcement order has been granted by the President of the District Court within whose jurisdiction the vessel is situated or expected.

(2) Is there a distinction between claims which give rise to a maritime lien and other types of claim?

The maritime lien is not a concept of Dutch law. Instead, under Dutch law one speaks of "priority-right". The priority-right resembles the maritime lien in many aspects but a person with a common law background should not assume that the two concepts are identical.

There is a distinction between claims which give rise to a maritime lien and other types of claims.

Other types of claims are claims not included in the priorities system and are in the first place those which are not mentioned as a priority-right in a statutory provision, such as possessory liens.

In nearly all cases of an enforced sale, the proceeds of the sale will be exhausted by maritime liens and the claims of the mortgagees of the vessel. Therefore, no payments will be made on lower-ranking claims such as those of a foreign ships register, foreign registration fees, tonnage taxes, survey fees of a classification society, etc.

When a vessel is sold to a third party not by means of an enforced sale, there is a distinction since only claims such as crew wages, mortgage, collision damage and the like will "follow the vessel".

However, a buyer of a vessel in a judicial sale in The Netherlands acquires the vessel free of all liens, encumbrances and mortgages existing at the time of the sale. Only possessory liens, such as liens of a shiprepairer or a salvor, will "stick" to the vessel. The possessory lien is enforced by the claimant simply by keeping possession of the vessel until his claim is paid and/or security has been given.

(3) (a) What pleadings, affidavits and documents must be presented to the court when applying for an arrest and in what language?

The lawyer of the claimant should file a petition for leave to arrest with the President of the District Court in whose jurisdiction the vessel is situated. No affidavits or documents are required to be presented with this petition.

The petition should of course be in the Dutch language. Supporting documentation may be attached to the petition and—depending on which President of the District Court deals with the petition—Dutch, English and German will be accepted.

In the petition for leave to arrest the claimant should describe the amount of the claim, the grounds for the claim, etc.

(b) Which documents must be notarised or otherwise authenticated?

None for a conservatory arrest on a vessel. In the case of an arrest for enforcement made by virtue of an enforceable document, this document should be presented and be notarised or otherwise authenticated.

(4) Is it possible to arrest a ship solely in order to obtain security for a claim which will ultimately be determined in another jurisdiction?

Yes. It is advisable for the lawyer to mention this in the petition for leave to arrest the vessel. This is because Dutch law requires that with the petition the claimant request the President of the District Court to set an ultimate date for issuing a writ of summons.

Unless the main proceedings have already been started the President of the

District Court will therefore order a date by which the main proceedings/arbitration, etc. have to be started.

(5) What kind of security is normally acceptable to enable the ship to be released from arrest?

A bank guarantee from a Dutch bank or a branch office of a first class foreign bank or a club guarantee from a first class P & I Club.

The security should be for the amount of the claim increased by 30 per cent for costs and interest.

(6) In what circumstances can a claimant be made to give security and what security is acceptable?

Under Dutch law the President of the District Court may demand security from a claimant although this hardly ever occurs. The security could be in the form of a bank guarantee or club letter as described under (5).

(7) In the event that the arrest was ultimately shown to have been wrongful, can a claim be made for wrongful arrest and what must be established in order to successfully maintain such a claim?

Yes, a claim for damages can be made in case of wrongful arrest. The claimant must then only prove damages and the actual amount of damages, since a wrongful arrest automatically means that the wrongful arrestor is liable.

(8) What are the court fees which must be paid in order to make an arrest? Are they recoverable in the event of a successful claim?

At present Dfls. 140. Those court fees are indeed recoverable in the event of a successful claim.

In addition to the court fees, bailiff costs amounting to Dfls. 600–1,500 should be paid. A bailiff effectuates the actual arrest.

(9) How are the lawyers' fees calculated? If possible please estimate the costs of a typical arrest.

The lawyers' fees are calculated per hour. The costs of a typical arrest range between Dfls. 1,200 and Dfls. 2,000 depending on the amount of the claim as well as the time invested.

(10) Are all or any part of the lawyers' fees recoverable in the event of a successful arrest?

At least part of the lawyers' fees are recoverable in the event of a successful arrest. However, many lawyers in The Netherlands claim in the petition for leave to arrest out-of-court costs and in most cases these costs are recoverable.

(11) How quickly can a ship be arrested after the local lawyer is fully instructed?

Two to three hours, provided the lawyer can convince the President of the District Court that the vessel will be leaving the jurisdiction of the District Court shortly. Of course the time factor is also influenced by the bailiff who effectuates the actual arrest.

(12) Is there a minimum amount in dispute for which a ship may be arrested?

Not really. The Presidents of the District Courts are reluctant to grant leave for arrest on larger vessels for amounts below Dfls. 10,000.

However, if the lawyer explains in the petition for leave to arrest the necessity of arresting a ship for a smaller amount, no doubt the President will grant leave to arrest.

(13) Is it possible to arrest a sister ship or a ship in "associated ownership"?

A sister ship may be arrested according to Article 3 of the International Convention 1952 as well as according to general Dutch law.

An arrest of a ship in "associated ownership" is only possible if the court allows a "piercing of the corporate veil". However, at this point Dutch jurisprudence is very strict. Therefore "piercing" hardly ever occurs in The Netherlands.

(14) What is the order of priorities in the event of the distribution by the court of the proceeds of sale of the ship?

The Dutch system of priorities is mainly based on statutory law. Under Dutch international private law, the law governing a claim determines whether a claim exists and the amount of the claim.

The system of priorities is determined by the law of the state where the vessel is registered. However, if under the law of the flag state of the vessel a claim ranks in priority to a mortgage, it will only be awarded that rank in the distribution proceedings following an enforced sale if Dutch law recognises a similar priority right.

One should be aware that the Dutch statutory provisions regarding priorities will always give rise to questions of qualification and interpretation, especially in view of the order/ranking of priorities.

In general the following order/ranking of priorities can be given:

A. First priority claims

1. Costs and expenses of the sale such as court fees, costs of lay-up of the vessel during the period of the actual sale proceedings, lawyers' fees;
   costs of wreck removal;
2. costs of preservation of the vessel after the arrest of the vessel;
3. crew wages and emoluments over the last 12 months;
4. salvage claims;
   claims for contribution in general average.

In the same class all liens rank equally, provided that claims for salvage and contribution in general average rank amongst themselves in the inverse order of time in which they arose.

B. Mortgages

Under Dutch law the priority of mortgages amongst each other is determined by the time of recording.

Mortgages always rank lower to maritime liens irrespective of the date on which the claim arose.

Mortgages will rank lower to rights which have been recorded against the vessel before the mortgage was recorded.

C. Claims of a lower priority against the vessel

1. Claims against the owner or a bareboat charterer of the vessel pursuant to contracts entered into by the owner or bareboat charterer for commissioning the vessel or keeping it in commission; and
2. claims pursuant to contracts of carriage against the person deemed to be carrier pursuant to the statutory provisions relating to the carriage of goods; and
3. claims for collision, or damage caused by the vessel without collision; and
4. claims for which the owner may (otherwise) establish a limitation fund pursuant to an application made by him.

These claims have even ranking.[1]

(15) Are the claims in respect of which a ship may be arrested subject to a time bar (or prescription) and, if so, are these different according to the nature of the claim?

Claims in respect of which a ship may be arrested are indeed subject to a time bar. The time bars are different according to the nature of the claim.

1 The source of this has been the relevant chapters written by Mr Willem Verhoeven in the *Maritime Law Handbook*.

For instance, claims for collision damages become time barred two years after the collision. Claims for cargo damages become time barred one year after the date of delivery in the port of destination or one year after the date the goods should have arrived at the port of destination.

In general in The Netherlands it is advisable to take action within one year after the claim arose since priority rights extinguish after one year.

(16) Is it possible to apply for the arrest of a ship outside the normal working hours of the court?

Yes, provided the lawyer and the President of the District Court are convinced that the vessel will be leaving the jurisdiction of the District Court shortly.

(17) Please provide any other information which you believe is relevant in deciding whether or not to arrest a ship in your jurisdiction.

One should be aware that in comparison to other jurisdictions it is relatively easy to arrest vessels in The Netherlands. The Netherlands are therefore considered still to be an "arrest-haven".

Under Dutch law an arrest of a foreign vessel in principle creates jurisdiction of a Dutch court.

CHAPTER 24

NEW ZEALAND[1]

Preliminary note

The admiralty jurisdiction of the High Court of New Zealand is similar to the jurisdiction of the English High Court, and New Zealand's maritime law closely follows English precedents. Jurisdiction is governed by the Admiralty Act 1973, which is based on the Administration of Justice Act 1956 (U.K.).

(1) What are the types of claim for which a ship may be arrested in New Zealand?

Claims in respect of which there exists a maritime lien at common law.

Claims of the kinds listed in section 4(1) of the Admiralty Act 1973. Such claims are the following:

- (a) any claim to the possession of a ship or to the ownership of any share therein;
- (b) any question arising between the co-owners of a ship as to possession, employment, or earnings of that ship;
- (c) any claim in respect of a mortgage of or charge on a ship or any share therein;
- (d) any claim for damage done by a ship;
- (e) any claim for damage received by a ship;
- (f) any claim for loss of life or personal injury sustained in consequence of any defect in a ship or in her apparel or equipment, or of the wrongful act, neglect, or default of the owners, charterers, or persons in possession or control of a ship or of the master or crew thereof or of any other person for whose wrongful acts, neglects, or defaults the owners, charterers, or persons in possession or control of a ship are responsible, being an act, neglect, or default in the navigation or management of the ship, in the loading, carriage, or discharge of goods on, in, or from the ship or in the embarkation, carriage, or disembarkation of persons on, in, or from the ship;
- (g) any claim for loss of or damage to goods carried in a ship;
- (h) any claim arising out of any agreement relating to the carriage of goods in a ship or to the use or hire of a ship;
- (i) any claim in the nature of salvage (including claims for services rendered in saving life from a ship or an aircraft or in preserving its cargo, apparel, or

1 New Zealand position as at January 1996.

wreck pursuant to the provisions of sections 113 and 114 of the Maritime Transport Act 1994 or any maritime rules made in relation to salvage);

(j) any claim in the nature of towage in respect of a ship or an aircraft;

(k) any claim in the nature of pilotage in respect of a ship or an aircraft;

(l) any claim in respect of goods, materials, or services (including stevedoring and lighterage services) supplied or to be supplied to a ship in its operation or maintenance;

(m) any claim in respect of the construction, repair, or equipment of a ship or for dock or port or harbour charges or dues;

(n) [repealed];

(o) any claim by a master or member of the crew of a ship for wages, and any claim by or in respect of a master or member of the crew of a ship for any money or property which, under any of the provisions of the Maritime Transport Act 1994, is recoverable as wages or in the Court and in the manner in which wages may be recovered;

(p) any claim by a master, shipper, charterer, or agent in respect of disbursements made on account of a ship;

(q) any claim arising out of an act which is or is claimed to be a general average act;

(r) any claim arising out of bottomry;

(s) any claim for the forfeiture or condemnation of a ship or of goods which are being or have been carried, or have been attempted to be carried, in a ship, or for the restoration of a ship or any such goods after seizure, or for droits of Admiralty.

(See also sections 5(1) and (2) Admiralty Act 1973, which sets out rules similar to those of section 21 of the UK Supreme Court Act 1981.)

Admiralty jurisdiction is prescribed in the Admiralty Act 1973. Procedure is regulated by the Admiralty Rules 1975. The Rules are currently being reviewed.

New Zealand has not ratified the 1926, 1967 or 1993 Conventions relating to maritime liens or mortgages. New Zealand law follows English law and is different from those Conventions. Neither has New Zealand ratified the 1952 Brussels Convention relating to arrest; however, the jurisdiction provisions of the Admiralty Act 1973 largely follow that Convention.

(2) Is there a distinction between claims which give rise to a maritime lien and other types of claim?

For the purpose of arrest, no. Pursuant to section 5(1) of the Admiralty Act 1973, the jurisdiction of the High Court may be invoked by an action *in rem* against a ship in respect of which there is a maritime lien or charge under section 4(1) of the Act (or alternatively against a sister ship under section 5(2) of the Act).

The distinction is, however, important in determining the order of priorities of claims. Claims generally fall into three broad categories and will be ranked accordingly in the following order:

(a) maritime liens (claims for damage done by a ship, salvage, seamen's wages, master's wages and disbursements, and bottomry and respondentia);

(b) mortgages;
(c) ordinary claims *in rem* created by statute (i.e. maritime claims listed in section 4(1) Admiralty Act 1973 other than maritime lien claims), often referred to as "statutory liens".

Within the category of maritime liens and mortgages the ranking may depend upon the date when each of the various claims arose. Within the category of statutory liens the claims will rank *pari passu* with each other. The order of priorities is discussed in detail in (14) below.

(3) (a) What pleadings, affidavits and documents must be presented to the court when applying for an arrest, and in what language?

The party applying for the warrant of arrest files in the High Court:

(a) writ of summons *in rem*;
(b) application for warrant of arrest;
(c) affidavit in support of application for warrant of arrest;
(d) undertaking to indemnify the Registrar for fees, expenses and harbour dues. The Registrar may request that security be given in respect of such costs (usually in the form of a deposit of a sum of money into court);
(e) warrant of arrest; and
(f) the Registrar may also require the applicant to prepare and file a notice of the arrest, which the Registrar would then serve on the vessel or appropriate person.

The documents are in English.

(b) Which documents must be notarised or otherwise authenticated?

None; although the original signed documents listed in paragraph (3)(a) must be filed in the court.

(4) Is it possible to arrest a ship solely in order to obtain security for a claim which will ultimately be determined in another jurisdiction?

In practice, yes. The New Zealand court has *prima facie* jurisdiction over the *res* by virtue of its presence in New Zealand at the time of the application for warrant of arrest; and such jurisdiction will continue until successfully challenged. If the underlying action is stayed—for example on *forum non conveniens* grounds, or pursuant to the provisions of the New York Convention—then a stay will ordinarily only be ordered on the condition that adequate alternative security to the *res* is provided. The New Zealand courts follow *The "Rena K"* line of cases: see *The "Akademik Sholkalskiy"* [1995] 2 NZLR 743.

(5) What kind of security is normally acceptable to enable the ship to be released from arrest?

In practice, either:

(a) a payment into court of the amount of the plaintiff's claim, together with interest and the costs of arrest, on the basis of the plaintiff's reasonably arguable best case, but the plaintiff cannot demand security in an amount which exceeds the value of the *res* proceeded against; or
(b) letter of undertaking from an acceptable underwriter, usually in the form of a P & I Club letter of undertaking.

Where the vessel's owners are forced to apply for the vessel's release, such application can be made to either:

(a) the Registrar—
  (i) the vessel will be released only if the amount of the plaintiff's claim is paid in, together with interest and the costs of arrest, on the basis of the plaintiff's reasonably arguable best case; or
  (ii) upon security for like amounts being given to the satisfaction of the Registrar—either by letter of undertaking from an insurance company carrying on business in New Zealand, or a similar undertaking from the person required to give such security (being the party requesting the release of the vessel from arrest) together with at least two sureties acceptable to the Registrar.

  It is submitted that the Registrar would not require security to be given in an amount which exceeds the valueof the *res* proceeded against; or
(b) the court—
  the court can order a release on terms it thinks fit, depending on the circumstances of each case. However, the usual practice is to only order the release on the provision of sufficient security to cover the amount of the plaintiff's claim, together with interest and costs, on the basis of the plaintiff's reasonably arguable best case, but for not greater than the value of the *res*.

(6) In what circumstances can a claimant be made to give security, and what security is acceptable?

The claimant can be required to give security only in respect of the potential costs of the proceedings. On a successful application by a defendant that the plaintiff be made to give such security, security is given:

(a) by paying into court an amount determined by the court; or

(b) by giving to the satisfaction of the Registrar security for a like amount, by such number of sureties as the Registrar thinks proper.

(7) In the event that the arrest was ultimately shown to have been wrongful, can a claim be made for wrongful arrest and what must be established in order to successfully maintain such a claim?

For the arrest to have been "wrongful", it would need to be shown to be malicious or contrary to good faith. If proven, damages would usually be awarded.

(8) What are the court fees which must be paid in order to make an arrest? Are they recoverable in the event of a successful claim?

NZ$830, being the filing fee on the application for the issue of a warrant of arrest. This amount, together with the other costs of the arrest (including legal fees—see (10) below) are recoverable in the event of a successful claim.

In addition to court fees, the Registrar may request that security (in the form of a deposit) be given in respect of fees, expenses and harbour dues—see (3)(a)(d), above.

(9) How are the lawyer's fees calculated? If possible please estimate the costs of a typical arrest.

Usually on a time and attendance basis. The approximate cost of a typical arrest is NZ$1,500, excluding GST (value added tax) and disbursements (which include court filing fees). However, almost every arrest gives rise to other issues which require attention at additional expense.

(10) Are all or any part of the lawyer's fees recoverable in the event of a successful arrest?

Lawyer's fees are recoverable; however, in the absence of a contract providing for full recovery of solicitor/client costs, the usual practice is for costs to be awarded on a party and party basis by reference to a Scale which is significantly out of date. The court has a discretion to award costs in excess of Scale, but it would be rare to recover more than 50 per cent of actual costs incurred.

(11) How quickly can a ship be arrested after the local lawyer is fully instructed?

The same day. It should be noted that as it is the Registrar (and not the lawyer) who executes the warrant of arrest, it is not necessary that a lawyer in the same town as the vessel be instructed. In New Zealand arrest proceedings can be issued out of any High Court Registry, and the Registrar will attend to the immediate execution of the warrant, through local court officers, wherever the vessel might be.

(12) Is there a minimum amount in dispute for which a ship may be arrested?

No.

(13) Is it possible to arrest a sister ship or a ship in "associated ownership"?

Sister ships can be arrested if the conditions of the proviso to section 5(2) Admiralty Act 1973 are met. See also *Reef Shipping* v. *The Ship "Fua Kavenga"* [1987] 1 NZLR 550.

Except in the class of claims which may be brought irrespective of ownership, or where the claim may be brought against a ship which is under demise charter, it is necessary for the court to identify the beneficial owner of all the shares in the ship which is sought to be arrested in order to determine whether the *in rem* claim can be brought against the ship. "Beneficial owner" has its ordinary meaning of equitable owner, as held in *The "Congresso del Partido"* [1978] QB 500.

It is believed that the decision in *The "Banco"* [1971] P 137 allowing only one ship to be arrested for each separate claim, would be followed in New Zealand.

(14) What is the order of priorities in the event of the distribution by the court of the proceeds of sale of the ship?

New Zealand has retained jurisdiction which recognises the principles of general maritime law. Therefore, subject to individual equity in each case, the following ranking would apply in New Zealand:

(a) the harbour authority's statutory claim for dues backed up by possession under section 111 of the Harbours Act 1950;
(b) the expenses of the High Court Registrar in having the vessel arrested and preserving the security;
(c) the costs of the producer of the fund (being the costs of his action up to and including the arrest, and the costs of obtaining the order for appraisement and sale), regardless of where such claimant's substantive claim is ranked;
(d) seamen's wages (for which judgment had been obtained) pursuant to the provisions of the Maritime Transport Act 1994 but subject to prior salvage unless the subsequent wages were earned in preserving the *res*;
(e) master's wages (for which judgment had been obtained) pursuant to the provisions of the Maritime Transport Act 1994 but subject to

prior salvage unless the subsequent disbursements were incurred in preserving the *res*;

(f) master's disbursements (for which judgment had been obtained) pursuant to the provisions of the Maritime Transport Act 1994 but subject to prior salvage unless the subsequent disbursements were incurred in preserving the *res*;

(g) the damage lien subject to later salvage;

(h) life salvage; the priority over property salvage being determined by section 113 of the Maritime Transport Act 1994;

(i) property salvage (for which judgment had been obtained) pursuant to section 114 of the Maritime Transport Act 1994;

(j) the possessory lien including, where the claim relates to freight or cargo, the wharf or warehouse owner under the provisions of the Mercantile Law Act 1908, and the repairman and shipbuilders who retain possession;

(k) mortgages which pursuant to section 40 of the Shipping Registration Act 1992 rank *inter se* according to the date of registration and not according to the date of the mortgage itself. Unregistered mortgages are postponed to those of registered mortgages whatever the date the unregistered mortgage was created. Unregistered mortgages rank in order of date of their creation (registered mortgages in respect of a foreign ship have the same priority as a mortgage registered under the Shipping Registration Act: see section 70 of that Act);

(l) the statutory liens or statutory claims *in rem* which include all claims or questions specified under section 4(1) of the Admiralty Act 1973 which are not also maritime liens or, because of the circumstances, classified as possessory liens.

(15) Are the claims in respect of which a ship may be arrested subject to a time bar (or prescription) and, if so, are these different according to the nature of the claim?

The following limitation periods apply:

(a) cargo claims under bill of lading where Hague Rules or Hague-Visby Rules apply—one year (under the Hague-Visby Rules, this period can be extended by agreement);

(b) collision claims—two years;

(c) there is no limitation period in respect of maritime lien claims or statutory claims under section 4(1) Admiralty Act 1973. The normal limitation period for claims in contract and tort is six years. However, section 4(8) of the Limitation Act 1950 excludes admiralty actions *in rem* from the normal regime.

However, the doctrine of laches does apply in New Zealand; and a court may refuse in its discretion to permit an arrest to remain where by reason of delay it would be unjust to do so, or the court might hold that a maritime lien had been extinguished by laches.

(16) Is it possible to apply for the arrest of a ship outside the normal working hours of the court?

Yes—subject to availability of the Registrar and court officers to execute the warrant of arrest.

CHAPTER 25

NORWAY

(1) What are the types of claim for which a ship may be arrested in Norway?

Until recently, a ship could be arrested in connection with any monetary claim the creditor had against the shipowner. However, after Norway became a party to the Brussels Convention of 1952 in respect of the arrest of vessels and adopted the provisions therein, an arrest is now only permissible in connection with a "maritime" claim. Hence, it is not possible to arrest a ship in Norway for fee claims from agents, stevedores, shipbrokers, insurance brokers or other middlemen. Nor is it possible to arrest a ship in Norway for unpaid premiums with respect to hull insurance or P & I coverage.

(2) Is there a distinction between claims which give rise to a maritime lien and other types of claim?

Most claims which will normally give rise to a maritime lien are specifically mentioned in the Norwegian Maritime Act and a maritime claim (i.e. claims for wages) will thus entitle the creditor to arrest the ship. However, if the claimant has a claim which is secured against the vessel as a maritime lien under foreign law, but it is not specifically mentioned as a maritime claim in the Norwegian Maritime Act, the claim will not entitle the creditor to arrest a ship in Norway.

(3) (a) What pleadings, affidavits and documents must be presented to the court when applying for an arrest and in what language?

A pleading/application must be lodged with the court in the jurisdiction where the ship is presently located or is expected to arrive. In this pleading the merits of the case should be presented in such a way that the court can easily understand the substance of the claim and the reason for arresting the vessel. All relevant documentation should therefore be enclosed. Normally, affidavits are neither required nor allowed in Norwegian arrest proceedings. The court may always demand that foreign language documents are translated into Norwegian. However, the court will normally accept English documents.

(b) Which documents must be notarised or otherwise authenticated?

There are no requirements for notarisation or other authentication of documents in Norwegian arrest proceedings.

(4) Is it possible to arrest a ship solely in order to obtain security for a claim which will ultimately be determined in another jurisdiction?

It is possible to arrest a ship in Norway solely for the purpose of obtaining security for a claim which will ultimately be determined in another jurisdiction.

(5) What kind of security is normally acceptable to enable the ship to be released from arrest?

Cash security or an unconditional letter of guarantee from a Norwegian bank are always acceptable. Save by agreement between the parties, Club letters are not acceptable to the court. Nor is it acceptable in Norway to post a bond.

(6) In what circumstances can a claimant be made to give security and what security is acceptable?

It is not uncommon for the court to require that the claimant give security. This is especially true if the claimant is a foreign citizen or a foreign company. Further, the court will require security if the claimant has not justified his claim (but an arrest is still granted because there is a risk of damage/loss, etc. if an arrest is denied). The form of security will be the same as mentioned under (5) above.

(7) In the event that the arrest was ultimately shown to have been wrongful, can a claim be made for wrongful arrest and what must be established in order to successfully maintain such a claim?

If an arrest is ultimately found to be wrongful, the claimant must be prepared to pay damages for the economic loss which the owner has suffered as a result of the arrest. The liability for wrongful arrest is basically strict. Hence, it is not necessary to prove that the claimant acted negligently.

(8) What are the court fees which must be paid in order to make an arrest? Are they recoverable in the event of a successful claim?

Approximately NOK 1,250. It should be noted that the court will not consider the application for an arrest before the fees have been paid.

The fees are recoverable in the event of a successful claim.

(9) How are the lawyers' fees calculated? If possible please estimate the costs of a typical arrest.

Lawyers' fees are calculated by the hours billed and the complexity of the case.

The costs of a typical arrest depend on whether the arrest is granted after an oral hearing or without an oral hearing. With an oral hearing, which is the general rule, we would estimate the costs to an average of approximately NOK 20,000. Without an oral hearing, we would estimate the costs to an average of approximately NOK 10,000.

(10) Are all or any part of the lawyers' fees recoverable in the event of a successful arrest?

In principle, yes.

(11) How quickly can a ship be arrested after the local lawyer is fully instructed?

Within one to two days.

(12) Is there a minimum amount in dispute for which a ship may be arrested?

No.

(13) Is it possible to arrest a sister ship or a ship in "associated ownership"?

Yes. A claimant may arrest either the particular ship in respect of which the maritime claim arose or any other ship which is owned by the person who was, at the time when the maritime claim arose, the owner of the particular ship and who is personally responsible for the claim. If someone other than the registered owner of the particular ship in respect of which the maritime claim arose is personally responsible for the claim, the claimant may further arrest any ship which at the date of the commencement of the arrest proceedings is owned by the person who is personally responsible for the claim.

(14) What is the order of priorities in the event of the distribution by the court of the proceeds of sale of the ship?

The order of priorities is that maritime liens are covered first. The main rule is then that registered rights have higher priorities than unregistered rights and that priority between the registered rights is based on the time of entry into the daily journal of the ship register. It should be noted, however, that arrests (and executions) registered the same day as a voluntary created right will have higher priority regardless of the time of entry in the daily journal.

(15) Are the claims in respect of which a ship may be arrested subject to a time bar (or prescription) and if so are these different according to the nature of the claim?

Yes. For instance, if a claimant wants to arrest a ship for a cargo claim he must commence arrest proceedings within one year after the claim arose. otherwise, the general rule is that the claimant must commence arrest proceedings within three years after the claim arose.

(16) Is it possible to apply for the arrest of a ship outside the normal working hours of the court?

Yes, but the claimant must obtain the co-operation and goodwill of the court in order to achieve this.

(17) Please provide any other information which you believe is relevant in deciding whether or not to arrest a ship in your jurisdiction

Of the approximately 65 countries party to the 1952 Arrest Convention, Norway is one of the few that requires that the claimant must prove, in addition to justifying the maritime claim, that the owner's conduct gives reason to fear that, unless an arrest is obtained, enforcement of the claim will be either impeded or substantially more difficult to effect, or that it will have to be effected abroad. Thus, the fact that the debtor is under substantial pressure from his creditors will not in itself provide a legitimate ground for arrest. It should be noted, however, that an arrest of a ship is always permitted where there is a claim that has fallen due which is secured by a mortgage (or lien).

CHAPTER 26

PANAMA

(1) What are the types of claim for which a ship may be arrested in Panama?

Since Panama has a specialised Maritime Court, created in 1982, any claim related to acts of maritime commerce, traffic and transportation, occurring inside the jurisdiction of Panama, and any claim related to acts of commerce, traffic and transportation occurring outside Panama, provided the vessel is present in Panama, confer jurisdiction to the Maritime Court. All vessels transiting the Panama Canal, all vessels registered in Panama, and their owners are subject to the jurisdiction of the Maritime Court of Panama.

(2) Is there a distinction between claims which give rise to a maritime lien and other types of claim?

Yes, the Panamanian Maritime Code established two separate types of action. One to enforce maritime liens upon a vessel, cargo or freight, which could be named action *in rem* and another one the action *in personam* to enforce any maritime claim against the owner, or charterer. Panama being a place where thousands of vessels registered throughout the world pass through the Panama Canal, Panamanian law provides for several rules in the application of foreign law to maritime claims.

(3) (a) What pleadings, affidavits and documents must be presented to the court when applying for an arrest and in what language?

Panamanian law requires the filing of a complaint and a petition for arrest. *Prima facie* evidence (which is accepted via fax) is acceptable. Documents could be filed in any language; a local translation is normally attached to foreign documents.

(b) Which documents must be notarised or otherwise authenticated?

Panamanian law requires the filing of a Power of Attorney and a Certificate of Corporate Good Standing, notarised and authenticated. Panama adopted the Apostille Convention, so documents properly apostilled are acceptable to the Maritime Court.

(4) It is possible to arrest a ship solely in order to obtain security for a claim which will ultimately be determined in another jurisdiction?

Yes, Panamanian law permits the filing of a claim to obtain security for a claim which will ultimately be determined in another jurisdiction. In fact, claims subject to arbitration or to a forum selection clause do not prevent the Maritime Court from arresting a vessel. Once the vessel is arrested, the Court has the discretion to decide a motion for abstention, and send the claim to arbitration or to another forum. Security could be either sent along with the claim, or kept in Panama pending the final decision.

(5) What kind of security is normally acceptable to enable the ship to be released from arrest?

Panama permits the following as acceptable security: cash, certified cheques, bank guarantee letters, local insurance bonds and government bonds. Panamanian law also permits the parties to agree on any other type of security. Normally, among maritime law practitioners letters of undertaking issued by P & I Clubs are acceptable.

(6) In what circumstances can a claimant be made to give security and what security is acceptable?

In all arrest cases the claimant has to give security. The Panamanian system permits the filing of an arrest petition, to enforce a maritime lien or to provide the Court with jurisdiction over a foreign defendant upon depositing US$1,000. In cases where the arrest is only to obtain security the deposit is twenty to thirty per cent of the amount in dispute. In all cases the Maritime Court requires the claimant to file *prima facie* evidence in support of the claim, showing the entitlement of the claimant.

(7) In the event that the arrest was ultimately shown to have been wrongful, can a claim be made for wrongful arrest and what must be established in order to successfully maintain such a claim?

In Panama there are provisions to challenge the legality and validity of the arrest. Panama has adopted a Motion to Show Cause (known as *Apremio* in Spanish) where the Maritime Court could, upon cause, have an immediate hearing and decide whether there is a wrongful arrest. Where the Court decides the legality of the arrest, a claim for all costs and expenses could be filed.

(8) What are the court fees which must be paid in order to make an arrest? Are they recoverable in the event of a successful claim?

The deposit for arrest expenses in Panama is normally US$2,500. In cases of larger vessels the Court is entitled to request additional funds. The Marshal of the Maritime Court is authorised to request funds for custody and conservation of the vessel at any time. If the requested funds are not deposited, the arrest is lifted.

All funds deposited in relation to the arrest of a vessel are taxed as costs and charged to the defendants on top of the underlying claim.

(9) How are the lawyers' fees calculated? If possible please estimate the costs of a typical arrest.

The Maritime Court of Panama calculates initially, when issuing the arrest order, a percentage of the amount in dispute as temporary costs. At the time of judgment, the Court is required to consider this amount, adding it to the judgment. The estimated costs of a typical arrest are as follows: US$1,000 arrest security, US$2,500 for custody and conservation of the vessel (in the case of vessels of more than 7,500 grt another US$2,500 is to be included), US$1,000 to cover initial translation and other arrest expenses.

(10) Are all or any part of the lawyers' fees recoverable in the event of a successful arrest?

The Maritime Court sets a temporary costs amount based on a percentage of the amount in dispute. At the time of judgment the Court decides the amount of attorney fees, based on several factors such as the type of claim, the work done, the novelty of the legal issues, the procedural conduct of the parties. The judgment includes at least part of the attorney fees.

(11) How quickly can a ship be arrested after the local lawyer is fully instructed?

The Maritime Court of Panama is, by law, open to arrest and release vessels 24 hours per day, all year long. There are Court staff on duty at all times. Normally, it takes from four to six hours to obtain an arrest order. Any delay is due to the banks business schedule, since cash or certified cheques are to be attached to the arrest petition.

(12) Is there a minimum amount in dispute for which a ship may be arrested?

There is no minimum amount for which an arrest could be filed.

(13) It is possible to arrest a sister ship or a ship in "associated ownership"?

Under Panamanian law, Art. 17 permits the arrest of a vessel under the same ownership. This could be a sister ship arrest. In cases of vessels owned by associated ownership, only in particular circumstances could an arrest be filed. In cases of fraud or violation of public policy, the Court could pierce the corporate veil and arrest a vessel.

(14) What is the order of priorities in the event of the distribution by the court of the proceeds of sale of the ship?

In Panama the order of priorities is normally established by the law of the flag of the vessel. So the ranking of priorities and distribution of the proceeds is done in accordance with the law of the flag of the vessel.

(15) Are the claims in respect of which a ship may be arrested subject to a time bar (or prescription) and, if so, are these different according to the nature of the claim?

In Panama the time bar, or prescription, or the statute of limitation is decided by the substantive law applicable to the claim. The Panamanian Maritime Code has adopted Art. 557 to determine the law applicable to different types of maritime claims. The prescription of claims is decided by the substantive law applicable to each claim.

(16) Is it possible to apply for the arrest of a ship outside the normal working hours of the court?

The Maritime Court of Panama is, by law, open to arrest and release vessels 24 hours per day, all year long. There are Court staff on duty at all times, holidays and after hours. The claimant is liable to pay overtime to the Court Officers, limited to US$40 per individual.

(17) Please provide any other information which you believe is relevant in deciding whether or not to arrest a ship in your jurisdiction

In arrest of vessels why choose Panama and the Panama Canal

Panama and the Panama Canal are brand names to the world's maritime community. The Panama Canal handles approximately 13,500 transits every year, and over 155 million metric tons. Thousands of vessels call at Panamanian ports, not necessarily going through the Panama Canal. There are over 7,000 active vessels registered in Panama, and over 5,000 mortgages registered in Panama, both types of registration increasing monthly. There are thousands of Panamanian registered shipping companies.

For the solution of maritime disputes, either involving vessels present in the Panama Canal or registered in Panama, there is the Maritime Court of Panama, a specialist tribunal handling exclusively admiralty and maritime cases. Panama has a flexible system of maritime jurisdiction whereby all vessels going through the Panama Canal, calling at Panamanian ports, or registered in Panama are subject to the jurisdiction of the Court for any maritime claim incurred anywhere in the world.

In Panama, the Maritime Court of Panama has jurisdiction over all vessels transiting the Panama Canal, over all vessels calling at Panamanian ports, over all vessels registered in Panama, and over all companies registered in Panama, regardless of where the claim originated. The Maritime Court of Panama has the power to arrest any vessel transiting the Panama Canal, or present at any Panamanian port, as well as the power to enforce claims, or judgments, against Panamanian registered vessels and companies.

CHAPTER 27

POLAND

(1) What are the types of claim for which a ship may be arrested in Poland?

In Polish law, two types of detention of a vessel exist: temporary detention and detention (arrest) of a vessel by judicial process to secure a maritime claim.

- (a) Temporary detention performed by the maritime administration (the harbour master) on the basis of Art. 74 of the Polish Maritime Code, for a period not exceeding 72 hours. The types of claims are here:
  - (i) for the purposes of securing the claim against a vessel for harbour dues or damage caused to harbour works, docks or navigable ways as well as damage resulting from oil pollution of the environment;
  - (ii) a recovered wreck or other objects which have hindered navigation, for the purpose of securing the claim in respect of their removal.
- (b) Detention of a ship by judicial process to secure a maritime claim. Such a detention is made under the provisions of the Polish Code of Civil Proceeding (Arts. 730 *et seq.*) and provisions of the International Convention for the Unification of Certain Rules Relating to the Arrest of Sea-Going Ships, signed at Brussels, 10 May 1952, which has been adopted by Poland.

There is a distinction between pecuniary claims and non-pecuniary claims. The claims we are talking about are pecuniary claims.

Among these claims are claims not connected with maritime matters (claims) as well as maritime claims. The list of maritime claims has been specified in the above-mentioned Convention.

(2) Is there a distinction between claims which give rise to a maritime lien and other types of claim?

It is not necessary to have a maritime claim to arrest a vessel. It is also possible to arrest a vessel (on the basis of the Code of Civil Proceeding) to secure a non-maritime but pecuniary claim.

However, in practice it sometimes happens that the Polish courts are not ready to arrest a vessel when a maritime claim does not exist, even when such a possibility is legally authorised and lawful. For example, the court refused to arrest a vessel when the basis for the claim was unpaid P & I Club calls because it was not a maritime claim. However, the same court (but with another judge) allowed arrest of a vessel to secure a non-maritime claim for legal services which remained unpaid for by the shipowners—on the basis of the Code of Civil Proceeding.

(3) (a) What pleadings, affidavits and documents must be presented to the court when applying for an arrest and in what language?

All documents confirming the enforceable claim and demonstrating the liability of the shipowner must be presented. The types of documents depend on the nature of the claim. When it is, for example, a cargo claim (for loss of or damage to cargo) the main document is the bill of lading. The others are: survey certificate, notification of the damage/loss, valuation of the damage/loss.

When it is a claim connected with a charter, a charterparty and other relevant documents must be enclosed.

The main rule is that all documents presented should be in Polish.

It is not possible to move a case without written confirmation of payment of the court fees.

A power of attorney is necessary as well.

A sworn translation is suggested because not every judge accepts a lawyer's translation.

(b) Which documents must be notarised or otherwise authenticated?

It is unnecessary for documents to be notarised. It is sufficient for a lawyer authorised to manage the case on behalf of the claimant to confirm that the documents enclosed are in accordance with the originals.

The courts are even willing to accept fax copies of documents.

Generally speaking in the civil proceeding—under the regulations of the Polish Code of Civil Proceeding—to secure a pecuniary claim the claimant must prove:

— the credibility of the claim;
— that lack of security could make him unable to get an indemnity.

Theoretically, it is unnecessary to prove these for maritime claims (being under the provisions of the Brussels Convention). However, the courts often forget such a rule (mainly in the appeal proceedings) and expect to have such evidence as for other pecuniary claims.

(4) Is it possible to arrest a ship solely in order to obtain security for a claim which will ultimately be determined in another jurisdiction?

Yes, there is no legal objection to arresting a ship solely in order to obtain security for a claim which will ultimately be determined in another jurisdiction.

The Polish jurisdiction is based on the provisions of the Brussels Convention Relating to the Arrest of Sea-Going Ships and on regulations of the Code of Civil Proceeding. In the Code of Civil Proceeding it is provided, *inter alia*, that Polish jurisdiction is conferred when a debtor has property in Poland or the seat of the debtor's company (or at least a branch) is in Poland.

(5) What kind of security is normally acceptable to enable the ship to be released from arrest?

To enable a ship to be released from arrest it is normally acceptable to provide a bank guarantee as well as a deposit into court on the value of the claim.

Sometimes in the order to arrest the ship as collateral it is expressly stated that some kind of parallel collateral (security) is expected, but it depends whether such a request was mentioned in the application.

(6) In what circumstances can a claimant be made to give security and what security is acceptable?

In the civil proceeding a foreign claimant can be made to give security for the costs of the proceeding expected to be borne by the debtor, but in practice it does not happen because the arrest proceedings before the court of first instance happens without the presence of the debtor, who appears only in the appeal proceedings. The court itself demands no security besides the payment of court fees.

(7) In the event that the arrest was ultimately shown to have been wrongful, can a claim be made for wrongful arrest and what must be established in order to successfully maintain such a claim?

Such cases are rather rare. In the event that the arrest was ultimately shown to have been wrongful, a claim can be made on the basis that a tort has been committed. However, the onus of proving this is on the shipowners—which is a very difficult task. The principle is to prove a connection between the wrongful act (arrest) and damage to the shipowners. The legal basis for such a claim is the Polish Civil Code.

(8) What are the court fees which must be paid in order to make an arrest? Are they recoverable in the event of a successful claim?

To make an arrest the application for arrest must be accompanied by the following court fees—such payment should be evidenced as having been paid to the court's account. The court fees depend on the value of the claim and in arrest proceedings they amount to one-fifth of the following standard court fees:

(a) when a claim's value exceeds US$40,000 the fees are:
  — US$3,000 for the first US$40,000
  — five per cent of the excess over US$40,000

(b) when a claim's value is between US$20,000 and US$40,000 the fees are:
  — US$1,500 for the first US$20,000
  — six per cent of the excess over US$20,000.

When an application to arrest a ship is lodged during a proceeding, for example in the summons, no court fee is demanded from the plaintiff.

There are also the bailiff's fees, which are as follows:

(a) a constant fee—twelve per cent of the claim's value but not to exceed US$3,700;

(b) an additional lump sum—twelve per cent of the claim's value but not to exceed US$3,700.

The losing party in the case is obliged to repay his opponent's costs on his demand. The opponent must present his demand to the court.

In certain specially justified circumstances the court can award against the losing party only part of the costs or a release from costs.

If a party is conducting the case in an improper manner or is acting dishonestly the court can award a recovery of costs regardless of the result of the proceedings.

(9) How are the lawyers' fees calculated? If possible please estimate the costs of a typical arrest.

Lawyers' fees are calculated by mutual arrangement between lawyer and client. It is not possible to estimate an exact level. However, a general legal basis for lawyers' fees can be found in the Order of the Minister of Justice of June 1992, where it provides that lawyers' fees depend on the claim's value (regardless of the result of the proceeding) as follows:

(a) for claims between US$20,000 and US$40,000 the fees can be expected to be between US$800 and US$8,000

(b) for claims between US$4,000 and US$20,000 the fees can be expected to be between US$650 and US$4,000.

In practice, fees are not calculated at the minimum level. The above-mentioned limits do not exist if the case needs much time and effort spent on it by the lawyer and the value of the claim is high.

(10) Are all or any part of the lawyers' fees recoverable in the event of a successful arrest?

The lawyers' fees are recoverable in the event of a successful arrest as a part of the costs of the process only when the proceeding connected with the main claim are successful for the party. Should the proceeding end on the arrest of the ship the costs of it are borne by the creditor. However, when in an appeal the Court of Appeal releases the ship from arrest the losing party (the creditor) is obliged to pay back the costs (including the lawyers' fees).

(11) How quickly can a ship be arrested after the local lawyer is fully instructed?

After a local lawyer is fully instructed (and the documents are supplied and the court fees paid) a ship can be arrested in two days. This is an average period, because it is also possible to arrest a ship in one day.

(12) Is there a minimum amount in dispute for which a ship may be arrested?

According to Polish law there is no minimum amount in dispute for which a ship may be arrested.

(13) Is it possible to arrest a sister ship or a ship in "associated ownership"?

It is possible to arrest a sister ship. It is not possible to arrest a ship in "associated ownership".

(14) What is the order of priorities in the event of the distribution by the court of the proceeds of sale of the ship?

The Polish Code of Civil Proceeding provides the following order of priorities:

- (a) execution costs;
- (b) maintenance debts;
- (c) salaries, pensions, indemnities for injury;
- (d) taxes and other similar dues;
- (e) payments due to the State;
- (f) bank credit dues;
- (g) dues secured by a lien on a ship;
- (h) dues owing to the creditors who have carried out the arrest;
- (i) other dues.

This order of priorities is general and most of the items of this list are applicable.

(15) Are the claims in respect of which a ship may be arrested subject to a time bar (or prescription) and, if so, are these different according to the nature of the claim?

Yes. The claims for which a ship may be arrested are subject to a time bar (or prescription). These are different according to the nature of the claim.

(16) Is it possible to apply for the arrest of a ship outside the normal working hours of the court?

No. However, if the creditor applies during working hours it is possible to obtain an order to arrest the ship and have the bailiff seize her outside normal working hours.

(17) Please provide any other information which you believe is relevant in deciding whether or not to arrest a ship in your jurisdiction.

The jurisdiction for the arrest of ships has not been finalised. Therefore some of the statements are relative. Every judge is independent, so the court decision (order) on the arrest of a ship is dependent on the judge's practice, knowledge and experience. It is not unknown for the same court to issue quite different decisions and awards based on similar circumstances (for example, the nature of a claim).

The proceedings to arrest a ship in Poland are quite expensive. It is possible to obtain the arrest of a ship as quickly as obtaining the release of a ship before the Court of Appeal.

The calculation of fees and costs is approximate and is connected to the rate of the US dollar in Poland.

It is possible to discuss fees with lawyers in Poland. It is not very common to estimate lawyers' fees on an hourly basis.

CHAPTER 28

PORTUGAL

(1) What are the types of claim for which a ship may be arrested in Portugal?

Ships may, in principle, be arrested for all types of claims or debts for which the owners of ships are responsible, i.e. (i) either claims or debts arising out of breach of contracts such as unpaid crew wages, debts arising out of services or goods supplied to ships, cargo losses or damages, port expenses etc., or (ii) for claims or debts related to civil liability compensation arising out of damages in tort caused by the ships.

However, the general principle referred to above will not be applicable when the ship to be arrested flies the flag of a contracting state to the International Convention for the Unification of Certain Rules Relating to Arrest of Sea-Going Ships, Brussels, 10 May 1952. In this case the arrest will only be possible if the claim or debt is a *maritime claim* as defined in the Convention.

(2) Is there a distinction between claims which give rise to a maritime lien and other types of claim?

There is a distinction between claims which give rise to a *maritime lien* and other claims which arise out of maritime claims or ordinary claims.

Portuguese internal law contemplates various types of maritime liens such as court costs, salvage awards or remuneration for assistance, port expenses, officers and crew wages, expenses made at a port of call, repair costs, etc.

Portugal is also a party to the International Convention for the Unification of Certain Rules of Law Relating to Maritime Liens and Mortgages, Brussels, 10 April 1926, according to which law costs due to the state, officers and crew wages, remuneration for salvage and assistance, indemnities for collision and claims resulting from contracts entered into by the master away from the ship's home port are deemed maritime liens.

The maritime liens will be relinquished on judicial sale of the vessel or even in the case of a private sale but in the latter case the seller will have to take proper steps before a competent court to have the creditors duly notified of such sale in order that they may exercise their rights. The change of ownership title in cases other than the above ones will not affect the rights of the holders of a maritime lien but the elapse of the time will prevent the enforcement of the claim as a maritime lien if not exercised within the legal time limits.

(3) (a) What pleadings, affidavits and documents must be presented in court when applying for an arrest and in what language?

It is mandatory for the claimant to appoint a lawyer to whom a power of attorney must be granted although the law allows that the power of attorney can be presented to court at a later date in urgent matters like arrests.

The lawyer will have to submit a petition to the competent court together with documentary evidence of the claim, namely correspondence, invoices, etc., and in principle examination of witnesses will also be required so as to satisfy the court that the arrest petitioner has a *prima facie* claim against the debtor. In other words, the claimant has the burden of providing *prima facie* evidence of his claim, which evidence is discretionally assessed by the court. The petition must be drawn up in Portuguese and documentary evidence in foreign languages must be translated into Portuguese.

(b) Which documents must be notarised or otherwise authenticated?

In principle no notarisation or authentication is required for documents to be attached to the arrest petition although under certain circumstances it may be necessary for the lawyers to ask for notarised and authenticated powers of attorney.

(4) Is it possible to arrest a ship solely in order to obtain security for a claim which will ultimately be determined in another jurisdiction?

Portuguese courts are competent in respect of the arrest of any ship lying in Portuguese territorial waters irrespective of their flag, whether or not they have jurisdiction on the merits of the claim. The competent jurisdiction for the decision on the merits of the claim may be a foreign one and therefore it is possible to arrest a ship solely in order to obtain security.

(5) What kind of security is normally acceptable to enable the ship to be released from arrest?

Once the ship is arrested by the judge the owner is entitled to submit to the competent court a bank guarantee from a local bank to lift the arrest order (claimants are not bound to release the ship from arrest on the mere basis of the usual P & I Club letters of undertaking or any other sort of guarantee issued by a foreign guarantor if they so elect, although this is an acceptable practice).

(6) In what circumstances can a claimant be made to give security and what security is acceptable?

Portuguese law contemplates the possibility that the arrest petitioner is obliged to put up security, pursuant to Art. 620° of the Civil Code, if the court so decides. However, in practice, this discretionary power of the judge is rarely used.

(7) In the event that the arrest was ultimately shown to have been wrongful, can a claim be made for wrongful arrest and what must be established in order to successfully maintain such a claim?

Under the Portuguese Rules of Civil Procedure (Art. 406, para. 4, CCP), the owner of the detained or arrested ship may file wrongful arrest proceedings against the claimant in the court which ordered the arrest and ask for compensation to be awarded in its favour, but the mere failure of the legal action on the merits of the claim is not enough to bring about the censure of the arrest petitioner.

A judgment in favour of the owners in wrongful arrest proceedings will only take place if it can be established either that the claimant acted in bad faith or that he acted recklessly or with gross negligence, which will, of course, be a rare situation (e.g. the arrest is filed against the owner of a ship on the assumption that he is the debtor but it turns out that he is not, or the legal action on the merits of the claim is dismissed due to the plaintiff's neglecting to take adequate procedural steps to obtain a decision on the merits).

(8) What are the court fees which must be paid in order to make an arrest? Are they recoverable in the event of a successful claim?

The legal court costs depend on the amount claimed in the arrest petition submitted to court. It is therefore a matter to be assessed case by case, the rule being that the higher the amount of security claimed by the arrest petitioner the higher the court costs.

If the claimant succeeds in his claim most of the court costs will be recovered from the opposing party, provided the latter pays the final court cost levied upon him by the court officer when the proceedings come to an end.

(9) How are the lawyers' fees calculated?

Unlike court costs, lawyers' fees are not charged on the basis of any fixed sums or percentages. It is even forbidden by Portuguese law for lawyers to enter into arrangements of "quota litis", i.e. percentages of the claimed amount recovered, or even based upon "no cure no pay" agreements.

Lawyers' fees are therefore based on the time spent on the case, the complexity of the procedural steps taken—in some cases arrest decisions give rise to defences lodged either by the arresting party or by a third party with a legal title on the arrested ship—and also the degree of expertise used.

(10) Are all or any part of the lawyers' fees recoverable in the event of a successful arrest?

Counsel's fees are not recoverable from the losing party, although the claimant may include disbursements arising out of the legal steps to be taken against the debtor in the amount to be claimed but this item may be rejected by the court.

It must be noted that once the arrest injunction is issued by the judge, a bailiff or ship's custodian will be appointed by the court and his fees will, in principle, be borne by the arrest petitioner unless the arrest respondent is ordered to indemnify the arrest petitioner during the legal action on the merits.

(11) How quickly can a ship be arrested after the local lawyer is fully instructed?

A ship can be arrested reasonably quickly provided the lawyer has had the time to prepare an arrest petition before her arrival in a Portuguese port; the port in question must fall within the jurisdiction of the Admiralty Court (not all ports are within such jurisdiction). In the case referred to above, 24 hours will, in principle, be enough to lodge an arrest.

(12) Is there a minimum amount in dispute for which a ship may be arrested?

There is no minimum amount in dispute for which a ship may be arrested.

(13) Is it possible to arrest a sister ship or a ship in "associated ownership"?

The creditor or claimant may apply for the arrest of the ship concerning which the claim arose or for the arrest of any other ship within the same ownership, but no lifting of the corporate veil is allowed by Portuguese law as regards *associated ownership*.

As to chartered vessels it must be noted that the ship regarding which the claim arises can be arrested for a "maritime claim" even if the claim is connected with a request for services or supply of goods ordered by the charterer, as long as it can be established that the owner gave his consent directly or indirectly.

(14) What is the order of priorities in the event of the distribution by the court of the proceeds of sale of the ship?

The order of priorities when the court distributes the proceeds of the sale of the ship has not been thoroughly tested in court since the practice is for the various claimants to reach a reasonable agreement to avoid lengthy disputes. The international private law principles in force in Portugal indicate that the question should be decided pursuant to the ship's flag.

The maritime liens as defined in Portuguese law will rank prior to mortgages and ordinary credits.

(15) Are the claims in respect of which a ship may be arrested subject to a time bar (or prescription) and, if so, are these different according to the nature of the claim?

The claims for which a ship may be arrested are subject to a time bar (or prescription) but this depends on the nature of the claim in question (e.g. a claim for cargo damage will become time barred one year from the date of the claim whilst a claim arising out of a collision is subject to a two-year prescription period).

(16) Is it possible to apply for the arrest of a ship outside the normal working hours of the court?

It is not possible to apply for an arrest of a ship outside the normal working hours of the court.

(17) Please provide any other information which you believe is relevant in deciding whether or not to arrest a ship in your jurisdiction.

As pointed out above, Portugal ratified the International Convention for the Unification of Certain Rules Relating to the Arrest of Sea-Going Ships, Brussels, 10 May 1952, in 1957 and its full wording was enacted in the Official Journal together with the Decree whereby the ratification was authorised. Since no specific procedural rules were enacted, the procedure of arrest of ships is governed by the Portuguese Code of Civil Procedure (CCP) and the Civil Code (CC), which are applicable to all ships, irrespective of their flag.

The arrest proceedings are regarded as preliminary proceedings since the purpose of the arrest is to obtain security for a claim and not to obtain any decision on the merits of such claim.

The conditions required for an arrest, in addition to the *prima facie* evidence of the maritime claim, may bring about the danger that, at the time of the enforcement of the judgment obtained against the debtor, no assets are available anymore (Art. 691, para. 1, CC and Art. 403, para. 5, CCP).

The legal action on the merits of the claim will have to be filed with the competent court within the legal time limit, failing which the arrest may be lifted at the request of the owners. The owners of the vessel will then be served a writ of summons in order to submit a defence against the claim on the merits although they are also entitled to challenge the arrest order.

CHAPTER 29

SCOTLAND

(1) What are the types of claim for which a ship may be arrested in Scotland?

The only types of claims for which a ship may be detained in Scotland are set out in section 47 of the Administration of Justice Act 1956 and are effectively:

(a) damage done or received by any ship;
(b) loss of life or personal injury sustained in consequence of any defect in a ship or in her apparel or equipment, or of the wrongful act, neglect or default of the owners, charterers or persons in possession or control of a ship or of the master or crew thereof or of any other person for whose wrongful acts, neglects or defaults the owners, charterers or persons in possession or control of a ship are responsible, being an act, neglect or default in the navigation or management of the ship, in the loading, unloading or discharge of goods on, in or from the ship or in the embarkation, carriage or disembarkation of persons on, in or from the ship;
(c) salvage;
(d) any agreement relating to the use or hire of any ship whether by charterparty or otherwise;
(e) any agreement relating to the carriage of goods in any ship whether by charterparty or otherwise;
(f) loss of, or damage to, goods carried in any ship;
(g) general average;
(h) any bottomry bond;
(i) towage;
(j) pilotage;
(k) the supply of goods or materials to a ship for her operation or maintenance;
(l) the construction, repair or equipment of any ship;
(m) liability for dock charges or dues;
(n) liability for payment of wages (including any sum allotted out of wages under section 141 of the Merchant Shipping Act 1894, or

adjudged under section 387 of that Act by a superintendent to be due by way of wages) of a master or member of the crew of a ship;

(o) master's disbursements, including disbursements made by shippers, charterers or agents on behalf of a ship or her owner;

(p) any dispute as to the ownership or right to possession of any ship or as to the ownership of any share in a ship;

(q) any dispute between co-owners of any ship as to the ownership, possession, employment or earnings of that ship;

(r) the mortgage or hypothecation of any ship or any share in a ship;

(s) any forfeiture or condemnation of any ship, or of goods which are being, or have been, carried, or have been attempted to be carried, in any ship, or for the restoration of a ship or any such goods after seizure.

(2) Is there a distinction between claims which give rise to a maritime lien and other types of claim?

Claims which give rise to a maritime lien are those arising out of salvage, seamen's wages, bottomry and respondentia (both virtually obsolete) and damage done by a vessel, including collision. These claims give rise to a lien which permit an *in rem* action against the vessel itself and these claims have priority over other ordinary creditors.

(3) (a) What pleadings, affidavits and documents must be presented to the court when applying for an arrest and in what language?

The only documents required, other than a summons, are, if relevant, copy invoices, survey reports, etc., depending on the nature of the claim. No affidavits are required normally. The summons must be in English.

(b) Which documents must be notarised or othewise authenticated?

At the arrestment stage, no authentication of documentation is necessary and no affidavits are required.

(4) Is it possible to arrest a ship solely in order to obtain security for a claim which will ultimately be determined in another jurisdiction?

It is possible to arrest a ship solely to obtain security: (a) where the shipowner is domiciled within the EU, the claim is raised in his jurisdiction and thereafter arrestment is by way of a petition in terms of section 27 of the Civil Jurisdiction and Judgments Act 1982; (b) where the defender shipowner is domiciled outwith the EU, security can be obtained by arrestment in Scotland, then, by agreement, the Scottish court proceedings can be stayed and the dispute can be resolved in the most appropriate forum.

(5) What kind of security is normally acceptable to enable the ship to be released from arrest?

Acceptable security would be:

- (a) a standard form of Club letter;
- (b) a letter of guarantee from a bank or other acceptable financial institution with a place of business within the Scottish jurisdiction;
- (c) placing the sum on joint deposit receipt in the names of the parties' solicitors;
- (d) payment into court of sufficient funds to cover both the claim and interest and expenses.

(6) In what circumstances can a claimant be made to give security and what security is acceptable?

At any time during the course of a litigation the defendant shipowner may seek an order of the court requiring the claimant to give security for costs in the event that the defendant is successful. The court would grant such an application if the defendant demonstrated that there was doubt about the claimant's ability to meet these costs. Security in the form of a sum of money lodged in court or deposited on joint deposit receipt in the name of the respective parties' solicitors or a letter of guarantee from an acceptable financial institution would normally be acceptable.

(7) In the event that the arrest was ultimately shown to have been wrongful, can a claim be made for wrongful arrest and what must be established in order to successfully maintain such a claim?

A claim can be made for wrongful arrestment and if established would require the claimant to meet the costs of any delay occasioned to the vessel and any costs incurred. To maintain a claim for wrongful arrestment it is necessary to demonstrate that the arrestment was done with malice and that the claim had no probable cause, or was done without a warrant granted by the court.

(8) What are the court fees which must be paid in order to make an arrest? Are they recoverable in the event of a successful claim?

Court fees to be paid depend upon which court is used—the Supreme Court or the local Sheriff Court. For reasons we discuss below, we recommend the use of the Court of Session and the fee is presently £89 if the summons is warranted during normal hours or approximately twice that if out-of-hours.

These fees are recoverable.

(9) How are the lawyers' fees calculated? If possible, please estimate the costs of a typical arrest.

The lawyers' fees are typically based on an hourly rate and the fee element of the costs will depend upon the complexity of the claim and whether or not the work can be done during normal working hours or at night or over a weekend. Apart from the solicitors fees, there are also counsel's fees incurred in drafting the summons and, often the largest element of costs, the Messengers-at-Arms fees in effecting the arrestment. If the vessel to be arrested is located in one of the Outer Isles, costs rise dramatically.

A straightforward arrestment on the mainland would be about £1,500, while a complex matter involving the arrestment of a ship on the Islands over a weekend could cost about £6,000.

(10) Are all or any part of the lawyers' fees recoverable in the event of a successful arrest?

Fees are recoverable if a claim is successful, except for Messengers-at-Arms fees where the claim is *in personam* rather than *in rem*.

(11) How quickly can a ship be arrested after the local lawyer is fully instructed?

Within a day.

(12) Is there a minimum amount in dispute for which a ship may be arrested?

There is no minimum amount but the costs involved make arrestment for minor sums uncommercial.

(13) Is it possible to arrest a sister ship or a ship in "associated ownership"?

It is possible to arrest a sister ship where the shares in the sister ship are all owned by the same defendant against whom the claim is directed. An arrestment *in rem* cannot be made against a sister ship.

(14) What is the order of priorities in the event of the distribution by the court of the proceeds of sale of the ship?

Generally speaking, the following is the ranking of claimants:

(a) claims for salvage;
(b) claims for crew wages;
(c) claims in respect of damage done by a vessel;
(d) claims for Master's disbursements;
(e) mortgagees in order of registration of mortgages;
(f) unsecured creditors rank equally.

(15) Are the claims in respect of which a ship may be arrested subject to a time bar (or prescription) and, if so, are these different according to the nature of the claim?

Typical claims against a ship are time barred, or prescribed at different times as follows:

(a) collision claim—two years;
(b) cargo claims are subject to the terms of the contract of carriage but typically one year;
(c) all other pecuniary claims are five years, except for passenger claims for injury or death—two years, crew claims for injury or death—three years.

(16) Is it possible to apply for the arrest of a ship outside the normal working hours of the court?

It is possible to apply for the arrest of a ship 24 hours a day, seven days a week. Delays are sometimes experienced in locating the Duty Clerk and, where necessary, a judge, but such delays are unlikely to exceed two hours. If it is anticipated that an arrestment will be necessary, then the relevant personnel can be alerted and be made available.

(17) Please provide any other information which you believe is relevant in deciding whether or not to arrest a ship in your jurisdiction.

A claimant is not responsible for any costs that are incurred by the shipowner in respect of the arrestment, except where wrongful arrestment is successfully argued. A claimant is not responsible for costs incurred in respect of harbour dues, seamen's wages or to suppliers to the vessel while it remains under arrest, or any other similar costs. These parties will no doubt become claimants in the Fund if, or when, the vessel is sold but if, for example, the vessel proves unsaleable, then the claimant has no liability to those other parties.

CHAPTER 30

SINGAPORE

(1) What are the types of claim for which a ship may be arrested in Singapore?

The types of claim are:

(a) any claim to the possession or ownership of a ship or to the ownership of any share therein;
(b) any question arising between the co-owners of a ship as to possession, employment, or earnings of that ship;
(c) any claim in respect of a mortgage of or charge on a ship or any share therein;
(d) any claim for damage done by a ship;
(e) any claim for damage received by a ship;
(f) any claim for loss of life or personal injury sustained in consequence of any defect in a ship or in her apparel or equipment, or of the wrongful act, neglect, or default of the owners, charterers, or persons in possession or control of a ship or of the master or crew thereof or of any other person for whose wrongful acts, neglects, or defaults the owners, charterers, or persons in possession or control of a ship are responsible, being an act, neglect, or default in the navigation or management of the ship, in the loading, carriage, or discharge of goods on, in or from the ship or in the embarkation, carriage or disembarkation of persons on, in or from the ship;
(g) any claim for loss of or damage to goods carried in a ship;
(h) any claim arising out of any agreement relating to the carriage of goods in a ship or to the use or hire of a ship;
(i) subject to section 304 of the Merchant Shipping Act (which requires salvage disputes to be determined summarily by a District Court in certain cases), any claim in the nature of salvage (including any claim arising under section 11 of the Air Navigation Act relating to salvage to aircraft and their apparel and cargo);
(j) any claim in the nature of towage in respect of a ship [or an aircraft];
(k) any claim in the nature of pilotage in respect of a ship [or an aircraft];

(l) any claim in respect of goods, materials supplied to a ship for her operation or maintenance;
(m) any claim in respect of the construction, repair or equipment of a ship or dock charges or dues;
(n) any claim by a master or member of the crew of a ship for wages and any claim by or in respect of a master or member of the crew of a ship for any money or property which, under any of the provisions of the Merchant Shipping Act is recoverable as wages or in the Court and in the manner in which wages may be recovered;
(o) any claim by a master, shipper, charterer or agent in respect of disbursements made on account of a ship;
(p) any claim arising out of an act which is or is claimed to be a general average act;
(q) any claim arising out of bottomry;
(r) any claim for the forfeiture or condemnation of a ship or of goods which are being or have been carried, or have been attempted to be carried, in a ship, or for the restoration of a ship or any such goods after seizure, or for droits of Admiralty.

(2) Is there a distinction between claims which give rise to a maritime lien and other types of claim?

The following types of claim given rise to a maritime lien:

(a) salvage;
(b) collision damage;
(c) seamen's wages;
(d) master's wages and disbursements; and
(e) bottomry.

Where a maritime lien subsists in respect of a ship, the admiralty jurisdiction of the Singapore High Court can be invoked (and the ship arrested) by an action *in rem* against that ship notwithstanding any subsequent sale of the ship to a third party and notwithstanding that the purchaser had no notice of the lien and no personal liability on the claim from which the maritime lien arose.

Where no maritime lien subsists, the types of claims mentioned in (a), (b), (c) and (r) of the answer to question (1) above are enforceable by an action *in rem* against the ship in question; however, the other types of claims mentioned in the answer to question (1) above are enforceable by an action *in rem* against the ship in connection with which the claim arose only if the following conditions are satisfied:

(i) the person who would be liable on the claim in an action *in personam* was the owner or charterer of, or in possession or in control of, that ship at the time the cause of the action arose;

(ii) at the time when the action is brought (that is, when the writ of summons is issued) that ship is beneficially owned (demise charter is not sufficient) as respects all the shares therein by the person referred to in (i) above.

In addition, claims which give rise to a maritime lien take priority over most other claims in the distribution of the proceeds of sale of a ship (see the answer to question (14) below).

(3) (a) What pleadings, affidavits and documents must be presented to the court when applying for an arrest and in what language?
(b) Which documents must be notarised or otherwise authenticated?

The following documents in the English language must be presented:

(i) Writ of Summons *in rem*;
(ii) Warrant of Arrest;
(iii) Praecipe requesting issue of Warrant of Arrest;
(iv) Affidavit leading to the Warrant of Arrest;
(v) Undertaking to indemnify the Sheriff for the charges and expenses to be incurred;
(vi) Letter of authority and particulars (of the person who would be effecting service of the Warrant of Arrest and Writ).

The following additional documents (in the English language) are required in particular cases:

(vii) in the case of an action for possession of the ship or for wages, where the ship in question is a foreign ship belonging to a port of a state having a consulate in Singapore—a copy of a notice sent to the consul that the action has been begun;
(viii) in the case of a claim arising out of bottomry—the bottomry bond and a notarial translation thereof (if the bond is not in the English language).

The affidavit (item (iv)) and the notarial translation (item (viii)) must be sworn/affirmed before a commissioner for oaths.

(4) Is it possible to arrest a ship solely in order to obtain security for a claim which will ultimately be determined in another jurisdiction?

It is not open to a plaintiff, having invoked the admiralty jurisdiction of the Singapore High Court in an action *in rem*, to seek to have the matter determined in the courts of another jurisdiction.

Please refer to the answer to question (17) on the possibility of the defendant shipowner seeking to have the Singapore proceedings stayed. The defendant shipowner may also, at its discretion, agree to have the matter determined in another jurisdiction and to provide security for the proceedings in that other jurisdiction.

Where the matter in dispute is the subject of an international arbitration agreement (as defined in section 5 of the International Arbitration Act) or the subject of an agreement that the International Arbitration Act or the UNCITRAL Model Law on International Commercial Arbitration is to apply, section 6 of the International Arbitration Act provides that "any party to the agreement may, at any time after appearance and before delivering any pleadings or taking any other steps in the proceedings, apply to that court to stay the proceedings". A plaintiff, being a party to the agreement, may rely on this provision to apply for a stay of admiralty proceedings. If the court stays the proceedings, the court may order that the ship arrested be retained as security for the satisfaction of any award made on the arbitration or that the stay be conditional on the provision of equivalent security for the satisfaction of any such award. It is however unclear as to how the costs of the proceedings would be allocated.

(5) What kind of security is normally acceptable to enable the ship to be released from arrest?

Security is normally provided by way of a letter of guarantee issued by either a first class Singapore bank or certain P & I Clubs in the appropriate wording. Bail bonds are acceptable but not usual.

(6) In what circumstances can a claimant be made to give security, and what security is acceptable?

Before a warrant of arrest is issued and executed, a written undertaking to indemnify the Sheriff and to provide the Sheriff with sufficient funds as and when required by the Sheriff in respect of the charges and expenses that may be incurred in consequence of the arrest of the ship must be provided to the satisfaction of the court.

In addition, the plaintiff is required to give an initial deposit of a minimum of S$5,000 to the Sheriff as security for the Sheriff's expenses (security guard charges, launch charges, cost of provisions, fresh water and fuel, agency fees, etc.). Once the initial deposit has been utilised, the Sheriff will require further deposits.

Apart from the foregoing, the Singapore High Court has a discretion to order that the plaintiff give security for the defendant shipowner's legal costs in the following circumstances:

(a) the plaintiff is ordinarily resident out of Singapore;
(b) the plaintiff (not being a plaintiff who is suing in a representative capacity) is a nominal plaintiff who is suing for the benefit of some other person and there is reason to believe that he will be unable to pay the costs of the defendant if ordered to do so;

(c) the plaintiff's address is not stated in the writ or other originating process or is incorrectly stated therein; or
(d) the plaintiff has changed his address during the course of the proceedings with a view to evading the consequences of the litigation.

Security for costs is normally provided by way of a guarantee issued by a Singapore bank.

(7) In the event that the arrest was ultimately shown to have been wrongful, can a claim be made for wrongful arrest and what must be established in order to successfully maintain such a claim?

In order to make a claim for wrongful arrest, it must be established that the plaintiff acted with gross negligence or malice.

(8) What are the court fees which must be paid in order to make an arrest? Are they recoverable in the event of a successful claim?

The stamp fees payable are:

(i) Writ of Summons—S$150.
(ii) Praecipe requesting the Warrant of Arrest—S$50.
(iii) Warrant of Arrest—S$100.
(iv) Affidavit leading to the Warrant of Arrest—S$20 oath fees plus S$5 per exhibit plus S$1 per page (subject to a minimum of S$10)
(v) Undertaking—S$50.

In the event of a successful claim, the plaintiff will normally (subject to the court's discretion) be awarded costs. If costs are awarded to the plaintiff, these stamp fees form part of the plaintiff's disbursements and are normally recoverable.

Further, an initial deposit of a minimum of S$5,000 for the Sheriff's expenses has to be given and further deposits will be required once the initial sum of S$5,000 has been utilised (refer to the answer to question (6)).

(9) How are the lawyers' fees calculated? If possible please estimate the costs of a typical arrest.

Lawyers' fees are based on work done and are *not* calculated on the basis of the claim amount.

The fees for effecting an arrest alone are usually about S$10,000 to S$12,000 per vessel (exclusive of disbursements).

(10) Are all or any part of the lawyers' fees recoverable in the event of a successful arrest?

As mentioned in the answer to question (8), in the event of a successful *claim*, the plaintiff will normally (subject to the court's discretion) be awarded costs. If costs are awarded to the plaintiff, the plaintiff will generally be able to recover about two-thirds of the lawyers' fees.

(11) How quickly can a ship be arrested after the local lawyer is fully instructed?

Provided all the requisite documents (e.g. charterparty, bill of lading, etc.) have been provided, the necessary preparations and searches can be completed in half a day.

However it should be noted that if the preparations and searches are completed after office hours, it would not be possible to find a commissioner for oaths before whom to swear/affirm the affidavit and the Registry of the Singapore High Court would be closed. In that event, the arrest may have to be effected on the next working day. (Please refer to the answer to question (16) for the possibility of arresting after office hours.)

Further, the Registry of the Singapore High Court requires "identification numbers" of parties to be stated in all cause papers. In the case of a company, its identification number is its registration number in its country of registration. It would be helpful if the plaintiff can provide its identification number at the time of giving instructions.

(12) Is there a minimum amount in dispute for which a ship may be arrested?

There is no minimum amount. However the court may take into consideration the amount of the claim when exercising its discretion on the question of costs.

(13) Is it possible to arrest a sister ship or a ship in "associated ownership"?

It is possible to arrest a sister ship if the following conditions are satisfied:

(i) the person who would be liable on the claim in an action *in personam* was the owner or charterer of, or in possession or in control of, the ship (in connection with which the claim arose) at the time the cause of the action arose;

(ii) at the time when the action is brought (that is, when the writ of summons is issued), the sister ship (which is to be arrested) is beneficially owned (demise charter is not sufficient) as respects all the shares therein by the person referred to in (i) above.

Apart from the foregoing, it is not possible to arrest a ship in "associated ownership".

(14) What is the order of priorities in the event of the distribution by the court of the proceeds of sale of the ship?

The order of priorities is generally (subject to the discretion of the court) as follows:

(i) the Sheriff's costs and expenses of the arrest, custody and sale of the ship (including the Sheriff's commission);
(ii) the legal costs of the arresting party and the party which obtained the order for appraisement and sale;
(iii) common law possessory liens (but subject to all maritime liens which attach prior to (and possibly statutory liens where the writ *in rem* was issued prior to) the assumption of possession);
(iv) maritime liens (the ranking of maritime liens *inter se* depends upon a number of factors);
(v) claims of mortgagees (but subject to statutory liens where the writ *in rem* was issued prior to the mortgage);
(vi) all other claims *in rem* (which are treated as ranking *pari passu*).

(15) Are the claims in respect of which a ship may be arrested subject to a time bar (or prescription) and, if so, are these different according to the nature of the claim?

Under domestic Singapore law, the following are some of the time limitations which generally apply to actions *in rem*:

(i) cargo claims in respect of which the Hague-Visby Rules apply—time bar: one year from date of delivery of goods (or date when they should have been delivered);
(ii) claims against a ship or her owners in respect of any damage or loss to another vessel, her cargo or freight, or any property on board her, or damages for loss of life or personal injuries suffered by any person on board her, caused by the fault of the former vessel, whether such vessel be wholly or partly in fault, or in respect of any salvage services—time bar: two years from the date when the damage or loss or injury was caused or the salvage services were rendered (subject to extension by the court in appropriate circumstances);
(iii) contribution in respect of an overpaid proportion of any damages for loss of life or personal injuries by virtue of section 3 of the Maritime Conventions Act 1911—time bar: one year from the date of payment (subject to extension by the court in appropriate circumstances);
(iv) certain claims in respect of liability for oil pollution (incurred under section 3 of the Merchant Shipping (Oil Pollution) Act, Cap 180)—time bar: three years after the claim arose *and* six years after the occurrences resulting in the discharge or escape of oil;
(v) claims for wages of seamen in contract—time bar: six years from the date on which the cause of action accrued;
(vi) other claims—whilst the legal position is not entirely clear, any contemplated claims in contract or tort should be brought within

six years (*three years* if damages in respect of personal injuries are claimed) from the date on which the cause of action accrued.

It should be noted that apart from the provisions of domestic Singapore law, actions may be time barred by virtue of contractual provisions or the provisions of the proper law (if different from Singapore law) applicable.

(16) Is it possible to apply for the arrest of a ship outside the normal working hours of the court?

The normal working hours of the court are:

Mondays to Fridays: 9.00 a.m. to 4.00 p.m.
Saturdays: 9.00 a.m. to 12 noon

The duty registrar would normally accede to requests to make himself/herself available up to 6.00 p.m. on weekdays and 1.00 p.m. on Saturdays provided there is firm instruction to arrest a ship and the additional time is required for the preparation of the necessary documents. However it should be noted that this is entirely at the discretion of the duty registrar. There is also the necessity of getting a commissioner for oaths so that the affidavit leading to the warrant of arrest can be sworn/affirmed.

In cases of urgency, it is possible to page the duty registrar to seek his/her assistance to issue the necessary papers. Even if the duty registrar can be contacted and consents to hearing the application, the process of getting the necessary papers issued would take more time than during office hours because the duty registrar would have to perform the various administrative/ records tasks (which are normally done by the registry staff) himself/herself. This procedure should not be resorted to unless the arrest is extremely urgent *and* totally unexpected.

(17) Please provide any other information which you believe is relevant in deciding whether or not to arrest a ship in your jurisdiction.

It is necessary to ascertain whether there is any applicable agreement relating to jurisdiction/arbitration which would enable the defendant shipowner to apply for a stay of the Singapore proceedings. If the defendant shipowner succeeds in its application for a stay of the Singapore proceedings, costs would normally be ordered against the plaintiff (except in the case of a stay pursuant to section 6 of the International Arbitration Act (please refer to the answer to question (4)) where the position is yet unclear).

CHAPTER 31

SOUTH AFRICA

(1) What are the types of claim for which a ship may be arrested in South Africa?

The Supreme Court of South Africa has jurisdiction to hear and determine any *maritime claim*, as defined in the Act, irrespective of the place where the claim arose, of the place of registration of the ship concerned or of the residence, domicile or nationality of its owner. Examples of maritime claims as defined in the Act, are the following:

(a) any claim relating to the ownership or possession of a ship;
(b) any claim in respect of a mortgage, hypothecation, right of retention, pledge or charge on a ship;
(c) any claim relating to damage caused by or to a ship, whether by collision or otherwise;
(d) any claim relating to loss of life or personal injury caused by a ship or any defect in a ship;
(e) any claim relating to the loss of or damage to goods carried or which ought to have been carried in a ship;
(f) any claim relating to the carriage of goods in a ship or any agreement for or relating to such carriage;
(g) any claim relating to any charterparty or the use, hire, employment or operation of a ship;
(h) any claim in the nature of salvage, towage or pilotage;
(i) any claim relating to the supply of goods or rendering of services to a ship;
(j) any claim arising from agency, whether as ships, clearing, forwarding or any other kind of agent;
(k) any claim relating to general average;
(l) any claim relating to marine insurance or any policy of marine insurance including the protection and indemnity by any body of persons of its members in respect of marine matters;
(m) any claim relating to a maritime lien.

The above list of claims is not exhaustive and we have simply highlighted those maritime claims which we believe to be most relevant.

In terms of the Act, a maritime claim may be enforced either by an action *in personam*, which is an action instituted against the owner of the asset/vessel, or by an action *in rem*, which is instituted against the asset/vessel itself. In order to proceed by way of an action *in personam*, it is necessary for a claimant to establish jurisdiction, which is often done by means of an attachment of a ship either whilst she is in a South African port or whilst she is within the territorial waters of the Republic adjacent to the coastline of the court's area of jurisdiction. It is not, however, always necessary to make an attachment of a ship in order to proceed by way of an action *in personam*, because it may well be that the defendant has further assets within the court's jurisdiction which may be attached to found or confirm jurisdiction, or the defendant may reside within the court's jurisdiction.

Where an action *in rem* is concerned, it is necessary that proceedings be instituted by way of an arrest, within the area of jurisdiction of the court, of the property in respect of which the claim lies. The property may be the ship itself or its equipment, furniture, stores, bunkers, cargo, freight or any container, provided that, in the case of a container, the claim relates to the use or carriage of that container.

(2) Is there a distinction between claims which give rise to a maritime lien and other types of claim?

At a practical level there is no real distinction between claims which give rise to a maritime lien and other types of maritime claims, because both are defined as maritime claims in terms of the Act. A slight distinction is drawn between a maritime lien and other maritime claims in the context of an *in rem* arrest, since the Act provides that a maritime claim may be enforced by an action *in rem* either if the claimant has a maritime lien over the property to be arrested or if the owner of the property to be arrested would be liable to the claimant in an action *in personam*. For all intents and purposes, however, provided one has a maritime claim and the owner of the property to be arrested would be liable in an action *in personam*, then whether or not the maritime claim is of the nature of a maritime lien, one may enforce the maritime claim by an action *in rem* and proceed with an arrest of the vessel as described above.

It is, however, important to note that a maritime claim does not arise *in vacuo* and therefore, in the absence of a maritime lien, it is necessary to establish the indebtedness of the debtor (e.g. a shipowner) by furnishing proof of the underlying contract between the claimant and that shipowner. In the case of a maritime lien, however, the lien itself gives rise to a maritime claim and it is not necessary for the claimant to have an underlying contract before it is able to proceed *in rem* against the vessel. The traditional maritime liens of wages, salvage, collision and bottomry are recognised under South African law.

(3) (a) What pleadings, affidavits and documents must be presented to the court when applying for an arrest and in what language?

The pleadings, affidavits, documents and the like which must be presented to the court when applying for an arrest depend upon the type of arrest itself. Firstly, if one proceeds by way of an *in rem* arrest, as described above, one is simply required to prepare a summons, warrant of arrest and certificate. The summons which is prepared sets out the details of the plaintiff and the defendant vessel as well as the nature and amount of the claim. The warrant of arrest instructs the sheriff to arrest the vessel and the certificate is signed by a solicitor practising within the provincial division of the court where the arrest is to take place. The certificate reflects the source of the arresting solicitor's knowledge, sets out which category of maritime claim the claim falls into and confirms that no security or undertaking has been furnished with regard to the claim. These documents are then issued by the registrar of the court, without requiring appearance before a judge, and the sheriff is then furnished with the summons and warrant of arrest for service on the master of the vessel, the vessel itself and the port captain, whereafter the vessel is under arrest and can only be released from arrest by the sheriff.

Secondly, if one proceeds by way of an action *in personam* and one wishes to make an attachment of the vessel to found or confirm the court's jurisdiction, then a substantive application to court is necessary and the matter must be presented before a judge. Application proceedings are brought through notice of motion with supporting affidavits and one must, *inter alia*, satisfy the court that the vessel is owned by the defendant. It should be noted that this application may be opposed by the shipowner, in which case it may take some time to be finalised. An attachment of this kind involves far more paperwork and is more time-consuming that an *in rem* arrest.

Thirdly, if the arrest is a security arrest, which is dealt with more fully under question (4) below, a substantive application must once again be made to the court by notice of motion and supporting affidavits. Such application may be brought urgently but may well be opposed by the shipowner. Once again, the matter must be argued before a judge of the Supreme Court during court hours or, before a duty judge, if the matter is brought urgently after hours.

In all three cases above, the papers are prepared in English and in the latter two cases, the matters will be argued before a judge in English. If an affidavit is written in a language other than English, then a sworn translation must accompany the affidavit, duly authenticated in terms of the laws of the country where the affidavit is deposed to.

It is necessary for the local solicitor to be furnished with the necessary documenation evidencing the cause of action giving rise to the claim so that he can arrest/attach the vessel. Copies of relevant invoices, charterparties, bills of lading and the like must be forwarded to the local solicitor and faxed copies of these documents are generally sufficient, provided they are legible, and it is not necessary to authenticate the documents. A further important point to note is that in matters of urgency, the local solicitor is entitled to depose to an affidavit on behalf of the claimant on instructions from the foreign solicitor/client. Generally, however, the courts will require an affidavit from the claimant or foreign solicitor if the matter is not urgent.

(b) Which documents must be notarised or otherwise authenticated?

In the case of an *in rem* arrest, it is not necessary for the documents to be notarised and it is simply a matter of the solicitor signing the summons, warrant of arrest and certificate whereafter the registrar will issue the arrest papers.

In the case of a substantive application to court either for an attachment to found or confirm jurisdiction in an action *in personam*, or for a security arrest, the affidavits must be signed before a commissioner of oaths. If the affidavit is deposed to by a person in a foreign country, then the document must be fully authenticated in terms of the laws of that country, before it is admissible in evidence in a South African court. Furthermore, as noted above, if the affidavit is in a language other than English, then a duly authenticated sworn translation of it must be placed before the court.

(4) Is it possible to arrest a ship solely in order to obtain security for a claim which will ultimately be determined in another jurisdiction?

A very important provision of the Act is that which provides for the arrest of a vessel in South Africa to obtain security for any foreign arbitration or court proceedings which are contemplated, pending or proceeding in a foreign jurisdiction. In order to obtain such security, it is necessary that the claimant has an action *in rem* against the ship in question or an associated ship, or an action *in personam* against the owner of the ship. Furthermore, and in terms of decided case law, the claimant must establish at a *prima facie* level that he has a cause of action enforceable in the nominated foreign forum and that he has a genuine and reasonable need for security in respect of the claim.

As discussed above, the procedure by which one makes a security arrest is through a substantive application to court, which necessitates the presentation of the matter before a judge. It was initially expected that this provision coupled with the provision relating to the arrest of associated ships, which is more fully dealt with later, would meet some resistance from members of the bench, particularly in light of an earlier statement by a Supreme Court judge to the effect that South African courts should not allow themselves to be "transformed into some sort of judicial Liberia or Panama" or to be "turned into a court of convenience for the wandering litigants of the world". However, the learned judge's fears have fortunately not materialised and provided one can establish the above requirements, the courts will grant an order for the arrest of a vessel as security for a claim in a foreign forum.

(5) What kind of security is normally acceptable to enable the ship to be released from arrest?

Acceptable security to enable a ship to be released from arrest takes the form of either a letter of undertaking, which is usually provided by a P & I Club or by local solicitors representing the P & I Club or shipowner's interests, or a suitable bank guarantee. It is the usual practice of local solicitors representing cargo interests to come to an agreement with either the P & I Club or solicitors representing them or shipowner's interests, as to the wording acceptable in the letter of undertaking. Should the parties be unable to reach agreement about an acceptable form of wording in the letter of undertaking, then only a suitable bank guarantee will ensure the vessel's release from arrest.

In the case of an *in rem* arrest the security which is obtained by the claimant is limited to the value of the arrest which is arrested, whereas in the case of an attachment to found or confirm jurisdiction in an action *in personam* the claimant is entitled to security for the full value of the claim.

(6) In what circumstances can a claimant be made to give security and what security is acceptable?

There is a provision in the Act relating to counter-security in terms of which a defendant is entitled to require the plaintiff to provide security for a counterclaim which the defendant intends instituting against the plaintiff, based on the wrongful arrest of the ship, or otherwise. In practice, however, this provision is seldom used and it is generally not common for a plaintiff to be called upon to provide counter-security.

In the event that a claimant is ordered to furnish counter-security, it would take the form of either a letter of undertaking, subject to agreement between the parties, or a bank guarantee.

A further important point to note is that in terms of the Supreme Court rules, a *peregrinus* (foreign) plaintiff can be required by the defendant to furnish security for the defendant's costs in the matter.

(7) In the event that the arrest was ultimately shown to have been wrongful, can a claim be made for wrongful arrest and what must be established in order to successfully maintain such a claim?

In terms of the Act, any claimant "who makes an excessive claim or requires excessive security or without reasonable and probable cause obtains the arrest of property or an order of court, shall be liable to any person suffering loss or damage as a result thereof for that loss or damage".

It is therefore clear that in order to establish that an arrest was wrongful, the defendant would have to show that either the plaintiff's claim or the security required by the plaintiff was excessive or that the arrest was made in circumstances without reasonable and probable cause. Examples of circumstances in which an arrest would be regarded as wrongful would be where the plaintiff refuses security which is clearly adequate, or where the plaintiff fails to make reasonable enquiries with regard to a claim and thereafter arrests the wrong vessel. In practice, however, there has been very little litigation on this issue but the right to proceed against a claimant who has wrongfully arrested a vessel does exist.

(8) What are the court fees which must be paid in order to make an arrest? Are they recoverable in the event of a successful claim?

Whether one proceeds by way of an *in rem* arrest, security arrest or an attachment to found or confirm jurisdiction in an action *in personam*, the court fees remain the same in that one is required to put revenue stamps on either the summons or the notice of motion, as the case may be, in the sum of US$20. Should the claimant be successful in his claim, then these costs are recoverable from the defendant.

The Sheriff, who is an officer of the court, is required to serve both the arrest and release papers on the vessel. Although it is difficult to quantify the Sheriff's fees because they may vary, depending upon the urgency of the matter, it can generally be said that the Sheriff's fees for the arrest and release of a vessel will be about US$350.

(9) How are the lawyers' fees calculated? If possible, please estimate the costs of a typical arrest

As in England, the South African legal profession is split with solicitors practising at the side-bar and barristers practising at the bar. Legal fees for both professions are calculated on the basis of the time taken to complete a particular piece of work charged at an hourly rate. The legal fees of both professions are unaffected by the success of the claim, in that contingency fees are regarded as unethical in South Africa, although a portion of the fees (between fifty per cent and sixty per cent) may be recoverable from the defendant if a costs order is granted in favour of the claimant.

The amount that a potential claimant is likely to incur with regard to legal fees will obviously vary depending upon the type of arrest/attachment. In the case of an *in rem* arrest, it is a case of the solicitor preparing the papers and issuing them to the Sheriff who will effect service of the papers on the vessel. In such circumstances, the solicitor's fees for arresting the vessel will range from approximately US$750 to US$1,200.

In the case of a security arrest or an attachment of the vessel to found or confirm jurisdiction, the fees will be higher because the matter must be presented before a judge. Although solicitors now have right of appearance in the Supreme Court the degree of complexity of maritime matters generally demands that a suitably qualified barrister appear on behalf of the claimant and this incurs both solicitor's fees and counsel's fees. Furthermore, it may be necessary for the solicitor to depose to the affidavit in support of the applicant's claim and this is generally a far more time-consuming exercise than simply preparing arrest papers *in rem*. A further consideration is that such applicants may well be opposed by the shipowners, which will necessitate the preparing of further affidavits, heads of argument and counsel appearing in court to present the applicant's case.

It is understandably, therefore, very difficult to estimate the legal fees that would be incurred in a security arrest or an attachment to found or confirm jurisdiction in an action *in personam*. Generally speaking, the hourly charge out rate of a solicitor who is a partner will vary between US$200 and US$250 and that of an assistant between US$125 and US$160. If the matter is opposed, then the legal fees will vary depending upon the length of time taken, charged at the above rates.

The costs of an attachment/arrest where the application is heard unopposed will range from approximately US$2,000 to US$3,000.

(10) Are all or any part of the lawyers' fees recoverable in the event of a successful arrest?

The extent to which an arrest may be regarded as successful or not depends on a number of factors. Perhaps the most important factor is the extent to which the arresting party is able to obtain sufficient and proper security for its claim against the defendant. Once the vessel has been arrested by the claimant, it is usual for the defendant to either settle the claim, in which instance legal costs would form part of the settlement between the parties, or to furnish suitable security for the claim, which security will cover the full quantum of the claim as well as interest and legal costs. It must be remembered that, in the case of an *in rem* arrest, the amount of security is limited to the value of the property arrested and therefore, in circumstances where the value of the arrested property is less than the claimant's full claim, interest and costs, the claimant will clearly not have sufficient and proper security for its claim. In the case of an *in personam* attachment, however, the claimant is entitled to security for its full claim, interest and costs. In this sense, the arresting party is able to obtain security for its costs in the matter but, failing settlement, it is necessary for the claimant to be successful in its action in court and to obtain an order for costs in its favour, before it is entitled to recover its legal fees from the defendant.

If it so happens that the claimant is unsuccessful in its action, although it was successful in arresting the vessel at the outset of the action, it will not be entitled to recover legal costs from the other side and its security for the quantum, interest and costs of the claim will fall away. In such circumstances it may well be that the claimant is ordered to pay the defendant's costs incurred in the arrest.

A further possibility is that once the ship has been arrested, and no security has been furnished nor an appearance to defend entered on behalf of the defendant, the claimant makes application to court for the sale of the vessel. Assuming that the court orders the sale of the vessel and it is thereafter sold in accordance with the court order, and a fund established from the proceeds of the sale, then the claimant is entitled to recover its legal costs in arresting the vessel and making application for the sale thereof, from the fund.

In summary, therefore, the extent to which legal fees are recoverable by the claimant really depends upon the claimant's success in the action or application proceedings after the vessel has been arrested and is not determined by the arrest itself, although the arrest/attachment may be a necessary step in the proceedings and is certainly necessary for the claimant to obtain security for its proceedings. A further point to note is that the court may grant an order for costs on a party and party basis, which amount will fall short of the solicitor/own client fee charged by the solicitor. Although it is difficult to provide an exact percentage, it can generally be stated that approximately fifty per cent to sixty per cent of the legal fees are recoverable in such instance.

(11) How quickly can a ship be arrested after the local lawyer is fully instructed?

The speed of an arrest in South Africa of necessity depends upon the nature of the arrest itself. In the case of an *in rem* arrest, the papers can be prepared within approximately 30 minutes, issued within a further 20 minutes and then handed to the Sheriff within a further 30 minutes for service. Assuming that the Sheriff is instructed to arrest the vessel as a matter of urgency, this can generally be done in the space of about 30 minutes after the Sheriff has been furnished with the papers, depending largely on the vessel's position in the port. A problem which may be encountered by an arresting claimant is the availability of the Sheriff at the time of the arrest although there is always a Duty Sheriff to attend to after hours arrests.

The Sheriff's course of action in arresting a vessel is first to proceed to the port captain to serve the warrant of arrest on him, which ensures that the vessel cannot thereafter leave the port. The Sheriff then proceeds to the vessel itself and serves the summons and warrant of arrest on the master or mate of the vessel as well as on a conspicuous part of the vessel itself.

If all parties carry out their functions as a matter of urgency, then, at best, an *in rem* arrest can be effected within one and a half hours of the local solicitor being fully instructed. In this regard, it is important to note that the registrar's office hours are from 9.00 a.m. to 1.00 p.m. and from 2.00 p.m. to 3.00 p.m. during the day. One cannot arrest a vessel without the registrar issuing the papers, and if the instruction falls outside the registrar's office hours, then it is incumbent upon the local solicitor to locate the duty registrar to issue the papers. This often proves to be a very time-consuming exercise and furthermore, although the Sheriff's office remains open in the afternoon until 4.00 p.m., the local solicitor would also have to locate a Duty Sheriff to effect service of the papers after hours. It is therefore important for international claimants to bear in mind that it may well take longer than one and a half hours to arrest a vessel in South Africa where such arrest must be effected after hours.

In the case of a security arrest or an attachment to found or confirm jurisdiction in an action *in personam*, it takes far longer to effect an arrest due to the type of papers which must be prepared by the local solicitor and because one must appear before a judge to obtain an order for such an arrest. The nature of the proceedings makes it very difficult to estimate a time within which such an arrest can be effected but, generally speaking, provided the papers are prepared expeditiously and make out a case for the relief sought and further that there is no opposition to the application, such an arrest may be effected in approximately four to five hours. It is important to note that this is a best case scenario and if such an arrest were to take place after hours, then it would necessitate an appearance before the judge on duty, which would delay the arrest proceedings. Once the judge has granted an order for the arrest of the vessel, then it is still necessary for the Sheriff to serve the order on the port captain, the master or mate and the vessel itself and this would also take a further 30 minutes as indicated. All in all, therefore, an arrest of this nature could at best be carried out in approximately four to five hours.

The aforesaid times will run from the time the solicitor is provided with all the documentation and information necessary to effect the arrest/attachment.

(12) Is there a minimum amount in dispute for which a ship may be arrested?

In the South African court structure, different monetary amounts give rise to proceedings in different courts. In the case of maritime matters, however, the Supreme Court has exclusive jurisdiction to hear the matter, provided one has a maritime claim, and one is not entitled to enforce a maritime claim in the lower courts. In the circumstances, it is the nature of the claim itself rather than the amount in dispute which determines whether a ship may be arrested. Provided the claimant has a maritime claim, he is entitled to arrest a ship irrespective of the monetary amount of the claim and the claimant is entitled to enforce the claim in the Supreme Court.

(13) Is it possible to arrest a sister ship or a ship in "associated ownership"?

A unique feature of South African admiralty law is that the Act makes provision for the arrest of an associated ship instead of the ship against which the claim lies. The Act, which was amended in 1992, essentially provides for two types of associated ship arrests.

Firstly, one is entitled to arrest what can be termed a conventional sister ship, i.e. a ship which is owned by the same person or company which owns the ship against which the claim arises. The relevant time when the association between the vessels must exist is at the time when the action is commenced by the claimant and not, as it appeared to be under the original definition, at the time when the maritime claim arose. Therefore, if two ships are owned by the same person or company at the time the claimant commences his action and ship A is the ship against which the claim arises whilst ship B is her sister ship, then the claimant may arrest ship B when she calls at a South African port to enforce the claim.

The second type of associated ship is a ship which is owned by a company which is controlled by the same person(s). The initial position was that it was the ownership/control of the shares in the company which determined the extent to which it controlled the vessels, but after the 1992 amendment and recent case law on the point the element of control is no longer simply determined by the control or ownership of shares in a company. In essence, it is the control of the company, rather than the control of shares in a company, which determines the association of the vessels. Therefore, if two ships are controlled by the same company or by different companies which are controlled by one holding company or by the same shareholders/managers/directors, then, provided this element of control is evident at the time of instituting action, one may arrest ship B in South Africa as an associated ship of ship A being the vessel against which the claim arose.

It is important to note that the onus of proving association rests on the claimant and it is the claimant who must therefore satisfy the court, on a balance of probabilities, that the necessary ownership or control was present at the time of instituting action which would bring the two ships within the definition of association as provided for in the Act.

A further interesting provision is that where a vessel is chartered or sub-chartered and the charterer or sub-charterer and not the owner of the vessel is alleged to be liable in respect of a maritime claim, then the charterer or sub-charterer is, for the purposes of the provisions relating to association, deemed to be the owner of the vessel. Therefore, if a vessel is chartered to a company and a claim arises against that company, then a vessel owned by that company may be arrested in a South African port as an associated ship.

(14) What is the order of priorities in the event of the distribution by the court of the proceeds of the sale of a ship?

The ranking of claimants against a fund which is estimated subsequent to a vessel being judicially sold, is determined in accordance with section 11 of the Act and the court does not have the power to vary the ranking specified therein. The ranking of claimants is as follows:

(a) a claim in respect of costs incurred to preserve the property or to procure its sale;
(b) a claim to a preference based on possession of property;
(c) a claim which arose not earlier than one year before the commencement of proceedings to enforce it or before the submission of proof thereof and which is a claim;
  (i) relating to the employment of any master, officer or seaman of a ship;
  (ii) in respect of port, canal, other waterways and pilotage dues;
  (iii) in respect of loss of life or personal injury;
  (iv) in respect of loss of or damage to property;
  (v) in respect of the repair of a ship or the supply of goods or the rendering of services to a ship;
  (vi) in respect of the salvage of a ship, wreck removal and any contribution in respect of general average;
  (vii) in respect of premiums owing under any policy of marine insurance with regard to a ship;
  (viii) in respect of contributions with regard to the protection and indemnity of members;
(d) a claim in respect of any mortgage, hypothecation or right of retention and any other charge on a ship;
(e) a claim in respect of any maritime lien not specifically mentioned above;
(f) any other maritime claim.

(15) Are the claims in respect of which a ship may be arrested subject to a time bar (or prescription) and, if so, are these different according to the nature of the claim?

Claims in terms of which a ship may be arrested are subject to prescription periods and these periods vary depending upon the nature of the claim. Firstly, any claim in respect of a bill of lading is subject to a one-year prescription period in terms of the Hague/Hague-Visby Rules.

Secondly, with regard to claims arising out of a charterparty, the prescription period is determined in accordance with the proper law of the contract. It may well be that the applicable law is agreed upon in the terms of the contract, in which case the prescription period is determined in accordance with that law. If, however, the parties do not provide for the applicable law, then the law where the cause of action arises will generally prevail. In this regard, should the cause of action arise within the jurisdiction of South African law, then a prescription period of three years applies.

Thirdly, with regard to a tort (delict) the prescription period is determined in accordance with the law applicable where the cause of action arises.

Should the cause of action arise within the jurisdiction of the South African court, then the applicable prescription period is three years.

It is also important to note that, in terms of the Act, where one has issued *in rem* papers or where security has been furnished to prevent an arrest or attachment, then service of process must be effected within 12 months, failing which the proceedings or the security shall lapse and be of no force and effect.

(16) Is it possible to apply for the arrest of a ship outside the normal working hours of the court?

As discussed above, it is possible to arrest a ship outside the normal working hours of the court. As we have noted, the registrar's office is open from 9.00 a.m. to 1.00 p.m. and 2.00 p.m. to 3.00 p.m. whilst the Sheriff's office is open for a further hour until 4.00 p.m.

It is possible to arrest/attach a ship at any time as there is always a Duty Registrar, Duty Sheriff and duty judge available for after hours court work. In the case of an *in rem* arrest, the local solicitor prepares the papers and travels to the Duty Registrar's house for issue of the papers. Thereafter, the local solicitor arranges to meet the Duty Sheriff and furnishes him with the necessary papers for service. The Sheriff then attends to the arrest of the vessel and contacts his instructing solicitors to confirm its arrest.

In the case of a security arrest or an attachment to found or confirm jurisdiction in an action *in personam*, it is necessary to present the matter before a duty judge. This can be arranged by contacting the judge's secretary, or the judge directly, depending upon the hour of the arrest, and arrangements are made for the judge to consider the matter. Once the judge has granted an order, then the local solicitor contacts the Sheriff to make arrangements for service of the order on the vessel as aforesaid.

(17) Please provide any other information which you believe is relevant to deciding whether or not to arrest a ship in your jurisdiction

There are a number of factors which, we believe, make South Africa a favourable jurisdiction within which to arrest vessels.

Firstly, one is able to arrest a vessel as security for proceedings in a foreign forum. Secondly, one is able to arrest an associated vessel in South Africa and the Act makes it possible to pierce the corporate veil by highlighting the issue of control, as opposed to ownership, as the relevant factor in determining the association of different vessels.

Further important points are the speed at which an arrest can be effected in South Africa and that it is not necessary for the claimant to furnish the court with a deposit prior to arresting a vessel. Furthermore, it is not necessary for the local solicitor to be furnished with a power of attorney and the arresting party is not liable for the port costs of the vessel whilst she is under arrest.

Another advantage of the South African maritime jurisdiction is that one is entitled to proceed with an application for the judicial sale of a ship without the necessity of taking default judgment against the shipowners. As mentioned above, once a ship has been arrested and no appearance to defend has been filed on the part of the defendant, any arresting creditor is thereafter entitled to make application to court for the judicial sale of the vessel. Assuming that the application for the sale of the vessel is unopposed, it normally takes approximately six weeks from the date of the application to the date of the sale of the vessel. Once the vessel is sold, a fund is duly constituted under the control of the registrar of the Supreme Court and creditors must then lodge their respective claims with the referee appointed to consider and report to the court on the various claims. Once the referee has submitted his report to the court, it is open for any claimant to make application to court for payment out of the fund in terms of the referee's recommendations. Thereafter, the relevant bank will effect payment of the creditor's claim, interest and costs in accordance with the court order and in terms of the registrar's authorisation. In this way, the Act has provided claimants with an effective means of enforcing their claims against the vessel and, generally speaking, they are able to obtain payment of their claims within three to four months of bringing the application for the sale of the vessel.

Finally, South Africa's coastline is strategically positioned and many vessels, including liner services, pass through the territorial waters of South Africa every year. Local solicitors monitor vessel movements and keep a close watch for any vessels which they may be required to arrest on the basis of either direct or associated claims.

South African maritime law has its basis in English law but has developed its own unique features since the Admiralty Jurisdiction Regulation Act was passed in 1983 and subsequently amended, which has added a distinct flavour to our maritime law and has finely balanced the jurisdictional requirements of South African law with the need to handle maritime matters as expeditiously and effectively as possible.

CHAPTER 32

SPAIN

(1) What are the types of claim for which a ship may be arrested in Spain?

Spanish law on ship arrest applicable to international relationships is constituted by the International Convention for the Unification of Certain Rules Relating to the Arrest of Sea-Going Ships, Brussels, 10 May 1952 and by the 1967 Act which implements the application of the Convention in Spain. Therefore, the claims which grant the right of arrest are those included in the categories of Article 1 of the Convention, namely:

(a) damage caused by any ship either in collision or otherwise;
(b) loss of life or personal injury caused by any ship or occurring in connection with the operation of any ship;
(c) salvage;
(d) agreement relating to the use of any ship whether by charterparty or otherwise;
(e) agreement relating to the carriage of goods in any ship whether by charterparty or otherwise;
(f) loss of or damage to goods including baggage carried in any ship;
(g) general average;
(h) bottomry;
(i) towage;
(j) pilotage;
(k) goods or materials wherever supplied to a ship for her operation or maintenance;
(l) construction, repair or equipment of any ship or dock charges and dues;
(m) wages of masters, officers or crew;
(n) master's disbursements, including disbursements made by shippers, charterers or agents on behalf of a ship or her owner;
(o) disputes as to the title to or ownership of any ship;
(p) disputes between co-owners of any ship as to the ownership, possession, employment or earnings of that ship;
(q) the mortgage or hypothecation of any ship.

(2) Is there a distinction between claims which give rise to a maritime lien and other types of claim?

Spanish law on maritime liens is constituted by two different systems:

(a) Domestic system: relevant provisions of the Spanish Commercial Code (Arts. 580–584) and the 1893 Ship Mortgage Act (Arts. 31 *et seq.*).
(b) Uniform system: the 1926 Brussels Convention on mortgages and maritime liens.

However, it can be said that the uniform system of the 1926 Convention has somehow displaced the domestic system to such an extent that the domestic system is only applied to marginal cases where the vessel involved does not belong to a contracting state. This question is, however, not free from discussion and some Spanish authors consider that the Convention has repealed the system of the Commercial Code and of the 1893 Ship Mortgage Act.

Having said that, if we focus on the provisions of the 1926 Convention, it can be observed that not all those "maritime claims" provided by Article 1 of the 1952 Convention give rise to a "maritime lien" under Articles 2 and 3 of the 1926 Convention.

Nevertheless, from a practical point of view, when it comes to arresting a ship, it is sufficient to allege a "maritime claim" and the arrest of the offending ship will be allowed by the court, even if (a) she is not owned by the debtor and (b) the alleged maritime claim does not give rise to a "maritime lien". Obviously, the arrest will be granted without prejudice to the remedies available to owners to release her from arrest. Thus, a shipowner not liable for a claim in respect of which his vessel has been arrested by a third party would be able to institute the so-called "ownership proceedings" in order to release her from the arrest.

(3) (a) What pleadings, affidavits and documents must be presented to the court when applying for an arrest, and in what language?
(b) Which documents must be notarised or otherwise authenticated?

A *writ* (arrest application) drafted according to the circumstances of each case must be filed by a "Procurator" (representative of each party before the court) together with a *Power of Attorney* (hereinafter referred to as "POA"). The POA has to be issued by the legal representative of the claimants before a notary public according to the law of the country where it is issued. The POA also needs to be legalised by means of an apostille as required by the 1961 Hague Convention concerning suppression of the legalisation requirement for foreign documents. If the country where the claimants are domiciled has not ratified the Convention, the notary's signature will have to be legalised by the Spanish Consulate in the country of issue. If the POA is issued in Spain the above legalisation formalities will not be necessary.

Furthermore, the claimants will have to provide a *counter-security* to cover any eventual damages that might be caused to the owners as a consequence of the arrest. There is no fixed quantum of the counter-security as this is always decided by the judge discretionally.

(4) Is it possible to arrest a ship solely in order to obtain security for a claim which will ultimately be determined in another jurisdiction?

Yes. Naturally, the claimants will have to commence proceedings on the merits within the period fixed in the Spanish Procedural Law (20 days) or by the arresting court under Art. 7(2) and 7(3) of the 1952 Convention in case the arresting court has no jurisdiction to hear the claim upon its merits.

(5) What kind of security is normally acceptable to enable the ship to be released from arrest?

In the event that there is no agreement between the parties about the nature and amount of the security, the Spanish courts normally request a bank guarantee; a deposit in cash would of course be acceptable too. In exceptional circumstances, some judges are happy to admit a bond issued by a first class insurance company.

(6) In what circumstances can a claimant be made to give security and what security is acceptable?

Pursuant to Art. 1.2 of the Spanish 1967 Act any claimant must provide counter-security to arrest a ship. The amount of this counter-security is discretionally fixed by the court in each case. As for the security to lift the arrest, this must be provided through a bank guarantee. A cash deposit would also be admitted.

(7) In the event that the arrest was ultimately shown to have been wrongful, can a claim be made for wrongful arrest and what must be established in order to successfully maintain such a claim?

Under Article 6 of the 1952 Brussels Convention, Spanish domestic law is the law applicable to disputes relating to arrestors' liability. It provides that the arrestors are obliged to indemnify damages and costs when:

(i) the proceedings on merits have not been instituted within the period granted by the court in the arrest order (ex Art. 1411 SPL);
(ii) an opposition to the arrest is accepted by the court (ex Art. 1416 SPL). Under Arts. 2 and 3 of the 1967 Act, the causes of opposition are:

— that the maritime claim alleged is not included in those enumerated by Article 1 of the Convention;
— that the cause of the "maritime claim" has not been alleged;
— that no counter-security has been provided; and
— that the limits of Article 3 of the Convention with respect to the vessel arrested have not been taken into account;

(iii) when the claim brought by the arresting party in the proceedings on merits is dismissed by the court with jurisdiction on the merits.

Any claim for damages and costs should be submitted to the arresting court and the extent of such damages and costs must be duly proved. The judgment on damages will be enforced against the counter-security provided to obtain the arrest.

(8) What are the court fees which must be paid in order to make an arrest? Are they recoverable in the event of a successful claim?

No court fees are charged; but the arresting party has to bear the lawyers' and procurators' fees (legal costs). Lawyers' and procurators' fees relating to the arrest would be recoverable as far as the judgment delivered in the proceedings on merits would award such costs. Where an opposition to the arrest is submitted, the losing party will have to bear the lawyers' and procurators' fees of the opponents calculated according to the Rules of the respective Bar Associations of the place where the arrest is made.

(9) How are the lawyers' fees calculated? If possible please estimate the costs of a typical arrest.

The respective Bar Associations provide the rules to calculate the lawyers' fees, which are based on a scale over the amount involved. The costs of a typical arrest cannot be calculated in general. Nevertheless, by way of example, an arrest in Barcelona involving a "maritime claim" amounting to Ptas 10,000,000, including interest and costs, without any further step—like opposition—would be about Ptas 600,000. In addition, the procurators' fees would be around Ptas 125,000.

Lawyers' fees can be also fixed on a time basis by mutual agreement with clients. However, in any claim in court to recover fees as provided in (8) above, the rates of recovery will be calculated under the Rules of the Bar Association of the place of the arrest, which figures would be considered a maximum limit.

(10) Are all or any part of the lawyers' fees recoverable in the event of a successful arrest?

Yes, they may be recoverable in certain circumstances; please see the answer to question (8).

(11) How quickly can a ship be arrested after the local lawyer is fully instructed?

The time needed to arrest a vessel does not necessarily depend on the steps to be taken in court, since they can act very quickly when reasons of urgency are alleged; however, the most important aspects are (i) the time to prepare the POA and (ii) the provision of the counter-security, which ultimately depends on how quickly claimants' banks work. Shipping lawyers can act very quickly in all aspects and it can be said that the arrest may be obtained in a short period of time if there is no delay in providing the POA and the counter-security.

(12) Is there a minimum amount in dispute for which a ship may be arrested?

No, a vessel may be arrested by any "maritime claim" irrespective of its amount. Only there is a limitation applicable to claims not exceeding 8,000 Ptas; in such cases, the arrest cannot be applied separately from the proceedings on merits (Art. 1397 SPL), which in practice means that the arrest will only be possible in cases when the Spanish courts have jurisdiction to award on merits.

(13) Is it possible to arrest a sister ship or a ship in "associated ownership"?

The arrest of a "sister ship" is feasible within the limitation set out in Article 3 of the 1952 Convention. Thus, a claimant may arrest in Spain either the particular ship in respect of which the maritime claim arose, or any other ship which is owned by the person who was, at the time when the maritime claim arose, the owner of the particular ship.

However, no ship, other than the particular ship in respect of which the claim arose, may be arrested in respect of maritime claims arising out of disputes as to title to or ownership of any ship (Article 1(o)), disputes between co-owners of any ship as to the ownership, possession, employment or earnings of that ship (Article 1(p)) or the mortgage or hypothecation of any ship (Article 1(q)).

In principle, the arrest of a ship in "associated ownership" will be possible when she is the offending ship and when the ownership of the shares correspond to the same shareholders of the companies in associated ownership (Article 3(2) of the 1952 Convention).

(14) What is the order of priorities in the event of the distribution by the court of the proceeds of sale of the ship?

Two different situations must be considered, which are as follows.

(i) The arrested ship is flagged in a contracting state to the 1926 Convention

If this is the case, the order of priorities shall be that provided by Articles 2 and 3 of the Convention as follows:

(a) Law costs due to the state and expenses in the common interest of the creditors in order to preserve the vessel or to procure its sale and the distributiuon of the proceeds of sale; tonnage dues, light or harbour dues and other public taxes and charges of the same character; pilotage dues, the cost of watching and preservation from the time of the entry of the vessel into the last port.
(b) Claims arising out of the contract of engagement of the master, crew and other persons hired on board.
(c) Remuneration for assistance and salvage and the contribution of the vessel in general average.
(d) Indemnities for collision or other accident of navigation as also for damage caused to works forming part of harbours, docks and navigable ways; indemnities for personal injury to passengers or crew; indemnities for loss of or damage to cargo or baggage.
(e) Claims resulting from contracts entered into or acts done by the Master, acting within the scope of his authority, away from the vessel's home port, where such contracts or acts are necessary for the preservation of the vessel or the continuation of its voyage, whether the Master is or is not at the same time owner of the vessel, and whether the claim is his own or that of shipchandlers, repairers, lenders or other contractual creditors.

The mortgages, hypothecations and other charges on vessels referred to in Article 1 rank immediately after the secured claims referred to above.

(ii) The arrested ship is not flagged in a contracting state

This case is more complex. The Spanish conflict of law rules (Art. 10.2 of the Civil Code) refer to the national law of the flag of the vessel. In this regard, the application of the national law is subject to two requirements: (a) that one of the parties invokes such law and (b) that same is proved. In our opinion, if these two requirements are not met, the Spanish domestic system would be applied since Article 14 of the 1926 Convention excludes the application of its provisions to ships not belonging to contracting states. As we mentioned in the answer to question (2) above, this issue is not free from discussion as some maritime authors are of the opinion that the 1926 Convention has repealed the Spanish domestic system. The reason they think this is that in the case of a claim against a vessel belonging to a non-contracting state where the national law is not invoked and proved, the provisions of the Convention would apply.

That being said, our view is that two different situations should be distinguished:

(a) Application of the national law of the flag of the vessel if invoked and proved.

(b) Application of the Spanish domestic system (if the national law of the vessel is not invoked and proved). In turn, two situations must be considered in this case:

(1) If the vessel is not subject to a mortgage, the order of priorities stated by Art. 580 of the Spanish Commercial Code shall apply as follows:

1. amounts due to the Treasury justified by an Official Certificate issued by the competent Authority;
2. costs of legal proceedings approved by the judge or Tribunal;
3. pilotage, tonnage and port dues justified by Certificates issued by the collection Authorities;
4. salaries of the bailees and keepers of the ship as well as any other expense incurred in her preservation from her entry into the port until her sale, always provided they are justified and approved by the judge or Tribunal;
5. the rent of the warehouse where the ship's tackle has been kept as per contract;
6. salaries due to the master and the crew in the last voyage;
7. reimbursement of the cargo proceeds when being sold by the master to repair the ship, provided that the sale has been ordered by a court order and it has complied with the required formalities and recorded in the ship's registration certificate;
8. any part of the price of the ship not paid to the last seller, amounts due to the ship builders, when the ship has not sailed, and those due in respect of repairs and supplies of fuel and food in her last voyage;
9. the bottomry loan and the insurance premiums;
10. indemnities for loss of or damage to the cargo for which the ship is liable, always provided that same be so stated by a court judgment or an arbitration award.

(2) If the vessel is subject to a mortgage, the preceding order changes substantially so that the following credits will rank over the mortgage (Arts. 31 *et seq.* of the 1893 Ship Mortgage Act):

1. public taxes and charges due to the state, the Province or the Local Authorities for the ship's last voyage or during the previous year;
2. the pilotage, tonnage and port dues and the salaries of the master and the crew during her last voyage;
3. insurance premiums over the last two years;
4. the credits referred to in points 7 and 10 of Art. 580 of the Commercial Code (above).

The preceding credits will have preference even though they are not recorded in the Commercial Register.

Besides, the following credits will rank over the ship mortgage provided that certain complex formalities are met:

1. bottomry in the last voyage;
2. contribution of the vessel in general average in her last voyage;
3. loan credits assumed by the master in the last voyage;
4. litigious rights or credits recorded in the Register by court order before the registration of the mortgage.

(15) Are the claims in respect of which a ship may be arrested subject to a time bar (or prescription) and if so are these different according to the nature of the claim?

Under Spanish law some claims in respect of which a vessel may be arrested (Article 1 of the 1952 Convention) may be subject to a different time bar depending on the nature of the claim as follows:

(i) Claims subject to a six-month time bar

(a) Freight and inherent expenses (Art. 951 of the Commercial Code).
(b) General average contribution (Art. 951 of the Commercial Code).

(ii) Claims subject to a one-year time bar

(a) Cargo claims (Art. 952 of the Commercial Code and Art. 3.6 of the Hague and Hague-Visby Rules).
(b) Damage caused to a fixed or floating object (Art. 1968.2 of the Civil Code).
(c) Pilotage (Art. 952.3 of the Commercial Code).
(d) Supplies to a ship (Art. 952.1 of the Commercial Code).
(e) Shipbuilders and repairers' claims (Art. 952.1 of the Commercial Code).

(iii) Claims subject to a two-year time bar

(a) Collisions between vessels (Art. 953 of the Commercial Code). The two-year period will be counted from the date of the accident.
(b) Assistance and salvage (Art. 11 of the 1962 Salvage Act). The two-year period will run from the termination of the assistance of salvage.
(c) Towage (Arts. 18 and 11 of the 1962 Salvage Act). The period will be counted as for the salvage claims.

(iv) Claims subject to a three-year time bar

(a) Bottomry (Art. 954 of the Commercial Code).
(b) Claims for salaries due to master and crew (Art. 100 of the Merchant Marine Labour Act).

(v) Other claims

Any other claims not subject to any of the above time bars will be subject to the general 15-year time bar provided by Art. 1964 of the Civil Code.

(16) Is it possible to apply for the arrest of a ship outside the normal working hours of the court?

It is possible in theory. In fact, it is usual to apply in the writ for the court to deal with the arrest outside the normal working hours.

However, what happens in practice is that the court on duty will be too busy attending to urgent criminal cases and it is unlikely that it will deal with the arrest.

CHAPTER 33

SWEDEN

Introduction

The International Convention for the Unification of Certain Rules Relating to the Arrest of Sea-Going Ships ("the Arrest Convention"), signed at Brussels on 10 May 1952, has been ratified by Sweden and incorporated into the Swedish Maritime Code, which came into force 1 October 1994. The provisions in the Swedish Maritime Code in respect of arrest of vessels are, accordingly, based on the Arrest Convention, and they apply to vessels entered in the Swedish ship register or a corresponding foreign ship register. However, they do not apply to Swedish or non-registered vessels if the applicant has his residence or principal place of business in Sweden ("national claims"). Should the vessel be Swedish or non-registered and the applicant is Swedish, the general rules in the Code of Judicial Procedure will then be applicable. In the event the latter rules contain a different regulation in comparison to the rules of the Maritime Code, such difference will be specifically noted below.

(1) What are the types of claim for which a ship may be arrested in Sweden?

Vessels may be arrested only for maritime claims, and the Maritime Code contains a complete enumeration of claims which are to be regarded as maritime claims. This enumeration corresponds to Article 1 in the Arrest Convention. In respect of national claims vessels may be arrested for any type of pecuniary claim.

The provisions do not apply to arrest for claims concerning taxes and charges levied by the state or a municipality.

(2) Is there a distinction between claims which give rise to a maritime lien and other types of claim?

In order for an arrest to be granted by a court the applicant must prove that there is a risk that the respondent may remove or hide the property or take action which would make the enforcement of a subsequent judgment difficult. However, this is not required when claims give rise to a maritime lien.

In the event that there is a risk that the respondent may remove or hide or otherwise take action in respect of the property, the court may grant an interlocutory arrest immediately without first serving the application on the respondent.

(3) (a) What pleadings, affidavits and documents must be presented to the court when applying for an arrest and in what language?

The application must be made in writing in Swedish and should be in the form of a statement of claim as in an ordinary civil case. It must be personally signed by the applicant or his attorney stating, *inter alia*, the amount claimed.

(b) Which documents must be notarised or otherwise authenticated?

In order to have an application for an arrest granted the applicant must establish the possibility of a valid claim. Accordingly, it is not necessary to produce full proof of the claim. Swedish courts require only particulars of an incident or transaction which give rise to a claim against the owner of the vessel. At this stage it is unnecessary for documents to be notarised or otherwise authenticated.

(4) Is it possible to arrest a ship solely in order to obtain security for a claim which will ultimately be determined in another jurisdiction?

A vessel may be arrested for a claim which ultimately will be adjudicated in Sweden or a foreign jurisdiction, provided that the claim does not arise out of a contract referring to a foreign court whose decision cannot be enforced in Sweden.

An arrest of a foreign vessel in Sweden automatically gives the relevant Swedish court competence to try the dispute giving rise to the arrest, unless the dispute arises out of a contract providing for arbitration or for foreign jurisdiction. The applicant must file his statement of claim with the competent court, or initiate arbitration proceedings if the relevant agreement contains an arbitration clause, within one month from the date of the court's decision granting the arrest.

(5) What kind of security is normally acceptable to enable the ship to be released from arrest?

(6) In what circumstances can a claimant be made to give security and what security is acceptable?

In order to have an arrest granted by a Swedish court a security is normally required. The court, in its discretion, will decide on the nature of the guarantee to be provided and also the amount. A bank guarantee or a guarantee of equal security value will normally be required. When determining the required amount the court takes into consideration, *inter alia*, the value of the vessel and the daily cost for the vessel. The security must in general amount to SEK 150,000–400,000.

(7) In the event that the arrest was ultimately shown to have been wrongful, can a claim be made for wrongful arrest and what must be established in order to successfully maintain such a claim?

In order to maintain a claim for wrongful arrest the claimant must establish damage and that the damage in question was caused by the wrongful arrest.

(8) What are the court fees which must be paid in order to make an arrest? Are they recoverable in the event of a successful claim?

The application fee is SEK 450, which will be recoverable in the event that the court's final judgment is in favour of the applicant. The Enforcement District's fee amounting to SEK 1,000 for effecting the court's order for arrest will be invoiced to the respondent if the final judgment is in favour of the applicant.

(9) How are the lawyers' fees calculated? If possible please estimate the costs of a typical arrest.

Swedish lawyers usually invoice their clients for the actual time spent on the arrest. In view of the fact that the parties may file several pleadings with the court before the arrest is granted and that the complexity of arrests varies it is difficult to estimate the costs of an arrest. In less complicated matters the costs, in general, amount to SEK 10,000–20,000.

(10) Are all or any part of the lawyers' fees recoverable in the event of a successful arrest?

In the event that an application for arrest is withdrawn by the applicant because, for example, the respondent has settled the claim in question, the court will not award the applicant any remuneration for lawyers' fees in respect of the arrest. If the application for an arrest is followed by a statement of claim within the stipulated one-month period and the applicant is eventually successful, lawyers' fees will in general be recoverable.

(11) How quickly can a ship be arrested after the local lawyer is fully instructed?

An interlocutory arrest can be granted the same day.

(12) Is there a minimum amount in dispute for which a ship may be arrested?

No.

(13) Is it possible to arrest a sister ship or a ship in "associated ownership"?

An arrest may be imposed on any other vessel belonging to the person who, at the time the maritime claim arose, was the owner of the vessel to which the maritime claim refers.

(14) What is the order of priorities in the event of the distribution by the court of the proceeds of sale of the ship?

In the event an arrested vessel is sold the proceeds from such a sale will be distributed among the creditors as if no arrest had been imposed on the vessel. Accordingly, an arrest does not give a maritime claim any preference.

(15) Are the claims in respect of which a ship may be arrested subject to a time bar (or prescription) and, if so, are these different according to the nature of the claim?

Claims referred to in (1) above are subject to different time bars. For instance, cargo claims are time barred one year from the time that the goods were delivered or should have been delivered and several claims are time barred after two years from the day they arose. It should be noted that in respect of claims giving rise to a maritime lien, which are time barred after one year from the time when the claim arose, such claims will not be time barred in the event that before the expiry date an arrest or distraint of the vessel has been secured, followed by the forced sale of the vessel.

(16) Is it possible to apply for the arrest of a ship outside the normal working hours of the court?

It is almost impossible to achieve an arrest outside office hours.

CHAPTER 34

UNITED ARAB EMIRATES

(1) What are the types of claim for which a ship may be arrested in the United Arab Emirates?

Under Art. 115 of the UAE Maritime Code (Federal Law No. 26 of 1981) a vessel may be arrested in connection with a "maritime debt" as follows:

(a) damage caused by the vessel by reason of a collision or otherwise;
(b) loss of life or personal injuries occasioned by the vessel and arising out of the use thereof;
(c) assistance and salvage;
(d) contracts relating to the use or exploitation of the vessel under a charterparty or otherwise;
(e) contracts relating to the carriage of goods under a charterparty, bill of lading, or other documents;
(f) loss of or damage to goods or chattels being carried on board the vessel;
(g) general average;
(h) towage or pilotage of the vessel;
(i) supplies of products or equipment necessary for the utilisation or maintenance of the vessel, in whichever place the supply is made;
(j) construction, repair or fitting out of the vessel, and costs of it being in dock;
(k) sums expended by the master, shippers, charterers or agents on account of the vessel or on account of the owner thereof;
(l) wages of the master, officers and crew, and other persons working on board the vessel under a contract of maritime employment;
(m) a dispute as to the ownership of the vessel;
(n) a dispute in connection with the co-ownership of the vessel, or with the possession or use thereof, or with the right to the profits arising out of the use thereof;
(o) a maritime mortgage.

(2) Is there a distinction between claims which give rise to a maritime lien and other types of claim?

Yes. First of all, it is not possible to arrest the vessel in connection with a claim unless the claim falls within the definition of a "maritime debt". However, there is a separate category of claim known as "priority rights" which are equivalent to maritime liens and are set out in Art. 84 of the UAE Maritime Code as follows:

(a) Judicial costs incurred in protecting and selling the vessel, and distributing the proceeds thereof, as well as loading, lighthouse and port charges, and other dues and taxes of the same type, pilotage fees, compensation for damage caused to port installations, docks and navigation lanes, the costs of removing obstacles to navigation caused by the vessel, and costs of towing and maintenance of the vessel from the time of its arrival at the last harbour.
(b) Debts arising out of a contract for the employment of the master and crew, and other persons bound by a contract of maritime employment on board the vessel.
(c) Monies due for assistance and salvage, and the share of the vessel in general marine average.
(d) Compensation due for collisions and other navigational accidents, compensation due for bodily injuries to the passengers and crew, and compensation for loss of or damage to goods and possessions.
(e) Debts arising out of contracts made by the master, and operations carried out by him outside the port of registration of the vessel within the scope of his lawful powers for an actual requirement dictated by the maintenance of the vessel or the continuance of its voyage, whether or not the master is also the owner of the vessel, or whether the debt is due to him, or to persons undertaking supply, or lenders, persons who have repaired the vessel, or other contractors.
(f) Breakdowns and damage giving rise to a right of compensation in favour of the charterers of the vessel.
(g) All premiums for insurance effected on the hull, equipment and fittings of the vessel due in respect of the last insured voyage, in cases where the insurance was effected for that voyage, or for the last period of insurance if the insurance was effected for a specified period, but provided that in either case the total does not exceed the premium for one year.

(3) (a) What pleadings, affidavits and documents must be presented to the court when applying for an arrest and in what language?
(b) Which documents must be notarised or otherwise authenticated?

An arrest application must be filed with the UAE court with sufficient supporting documents to show a *prima facie* case. No affidavits are required. The local court advocate will need to file his power of attorney, which must be notarised.

According to Art. 4 of the Civil Procedure Code (Federal Law of No. 11 of 1992) the language of the court is the Arabic language and, as such, all applications are to be made in Arabic.

According to Section 13 of the Federal Evidence Act of 1992, all documents which are issued in a foreign jurisdiction need to be notarised, legalised and consularised by the UAE or GCC country embassy/consulate and authenticated. The UAE courts usually accept copies of such documents unless the defendants request that such notarised copies are obtained and the UAE court accedes to their request.

(4) Is it possible to arrest a ship solely in order to obtain security for a claim which will ultimately be determined in another jurisdiction?

Art. 22 of the Civil Procedure Code (Federal Law No. 11 of 1992), dealing with attachments of assets, appears to allow arrest for security only. There have since been arrests for security only under Art. 22, though not many. As there is no system of binding precedent in the UAE and the concept is still relatively new, it still remains unclear as to when the UAE courts will issue an arrest order for a vessel located in the UAE as security for a claim to be heard in a foreign jurisdiction.

(5) What kind of security is normally acceptable to enable the ship to be released from arrest?

Under the UAE law there is no specific requirement for any form of security to be provided for the vessel to be released. The requirement for security is left to the discretion of the court. However, it is common practice for a local bank guarantee to be provided for the full amount of the claim. P & I Club letters of undertaking are not usually accepted by the UAE courts.

(6) In what circumstances can a claimant be made to give security and what security is acceptable?

As mentioned above, the need to provide security is left to the discretion of the UAE courts. If security is to be provided by the claimant, this may take the form of a letter of undertaking from a local company, or a local bank guarantee to cover damages for wrongful arrest. The amount is within the discretion of the UAE courts but 20 per cent to 25 per cent of the claim amount is usually sufficient.

(7) In the event that the arrest was ultimately shown to have been wrongful, can a claim be made for wrongful arrest and what must be established in order to successfully maintain such a claim?

In a decision of the Dubai Court of Cassation, the court held that, for a claim for wrongful arrest to succeed, "wrongful intent" must be shown according to Art. 106 of the UAE Civil Code. To constitute "wrongful intent":

(i) the arrest must have been intended to cause damage to another person;

(ii) the person who carried out the arrest must have intended to obtain an illegal benefit. The benefit will be illegal if it was in violation of any of the Sharia Islamic principles or contrary to the law, public order or morals;

(iii) the benefit to the applicant from the arrest must have been small and disproportionate to the damage which resulted from the arrest;

(iv) the person who obtained the arrest must have by his conduct exceeded the bounds of usage and custom.

(8) What are the court fees which must be paid in order to make an arrest? Are they recoverable in the event of a successful claim?

The court fees vary in each Emirate. In Dubai the court fees for an arrest are three and three quarters per cent of the value of the claim, subject to a maximum of Dhs 15,000 and for the main court action seven and one half per cent of the value of the claim, subject to a maximum of Dhs 30,000. Court fees are usually recoverable in the event of a successful claim.

(9) How are the lawyers' fees calculated? If possible please estimate the costs of a typical arrest.
(10) Are all or any part of the lawyers' fees recoverable in the event of a successful arrest?

In the UAE the costs involved fall under three categories:

(i) Court fees

Court fees are payable on the commencement of a court action in the UAE and vary from Emirate to Emirate. By way of example, the court fees for commencing an action in Dubai are seven and one half per cent of the first Dhs 200,000 of the claim amount, six per cent of the next Dhs 100,000 and five per cent for any amount over Dhs 300,000 subject to a maximum of Dhs 30,000. In Abu Dhabi the court fees are five per cent of the claim amount for claims above Dhs 5,000 with a maximum court fee payable of Dhs 10,000. Further court fees are payable on appeals to the Court of Appeal (in Dubai one and one half per cent of the first Dhs 200,000 of the claim amount, one and one fifth per cent for the next Dhs 100,000 and one per cent for any amount over Dhs 300,000, subject to a maximum of Dhs 6,000) and Court of Cassation (in Dubai Dhs 1,500) as well as for bringing an action to attach assets (e.g. arrest a vessel) and to execute a final judgment. Court fees are usually recoverable by a successful litigant, though this is subject to the discretion of the court.

(ii) Lawyers' charges

Local court advocates' charges are normally calculated on the basis of a percentage of the value of the claim. There are two systems generally used by local court advocates. One system is a fixed fee which will cover all hearings before the Court of First Instance and all levels of appeal until final judgment or settlement. The other system is a fixed fee for acting before the Court of First Instance with 50 per cent of that fee payable on appeal to the Court of Appeal and 50 per cent of the Court of Appeal fee payable on appeal to the Court of Cassation. No contingency fees are allowed under the recent UAE Advocate's Law. Only a nominal amount of court advocate's fees, usually in the region of Dhs 500 to Dhs 1,500, may be recoverable by a successful litigant. Solicitors' charges are not recoverable.

(iii) Disbursements

As all pleadings are conducted in Arabic, all relevant and necessary documentation must be translated. Approximate translation costs are in the region of Dhs 70 to Dhs 100 per page. Such disbursement costs are not recoverable in court.

(11) How quickly can a ship be arrested after the local lawyer is fully instructed?

Provided all the legal and procedural requirements are complied with, the vessel can be arrested by an immediate order of the court on the day of the application. There can be a further delay, however, in typing the court order and serving it on the Port Police, Port Authority and the vessel.

(12) Is there a minimum amount in dispute for which a ship may be arrested?

There is no statutory *de minimis* provision under UAE law. However, we would expect the UAE courts to have regard to the reasonableness of the claim amount against which an arrest order is requested.

(13) Is it possible to arrest a sister ship or a ship in "associated ownership"?

Yes with regard to sister ships. The UAE courts tend to respect the concept of single ship-owning companies and, even if there was compelling evidence, an "associated ownership" arrest would be difficult.

(14) What is the order of priorities in the event of the distribution by the court of the proceeds of sale of the ship?

See the reply to question (2). Art. 84 sets out the list of priority debts. A mortgage will rank after priority debt (e) as per Art. 105 of the UAE Maritime Code.

(15) Are the claims in respect of which a ship may be arrested subject to a time bar (or prescription) and, if so, are these different according to the nature of the claim?

The UAE Maritime Code sets out a number of limitation periods relating to certain claims and the relevant periods may vary from six months to three years.

(16) Is it possible to apply for the arrest of a ship outside the normal working hours of the court?

No.

(17) Please provide any other information which you believe is relevant in deciding whether or not to arrest a ship in your jurisdiction.

There are limitations in certain circumstances on the right to arrest a state-owned vessel.

CHAPTER 35

UNITED STATES OF AMERICA

(1) What are the types of claim for which a ship may be arrested in the USA?

The arrest of a vessel in the United States of America ("the US") is governed by the Supplemental Rules for Certain Admiralty and Maritime Claims contained in the Federal Rules of Civil Procedure. Rule C of the Rules provides a claimant with an *in rem* action against the vessel to enforce any "maritime lien" such as necessary services furnished to the vessel, maritime torts and breaches of certain maritime contracts. Whether a claimant has a "maritime lien" for the purposes of Rule C is now provided for in the Maritime Lien Act, 46 USC §971 *et seq.* The Maritime Lien Act provides a lien to any person "furnishing repairs, supplies, towage, use of dry dock or marine railway or other necessaries to any vessel . . .". The following are examples of types of claims that have been determined by the courts to be valid maritime liens claims: by seamen for wages; tort claims for collision and personal injury; claims for repairs, supplies, wharfage, stevedoring, towage charges, etc., provided to the vessel; claims for cargo damage; and breach of certain maritime contracts.

(2) Is there a distinction between claims which give rise to a maritime lien and other types of claim?

A distinction has been made by the courts between a claim which gives rise to a maritime lien as defined by the Maritime Lien Act and those claims which, although maritime in nature, do not constitute a "lien". If a claim does not constitute a lien within the definition of the Maritime Lien Act, no arrest can be effectuated pursuant to Rule C. However, a claimant may have a remedy pursuant to Rule B of the Supplemental Rules for Certain Admiralty and Maritime Claims. Rule B allows for the attachment of a vessel provided the claim is maritime in nature, typically asserted as an *in personam* action against an owner of a vessel; that the property is within the jurisdiction of the court; and that the garnishee is not "present in the jurisdiction". Under Rule B there is no *in rem* claim, rather the vessel is being attached as security for an *in personam* claim against the owner.

(3) (a) What pleadings, affidavits and documents must be presented to the court when applying for an arrest and in what language?

In order to effect an arrest of the vessel, the claimant must file a Verified Complaint, an Affidavit setting forth the facts surrounding the claim, as well as a Warrant of Arrest. These documents can be prepared and executed by the claimant's attorney if the client does not maintain offices in the jurisdiction of the arrest. If the attorney is going to execute the Verified Complaint and Affidavit he needs copies of documents sufficient to form a "good faith" belief that the client has a valid claim.

(4) Is it possible to arrest a ship solely in order to obtain security for a claim which will ultimately be determined in another jurisdiction?

Yes.

(5) What kind of security is normally acceptable to enable the ship to be released from arrest?

Although it is customary for a claimant to accept a P & I Club Letter of Undertaking as security to enable a ship to be released from arrest, a claimant may demand that the security be in the form of a bond issued by an "A-rated" domestic insurance company or any other security acceptable to the court.

(6) In what circumstances can a claimant be made to give security and what security is acceptable?

A claimant may be ordered by the court to post counter-security if the defendant files a counter-claim. Counter-security can be in the form of a bond issued by an "A-rated" insurance company, or any other security acceptable to the court.

(7) In the event that the arrest was ultimately shown to have been wrongful, can a claim be made for wrongful arrest and what must be established in order to successfully maintain such a claim?

In the event that the arrest of a vessel proves to be a wrongful arrest, a plaintiff may be held liable for damages. However, in order for a vessel owner to obtain an award for damages, he must demonstrate that the plaintiff acted in bad faith, with malice, or was grossly negligent. This is an extremely difficult burden for the vessel owner and accordingly, awards for wrongful arrest are rare.

(8) What are the court fees which must be paid in order to make an arrest? Are they recoverable in the event of a successful claim?

In order to file an arrest, it is necessary to file a Summons and Complaint which has a filing fee of $120. In addition, the US Marshall's Office will require a deposit of approximately $5,000 in order to cover the costs of maintaining the vessel while under arrest. If a vessel is released shortly after the arrest, the Marshall will return the unused portion of the funds. In the event that the arrest is maintained for a considerable period of time, the US Marshall's Office will require further deposits to be made to maintain the vessel. The court fees as well as the cost of arrest are recoverable in the event of a successful claim.

(9) How are the lawyers' fees calculated?

In the United States, lawyers may take a case either on a contingent fee basis (no cure, no pay) or on an hourly basis. The actual time spent on effecting arrest is usually not substantial and can be completed in a few hours.

(10) Are all or any part of the lawyers' fees recoverable in the event of a successful arrest?

Under US law, attorneys' fees are usually not recoverable by the successful party unless extraordinary circumstances exist.

(11) How quickly can a ship be arrested after the local lawyer is fully instructed?

If the attorneys in the US are experienced in executing ship arrests, an arrest can be effected within a few hours.

(12) Is there a minimum amount in dispute for which a ship may be arrested?

No.

(13) Is it possible to arrest a sister ship or a ship in "associated ownership"?

Under Rule C of Supplemental Rules for Certain Admiralty and Maritime Claims, a claim can only be made against the vessel which was provided with the services. However, as stated above, if a claim is being made against the same owner, an attachment of the vessel may be possible under Rule B of the Supplemental Rules for Certain Admiralty and Maritime Claims provided the requirements for a Rule B attachment set forth above are met.

(14) What is the order of priorities in the event of the distribution by the court of the proceeds of sale of the ship?

The following is the order of the distribution by the court of the proceeds of the sale of the ship.

1. Claims arising from the care and operation of the ship while it is in the custody of the court through the US Marshall.
2. Claims by seamen for wages.
3. Salvage.
4. Tort claims for collision and personal injury, etc.
5. Liens for repairs, supplies, wharfage, stevedoring and "other necessaries".
6. Liens of cargo against the ship.

(15) Are the claims in respect of which a ship may be arrested subject to a time bar (or prescription) and, if so, are these different according to the nature of the claim?

Although there is no specific statutory time bar relating to the arrest of a ship, a court may find that the arrest is barred by the principle of laches. Laches is an equitable principle which would find that under the circumstances of the specific case, the plaintiff has waited too long to execute his lien rights. The period of time that must pass before laches applies will be dependent upon the specific facts of the case. It should be noted that the sale of the vessel does not extinguish the claim unless such sale was ordered by an Admiralty Court of competent jurisdiction.

(16) Is it possible to apply for the arrest of a ship outside the normal working hours of the court?

Yes. Arrangements can be made with the US Marshall to arrest a vessel any time of day or night. However, notice should be given to the Marshall in advance so that they can make appropriate arrangements.

(17) Please provide any other information which you believe is relevant in deciding whether or not to arrest a ship in your jurisdiction

As you can see from the aforementioned, arrest of a vessel in the US can be quickly and easily accomplished by an experienced maritime practitioner without the need for extensive filing of documents. Accordingly, ship arrests in the US can be a fast, cost-effective way to obtain a successful recovery of outstanding debts.

APPENDIX 1

INTERNATIONAL CONVENTION FOR THE UNIFICATION OF CERTAIN RULES RELATING TO THE ARREST OF SEA-GOING SHIPS, BRUSSELS, 10 MAY 1952

The High Contracting Parties,

Having recognised the desirability of determining by agreement certain uniform rules of law relating to the arrest of sea-going ships.

Have decided to conclude a Convention for this purpose and thereto have agreed as follows:

Article 1

In this Convention the following words shall have the meanings hereby assigned to them:

(1) "Maritime Claim" means a claim arising out of one or more of the following:

- (a) damage caused by any ship either in collision or otherwise;
- (b) loss of life or personal injury caused by any ship or occurring in connection with the operation of any ship;
- (c) salvage;
- (d) agreement relating to the use or hire of any ship whether by charterparty or otherwise;
- (e) agreement relating to the carriage of goods in any ship whether by charterparty or otherwise;
- (f) loss of or damage to goods including baggage carried in any ship;
- (g) general average;
- (h) bottomry;
- (i) towage;
- (j) pilotage;
- (k) goods or materials wherever supplied to a ship for her operation or maintenance;
- (l) construction, repair or equipment of any ship or dock charges and dues;
- (m) wages of Masters, Officers, or crew;
- (n) Master's disbursements, including disbursements made by shippers, charterers or agents on behalf of a ship or her owner;
- (o) disputes as to the title to or ownership of any ship;
- (p) disputes between co-owners of any ship as to the ownership, possession, employment or earnings of that ship;
- (q) the mortgage or hypothecation of any ship.

(2) "Arrest" means the detention of a ship by judicial process to secure a maritime claim, but does not include the seizure of a ship in execution or satisfaction of a judgment.

(3) "Person" includes individuals, partnerships and bodies corporate, Governments, their Departments, and Public Authorities.

(4) "Claimant" means a person who alleges that a maritime claim exists in his favour.

Article 2

A ship flying the flag of one of the Contracting States may be arrested in the jurisdiction of any of the Contracting States in respect of any maritime claim, but in respect of no other claim; but nothing in this Convention shall be deemed to extend or restrict any right or powers vested in any Governments or their Departments, Public Authorities, or Dock or Harbour Authorities under their existing domestic laws or regulations to arrest, detain or otherwise prevent the sailing of vessels within their jurisdiction.

Article 3

(1) Subject to the provisions of paragraph 4 of this Article and of Article 10, a claimant may arrest either the particular ship in respect of which the maritime claim arose, or any other ship which is owned by the person who was, at the time when the maritime claim arose, the owner of the particular ship, even though the ship arrested be ready to sail; but no ship, other than the particular ship in respect of which the claim arose, may be arrested in respect of any of the maritime claims enumerated in Article 1(1)(o), (p) or (q).

(2) Ships shall be deemed to be in the same ownership when all the shares therein are owned by the same person or persons.

(3) A ship shall not be arrested, nor shall bail or other security be given more than once in any one or more of the jurisdictions of any of the Contracting States in respect of the same maritime claim by the same claimant; and, if a ship has been arrested in any one of such jurisdictions, or bail or other security has been given in such jurisdiction either to release the ship or to avoid a threatened arrest, any subsequent arrest of the ship or of any ship in the same ownership by the same claimant for the same maritime claim shall be set aside, and the ship released by the Court or other appropriate judicial authority of that State, unless the claimant can satisfy the Court or other appropriate judicial authority that the bail or other security had been finally released before the subsequent arrest or that there is other good cause for maintaining that arrest.

(4) When in the case of a charter by demise of a ship the charterer and not the registered owner is liable in respect of a maritime claim relating to that ship, the claimant may arrest such ship or any other ship in the ownership of the charterer by demise, subject to the provisions of this Convention, but no other ship in the ownership of the registered owner shall be liable to arrest in respect of such maritime claims.

The provisions of this paragraph shall apply to any case in which a person other than the registered owner of a ship is liable in respect of a maritime claim relating to that ship.

Article 4

A ship may only be arrested under the authority of a Court or of the appropriate judicial authority of the Contracting State in which the arrest is made.

Article 5

The Court or other appropriate judicial authority within whose jurisdiction the ship has been arrested shall permit the release of the ship upon sufficient bail or other security being furnished, save in cases in which a ship has been arrested in respect of any of the maritime claims enumerated in Article 1(1)(o) and (p). In such cases the Court or other appropriate judicial authority may permit the person in possession of the ship to continue trading the ship, upon such person furnishing sufficient bail or other security, or may otherwise deal with the operation of the ship during the period of the arrest.

In default of agreement between the Parties as to the sufficiency of the bail or other security, the Court or other appropriate judicial authority shall determine the nature and amount thereof.

The request to release the ship against such security shall not be construed as an acknowledgment of liability or as a waiver of the benefit of the legal limitation of liability of the owner of the ship.

Article 6

All questions whether in any case the claimant is liable in damages for the arrest of a ship or for the costs of the bail or other security furnished to release or prevent the arrest of a ship, shall be determined by the law of the Contracting State in whose jurisdiction the arrest was made or applied for.

The rules of procedure relating to the arrest of a ship, to the application for obtaining the authority referred to in Article 4, and all matters of procedure which the arrest may entail, shall be governed by the law of the Contracting State in which the arrest was made or applied for.

Article 7

(1) The Courts of the country in which the arrest was made shall have jurisdiction to determine the case upon its merits:

- — if the domestic law of the country in which the arrest is made gives jurisdiction to such Courts;
- — or in any of the following cases namely:
    - (a) if the claimant has his habitual residence or principal place of business in the country in which the arrest was made;
    - (b) if the claim arose in the country in which the arrest was made;
    - (c) if the claim concerns the voyage of the ship during which the arrest was made;
    - (d) if the claim arose out of a collision or in circumstances covered by Article 13 of the International Convention for the unification of certain rules of law with respect to collisions between vessels, signed at Brussels on 23rd September 1910;
    - (e) if the claim is for salvage;
    - (f) if the claim is upon a mortgage or hypothecation of the ship arrested.

(2) If the Court within whose jurisdiction the ship was arrested has not jurisdiction to decide upon the merits, the bail or other security given in accordance with Article 5 to procure the release of the ship shall specifically provide that it is given as security for the satisfaction of any judgment which may eventually be pronounced by a Court having jurisdiction so to decide; and the Court or other appropriate judicial authority of the country in which the arrest is made shall fix the time within which the claimant shall bring an action before a Court having such jurisdiction.

(3) If the parties have agreed to submit the dispute to the jurisdiction of a particular Court other than that within whose jurisdiction the arrest was made or to arbitration,

the Court or other appropriate judicial authority within whose jurisdiction the arrest was made may fix the time within which the claimant shall bring proceedings.

(4) If, in any of the cases mentioned in the two preceding paragraphs, the action or proceedings are not brought within the time so fixed, the defendant may apply for the release of the ship or of the bail or other security.

(5) This Article shall not apply in cases covered by the provisions of the revised Rhine Navigation Convention of 17 October 1868.

Article 8

(1) The provisions of this Convention shall apply to any vessel flying the flag of a Contracting State in the jurisdiction of any Contracting State.

(2) A ship flying the flag of a non-Contracting State may be arrested in the jurisdiction of any Contracting State in respect of any of the maritime claims enumerated in Article 1 or of any other claim for which the law of the Contracting State permits arrest.

(3) Nevertheless any Contracting State shall be entitled wholly or partly to exclude from the benefits of this Convention any Government of a non-Contracting State or any person who has not, at the time of the arrest, his habitual residence or principal place of business in one of the Contracting States.

(4) Nothing in this Convention shall modify or affect the rules of law in force in the respective Contracting States relating to the arrest of any ship within the jurisdiction of the State or her flag by a person who has his habitual residence or principal place of business in that State.

(5) When a maritime claim is asserted by a third party other than the original claimant, whether by subrogation, assignment or otherwise, such third party shall, for the purpose of this Convention, be deemed to have the same habitual residence or principal place of business as the original claimant.

Article 9

Nothing in this Convention shall be construed as creating a right of action, which, apart from the provisions of this Convention, would not arise under the law applied by the Court which had seisin of the case, nor as creating any maritime liens which do not exist under such law or under the Convention on Maritime Mortgages and Liens, if the latter is applicable.

Article 10

The High Contracting Parties may at the time of signature, deposit of ratification or accession, reserve

(a) the right not to apply this Convention to the arrest of a ship for any of the claims enumerated in paragraphs (o) and (p) of Article 1(1), but to apply their domestic laws to such claims;

(b) the right not to apply the first paragraph of Article 3 to the arrest of a ship, within their jurisdiction, for claims set out in Article 1(1), paragraph (q).

Article 11

The High Contracting parties undertake to submit to arbitration any disputes between States arising out of the interpretation or application of this Convention, but this shall be without prejudice to the obligations of those High Contracting Parties who have agreed to submit their disputes to the International Court of Justice.

Article 12

This Convention shall be open for signature by the States represented at the Ninth Diplomatic Conference on Maritime Law. The protocol of signature shall be drawn up through the good offices of the Belgian Ministry of Foreign Affairs.

Article 13

This Convention shall be ratified and the instruments of ratification shall be deposited with the Belgian Ministry of Foreign Affairs which shall notify all signatory and acceding States of the deposit of any such instruments.

Article 14

(a) This Convention shall come into force between the two States which first ratify it, six months after the date of the deposit of the second instrument of ratification.

(b) This Convention shall come into force in respect of each signatory State which ratifies it after the deposit of the second instrument of ratification six months after the date of the deposit of the instrument of ratification of that State.

Article 15

Any State not represented at the Ninth Diplomatic Conference on Maritime Law may accede to this Convention.

The accession of any State shall be notified to the Belgian Ministry of Foreign Affairs which shall inform through diplomatic channels all signatory and acceding States of such notification.

The Convention shall come into force in respect of the acceding State six months after the date of the receipt of such notification but not before the Convention has come into force in accordance with the provisions of Article 14(a).

Article 16

Any High Contracting Party may three years after the coming into force of this Convention in respect of such High Contracting Party or at any time thereafter request that a conference be convened in order to consider amendments to the Convention.

Any High Contracting Party proposing to avail itself of this right shall notify the Belgian Government which shall convene the conference within six months thereafter.

Article 17

Any High Contracting Party shall have the right to denounce this Convention at any time after the coming into force thereof in respect of such High Contracting Party. This denunciation shall take effect one year after the date on which notification thereof has been received by the Belgian Government which shall inform through diplomatic channels all the other High Contracting Parties of such notification.

Article 18

(a) Any High Contracting Party may at the time of its ratification of or accession to this Convention or at any time thereafter declare by written notification to the Belgian Ministry of Foreign Affairs that the Convention shall extend to any of the territories for whose international relations it is responsible. The Convention shall six months after the date of the receipt of such notification by the Belgian Ministry of Foreign Affairs extend to the territories named therein, but not before the date of the coming into force of the Convention in respect of such High Contracting Party.

(b) A High Contracting Party which has made a declaration under (a) of this Article extending the Convention to any territory for whose international relations it is responsible may at any time thereafter declare by notification given to the Belgian Ministry of Foreign Affairs that the Convention shall cease to extend to such territory and the Convention shall one year after the receipt of the notification by the Belgian Ministry of Foreign Affairs cease to extend thereto.

(c) The Belgian Ministry of Foreign Affairs shall inform through diplomatic channels all signatory and acceding States of any notification received by it under this Article.

Done at Brussels, on May 10, 1952 in the French and English languages, the two texts being equally authentic.

APPENDIX 2

CONTACT DETAILS OF CONTRIBUTORS

Company Name/Address	*Telephone No:*	*Fax No:*
Algeria		
Omar Khelifa 6 Rue de L'Espoir Bd Krim Belkacem 16000 Alger Algeria	213 74-20-95/96	213 74-20-97
Argentina		
Jose D Ray Edye Roche, de la Vega & Ray 25 de Mayo 489 5th Floor 1339 Buenos Aires Argentina	54 313 6620/6617	54 313 7705
Australia		
Drew James Norton Smith & Co. Level 8, Gateway 1 Macquarie Place Sydney, New South Wales Australia	61 2-9930 7500	61 2-9930 7600
Belgium		
T. Kegels Kegels, Roosendaal, Keyzer, Straatman & Berckmans Mechelsesteenweg 136 B-2018 Antwerpen Belgium	32 3-237 0101	32 3-237 03 24

Company Name/Address	*Telephone No:*	*Fax No:*
Brazil		
Clyde & Co. Alameda faú. 1754-3rd Floor 01420 002 São Paulo-SP	55 11-3068 8466	55 11-280 6312
Chile		
Andrew J. Cave Cave y Compania Limitada Almirante Senoret 70 Edificio Capitania, 11th Floor Office 11 Casilla 1455, Valparaiso Chile	56-32 21 2304	56-32 25 4252
China, People's Republic of		
P. J. Murray Sinclair Roche & Temperley 1001 North Building Jin Jiang Hotel 59 Mao Ming Road Shanghai 200020 (S) P.R. China	86 21 635 12312	86 21 635 12056
Canada		
Owen Bird Twenty Ninth Floor Three Bentall Centre 595 Burrard Street Box 49130 Vancouver, B.C. B7X 1J5 Canada	604 688 0401	604 688 2827
Denmark		
Peter Schaumburg-Müller Advokaterne Ostergade 55 DK-1100 Kobenhavn K Denmark	45 33 13 1511	45 33 32 0338
Egypt		
Eldib & Partners Advocates 78 al Gomhouria Street Cairo Egypt	20 3 4820111	20 3 4821900

Company Name/Address	*Telephone No:*	*Fax No:*
England and Wales		
Andrew M. Jackson & Co. P.O. Box 47 Essex House Manor Street Hull, HU1 1XH Great Britain	01482 325242	01482 212974
France		
Geraldine Pageard Rembauville Bureau Martel Lalanne Lescop & Associés 161 Boulevard Haussmann 75008 Paris France	33 1 45 63 6336	33 1 45 61 4941
Germany		
Dr. Bartels Blaum Dettmers Rabstein Postfach 1064 40 28064 Bremen Germany	49 421 3660 10	49 421 3660 151
Greece		
John Hadjis John G. Hadjis Law Offices 6 Bouboulinas Street 18535 Piraeus Greece	30 42 25 301	30 42 25 300
Hong Kong		
Paul Fortune Ng & Partners Suite 1910, Swire House 11 Chater Road, Central Hong Kong	852 2521 8688	852 2525 0292
Ireland, Republic of		
McCann Fitzgerald 2 Harbourmaster Place Custom House Dock Dublin 2 Eire	353 1 829 0000	353 1 829 0010
Israel		
A. Kesary S. Friedman & Co. 31 Haatzmauth Road Haifa 33033 Israel	972 4 867 0701	972 4 867 0754

Company Name/Address	*Telephone No:*	*Fax No:*
Italy		
Pietro Palandri Studio Legale Mordiglia VIA XX Settembre 14/17 1612 Genova Italy	39 10 586 841	39 10 532 729
Japan		
Hidetaka Moriya Braun Moriya Hoashi & Kubota 911 IINO Building 1-1 Uchisaiwai-cho 2-Chome Chiyoda-ku, Tokyo Japan	81 3 3504 0251	81 3 3595 0985
Korea, Republic of (South)		
Rok Sang Yu Kim, Shin & Yu C.P.O. Box 3238 12th Floor, Leema Bldg #146-1 Susong-Dong Chongro-ku Seoul 110755 Korea	82 2 735 5822	82 2 739 6606
Malaysia		
Skrine & Co. Straits Trading Building No. 4 Leboh Pasar Besar 50050 Kuala Lumpur Malaysia	60 3 2945111	60 3 2934327
Malta		
Fenech & Fenech 198 Old Bakery Street Valletta VLT 09 Malta	356 241 232	356 221 893
The Netherlands		
Fred J. Langelaar Den Hollander Advocaten Oost Zanddijk 1 P.O. Box 206 3220 AE Hellevoetsluis (Rotterdam) The Netherlands	31 181 313444	31 181 322556

Company Name/Address	*Telephone No:*	*Fax No:*
New Zealand		
Nathan Gray Chapman Tripp Sheffield Young P.O. Box 993 Wellington 1 New Zealand	64 4 499 5999	64 4 472 7111
Norway		
Per M. Ristvedt Wikborg, Rein & Co. Kronprinsesse Marthas pl. 1 P.b. 1513 Vika 0117 Oslo Norway	47 22 82 7500	47 22 82 7501
Panama, Republic of		
Francisco Carreira-Pitti Carreira-Pitti P.C. Attorneys P.O. Box 6-10100 Eldorado Panama City Republic of Panama	507 269 2444	507 263 8290
Poland		
Kancelaria Adwokacka 81-368 Gdynia ul. Pulaskiego 8 Poland	48 27 21 86	48 21 03 62
Portugal		
J. Medeiros Cosme Medeiros Cosme Graça Sardinha Av. Fontes P. De Melo No. 17 16th Floor 1050 Lisboa Portugal	351 3563 431	351 3532 509
Scotland		
J. A. G. Lowe Henderson Boyd Jackson W.S. 19 Ainslie Place Edinburgh, EH3 6AU Scotland	0131 226 6881	0131 225 1103
Singapore		
Khattar Wong & Partners 80 Raffles Place #25-01, UOB Plaza 1 Singapore 048624	65 535 6844	65 534 4892

Company Name/Address	*Telephone No:*	*Fax No:*
South Africa		
Mike Posemann Adams & Adams P.O. Box 1538 Durban 4000 South Africa	27 31 304 3773	27 31 304 3799
Spain		
Eduardo Albors Albors, Galiano & Co. Nunez de Balboa, 46 28001 Madrid Spain	34 1 435 6617	34 1 576 7423
Sweden		
Magnus Sjodin Setterwalls Arsenalsgatan 6 11147 Stockholm Sweden	46 8 678 78 78	46 8 611 46 80
United Arab Emirates		
John Murkett Clifford Chance P.O. Box 9380 Dubai United Arab Emirates	971 4 31 4333	971 4 31 3990
United States of America		
Robert J. Brown Chalos & Brown 300 East 42nd Street New York New York 10017-5982 U.S.A.	212 661 5440	212 697 8999